Memletics® Accelerated Learning Manual

Sean Whiteley

D1710688

Affix serial number label
here. If missing, please
contact Memletics.com

Memletics® Accelerated Learning Manual (version 1.31.)

Contents

Preface

Welcome! Firstly, thanks for picking up this book. In this preface I outline some history of how this project started, and where I'd like to take it from here.

The roots of this project extend back to 1994, when I picked up a book called "SuperLearning" while in college. I tried some of the techniques in the book and, witnessing the effect on my grades, believed there was something worthwhile in accelerated learning.

Over the next few years I kept up an interest in accelerated learning. When the opportunity arose in 1998 to start flying, one of my main motivators was to try out some techniques and see how effectively they worked. Flying is a great way to prove the effectiveness of memory techniques. In the air it becomes obvious if you have learned something or not.

Well, some of those techniques did work, and worked well. My flight instructor at the time asked me where I had learned them. As I'd learned them from many sources, I instead suggested I write a few notes. Those notes turned into a thirty page booklet that I gave out to a small group of people.

After a pause in flight training because of work commitments, I returned to complete my private license. I extended some of the memory techniques I'd used previously, and tried some new ones. As a result I completed that stage of my license in close to the least number of hours the school had seen, especially for a part-timer flying on the weekends.

I felt others could use what I'd learned about memory. Again, work commitments took priority until in February 2002 I decided to reduce my work hours. I wanted to do some more activities unrelated to work.

During this time, I eventually decided to turn that thirty page booklet into something I could publish. Those thirty pages turned into two hundred and eighty single-spaced pages of content, too much for a single volume. I then separated the learning system from the flying content, and so you have in your hands my first book. Given the heritage of Memletics, you will understand why there are still many examples related to aviation in this book. I find the aviation examples often offer a clearer explanation of a principle or technique. I've included many examples from other areas, so I hope you don't find the aviation examples too excessive.

What's ahead for me? I'd like to write or co-write more materials that help others use Memletics for specific topics. However, my primary aim is to find ways to use technology to improve the way we learn and remember. In many ways we are still using technology from the fifteenth century when it comes to "knowledge transfer." This is the printed book. Information technology and the Internet help us create and spread information faster than ever before. Unfortunately though, we still don't have good technology that helps us transfer knowledge, skills and experience efficiently between individuals, organizations and generations. You can see people and generations repeatedly making the same mistakes.

This book does contain information on two newer technologies that do improve the way we learn and remember. These are simulators and programmed repetition software such as SuperMemo. These are just the start. I aim to find and communicate to you new technologies and methods that help you become a *high performance learner*. This book is just the start. There will be more versions and updates to come. Memletics will help you see where these developments fit.

I believe we are yet to find or develop the technology that allows us to reach the next stage of "knowledge transfer" between one another. When we do, it will change society as much as books and literacy have over the past six hundred years. Perhaps Memletics, in future research, will help us reach that next stage. This possibility creates a sense of adventure for me. By buying this book you support the adventure, and I thank you for that.

As this is my first major publication on what I've found, I encourage you to share your thoughts and findings through the book's website. I value your comments and suggestions. They can help shape the future direction of Memletics.

Lastly, I hope you find this journey of discovery as adventurous and enlightening as I have found it.

Sean

Sean Whiteley

Acknowledgements

Several people have helped me at various times during this project. I've appreciated their support and encouragement, and they have all helped make this book happen.

Firstly, thanks must go to my two flight instructors, Tim Clark and Scott Rawling. They continued to show interest, patience and understanding, especially when some of my techniques didn't work as effectively as I thought they would. Tim continues to provide feedback through being the first user of much of my material. Thanks also to Graeme Hodges and the staff at Civil Flying School in Moorabbin, Tony Smith my check-ride instructor, and David "Montie" Lester for inviting me to take that first flight.

Doug Edwards, author of "Fit to Fly," has provided me with comments, support, education and advice throughout the project. Many ideas have come from discussions with him.

Ruth King and Michael Sutcliffe have provided comments, contacts, support and encouragement from early in the project. Julian Fraser from QBE Aviation provided support and helped me spread my network further. Bill Mattes, of the Aviation Safety Foundation of Australia, has provided reviews, contacts and reference material, as well as "behind the scenes" support.

There are two reviewers of my first draft whom I haven't already mentioned. Darren Russ provided detailed feedback on both content and style. Keith Ryall provided perspectives from years of experience in the training profession. I'm still not sure how any of my reviewers found the motivation to get through that first draft.

Trent Mayberry provided me with the opportunity to spend more time on this project. He, with Andrew Weekes, dealt with the challenges of me working four days a week in gainful employment.

You, the reader, have provided me with motivation to make this book happen. If you weren't reading this book now, I would never have started!

Lastly and most importantly, thanks must go to my partner Kristen. She has contributed and supported in so many ways. Without her you would not be reading this book.

Introduction

Our memory underpins everything we think, say and do. Many of us consider it a basic brain ability that allows us to (sometimes) remember a shopping list, birthday or anniversary. Memory is far more fundamental than that. It supports basic activities such as breathing and movement, right through to complex activities such as performing surgery and flying an aircraft.

For such a fundamental skill, it's surprising that school does not teach us more about how to learn and how to use our memory well. Many people still consider learning a "hit and miss" affair. They hope that some of what they learn by rote sinks in to allow them to pass a test.

If you have ever tried to find out more about learning though, you probably found few guides on how to learn more effectively. Our brain doesn't come with a user's manual. You also may not have the time to find valuable information. A wide range of methods and techniques out there claim to improve memory. Many do not work. Some bad experiences may push you to stick to the ways you already know.

I believe this book answers the question "how do I improve my learning and memory?" Over the past few years, I've used flight training and other activities to help work out that answer for myself. In researching this book, I've reviewed more than thirty books, many articles and countless web references to add to and refine my knowledge. I've tried to avoid the unproven ideas and only include techniques shown to work by reputable organizations or direct experience. I've then turned that knowledge into an easy-to-understand system you can easily apply to any learning objective.

I call this learning system *Memletics*. Memletics combines the words *Memory* and *Athletics*. I chose this name because there many parallels between athletic skill and learning skill. Let's look at some of those.

While you may believe you have a poor memory, your brain's performance does not differ that much from the rest of the population. Think of your brain like your muscles. The strength and endurance of your muscles comes mostly from repeated exercise and training. Almost anyone can improve their fitness and strength through training. There isn't much variation between individuals at the muscle cell level, nor at the brain cell level. You mostly get fit, and lose fitness, at a similar pace as the rest of the population. We remember and forget at a similar pace. You don't have a poor memory, you just have an untrained memory.

You can improve your athletic fitness through many activities. Similarly, you can also improve your memory fitness through many activities. Some are easy, some are challenging. Just like athletic fitness, it takes time to build your memory fitness. You don't expect you can run a marathon the day after going for a jog for the first time in five years. Similarly, you can't learn one memory technique and suddenly your memory drastically improves.

Like improving your athletic fitness, improving your memory fitness has benefits in many areas of your life. Employment, relationships, confidence and leisure are a few. I strongly believe that in today's economic climate, *self-directed learners* have a great advantage over those who wait for the next organized course to come along. This book helps you become a self-directed learner.

The more varied your memory training, the more you can use your memory fitness in different ways. Comparing back to athletics, if you only learn one technique you are like someone who only does the javelin. If you instead learn several disciplines, you are like someone who can also run, swim and jump. Someone capable in these areas can also apply and enjoy their fitness in new sports, physical games, and other activities. Similarly, knowing several memory techniques allows you to enjoy the benefits of good memory in many other areas of your life, not just in your studies.

Athletics and Memletics do differ on a particular point though. Athletics typically focuses on a particular event. For example, an athletic meet, championship or even the Olympic Games. Memletics differs because it focuses on lifelong learning. Let me explain a little more. We often measure the effectiveness of a training course by how effectively we can perform certain skills at the end of the course. For example, we use an exam to test our learning. This measure of effectiveness does not consider how much we forget three months, six months or a year after training—usually the most important time! If we used long-term retention as the measure of success for today's courses, we would find that many rate poorly.

Memletics does not just focus on training for an exam or test. It provides you with techniques to help keep what you've learned in your immediately accessible memory for the long term—for the rest of your life if you wish.

You can apply Memletics to many goals involving some form of learning. In doing so you further develop your Memletic fitness. Indeed, if you don't already have a goal in mind I recommend you find one to help you learn Memletics at the same time. In the Overview chapter, I list many examples, however here are a few: Use it to learn professions such as flying, medicine and law. Use it to develop personal skills such as communication, presentation, leadership and consulting. School and college students can apply it to their studies. If you want to focus on pursuits unrelated to work, why not try your hand at sailing, photography, languages, cooking or wine appreciation? Lastly, Memletics works well with sports and other physical activities.

Throughout this book, you will find practical examples from some of these areas. I often use these examples to show how to apply a particular technique. Many of the examples are from learning to fly, however I've also included examples from public speaking, sailing, photography and others. The word *example* appears over four hundred times in this book.

At first, using Memletics may take more time. As a society we have tried to take shortcuts in learning. Memletics will help you relearn practices so you can learn any topic quickly. Once you learn how, the extra effort repays itself many times over.

This book is your Memletics training guide. Use it to help you develop Memletic fitness. The first chapter gives you an overview and then the following five chapters take you through Memletics in detail. You learn the fundamentals of the

Memletic State, Process, Techniques, Styles and Approach. Any worthwhile effort likely involves various challenges. Chapter seven of the book, "Deal with Challenges," provides examples on how you can overcome some common learning challenges. The last chapter, "Closing Comments" provides further ideas on how you can continue building your Memletic fitness, as well as some final words.

* * *

As you can see, you can apply Memletics in almost any area of your life. You may be still in school, in the middle of a career or retired. For younger individuals, Memletics provides a great head start in education. Those who are working can use Memletics to advance their career faster. Memletics can help you make the most of recreation time. For older individuals, Memletic fitness helps ward off the effects of ageing on the brain.

I want to mention one last parallel between athletic fitness and Memletic fitness. Like athletic fitness, your Memletic fitness doesn't improve if you don't *get up and do something*. Reading this book alone may slightly improve your Memletic fitness, however to get the benefits you need to start learning and using the system. A good memory comes from practice. As you read, start thinking of ways you can practice Memletics. How can you start to apply the system in your life? If you don't already have a goal in mind, start thinking of ideas.

Be excited about learning! Read on and find out how.

Using this book

The following tips will help you get the most from four useful features of this book—margin icons, sidebars and text boxes, references and the index.

Margin icons

(i) This book only uses one margin icon. It highlights an important point or caution. You can see an example to the left of this paragraph.

Sidebars and text boxes

I've included many sidebars and text boxes throughout this book. An example of a sidebar is on the right. A text box spreads across a page. You can tell it's a sidebar or text box because I've shaded them.

> **Example sidebar**
> These sidebars provide extra information. You won't miss core elements of Memletics if you skip them.

These boxes provide further useful information that doesn't necessarily belong in the main body of the book. You can choose to read these or skip them. You don't miss the essentials of Memletics if you do choose to skip them.

References

As you read you may notice that I reference books, software and websites, however the text contains few web page links or URLs. Instead, I'm keeping all the references on the Memletics website. I believe this approach is easier to use, it doesn't interrupt your reading and it helps me manage out of date or dead links.

Whenever I have more information on a particular topic available in the references, you see a small symbol. For example:

This sample paragraph has more information available on the web, such as text or website links. 🌐

If you would like to view that extra information, go to the book's reference pages at http://www.memletics.com/manual/references

Index

As there are many cross-references in the book, I've provided a comprehensive index.

Important notice

 This book is for informational purposes only. It's your sole responsibility to decide the usefulness, applicability, completeness and correctness of the content in this book. By reading this book you agree to the "Memletics Terms of Use" in the back of the book. If you do not accept this, don't read the book.

Acquire an overview of Memletics

Memletics draws together much of what we know about effective learning into an easy-to-apply system. This chapter provides you with an overview before you start learning about the individual parts of Memletics. This helps you learn Memletics faster. Having this overview also helps you understand links between the different parts of Memletics. You will soon begin to see the power of Memletics comes from both the individual parts and the whole system.

This chapter outlines the five parts of Memletics. These parts are the Memletic State, Memletic Process, Memletic Techniques, Memletic Styles and Memletic Approach:

- **The Memletic State.** How to make sure your brain cells, physical systems and mental systems are in the best state for learning.

- **The Memletic Process**. The steps you take to LEARN the knowledge needed for your goal.

- **The Memletic Techniques.** These techniques improve the speed and quality of your learning.

- **The Memletic Styles**. Use your stronger and secondary learning preferences to improve your overall learning.

- **The Memletic Approach.** Manage the overall learning journey by prior planning and then tracking along the way.

Don't worry too much about the details of each part at this point. In this chapter I just provide an overview of each part of Memletics. This is because there are many interrelationships between the five parts of the system. Having a broad understanding first helps you recognize those linkages as they arise in the following chapters.

You don't have to read the chapters in a sequential order. Read this overview chapter first, and then read the rest of the chapters in an order that suits you. If you prefer high-level detail first, progressively getting down into the details, read Approach, Styles, State, Process, and then Techniques. If you want the juicy details first, read Techniques, Process, State, Styles and Approach. Or, just read them as presented. It's up to you.

Memletic State is the right state for learning

Memletic State helps you ensure your cell state, physical state and mental state are in good condition for learning. It's harder to learn if your cells, body and mind do not perform well.

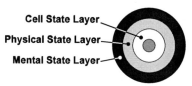

Cell state refers to the state of the cells, primarily neurons, which make up the brain. Physical state involves the different bodily systems that support life, such as breathing, blood circulation, sleep and general bodily health. Mental state involves mental processes that predominately occur in the mind, such as motivation, concentration, awareness and attitude.

Good learning state supports the building of the networks of neurons for the *material you learn*. At the same time, positive learning experiences build neural networks that improve *how you learn*.

What is "good condition?" Let's look at some examples:

- **Cell state.** The brain is a cell-based system and relies on essential materials such as oxygen, water, food and nutrients. These materials are essential for the proper functioning of neurons and other key brain cells (see text box page 16). Good cell state requires a good supply of all these during learning.

- **Physical state:** Your physical environment has a big impact on your body, so fresh air, right temperature, good light and correct furniture are important. Controlling your breathing and stress helps good state, as does getting enough rest and sleep. Longer term, good diet and exercise also have positive effects. Some dietary supplements can also increase brain performance.

- **Mental state:** Clearly defined goals and defined steps for achieving those goals are essential for motivation. Attention and concentration are critical for learning. Longer term, good mental health and "mental exercise" also improve your overall learning.

There are also some negative impacts on state, and I discuss these as well. For example, excess stress and tension are enemies of good state.

Memletic Process—the steps to LEARN

The Memletic Process provides steps to follow when learning new material. You use this process at varying levels of detail throughout

your learning. For example, you first use this process at a high level to understand the overall organization of your material. You then repeat the process at lower levels of detail until you are learning individual chunks of knowledge, such as a particular skill or fact. This approach provides a repeatable process you can refine to improve your overall learning performance.

The diagram above shows the five activities of the Memletic Process. These are:

- **Locate.** Firstly you find and prepare content for your learning goal. This may involve using standard books and manuals, however it could also involve getting notes from lectures, one-on-one tutoring sessions, the Internet and other references.

- **Explore.** Here you work through and understand your content. There are some general principles to follow, such as learning to a level deeper than needed. There are also some approaches relevant to particular learning styles that you may want to try.

- **Arrange.** Next you select which material you want to memorize, and prepare it for memorization. You select Memletic Techniques based on the type of knowledge you want to learn. This book has over twenty different techniques you can apply to various forms of content. You then prepare your content for use with those techniques.

- **Reinforce.** You then use those techniques to reinforce knowledge, skills and behaviors. Further reinforcing techniques help you lock in that material for the long term.

- **eNquire.** Lastly, you review both how well you learned your content, as well how well you applied Memletics along the way.

Notice how the first letters of these steps spell out LEARN (eNquire starts with the 'N' sound).

Don't feel like you have to stick rigidly to these activities. They sometimes overlap. For example, when you explore content you start to form ideas on the techniques to use to memorize it. You start to reinforce material when you explore and arrange it. You may need to rearrange some material during the reinforcing process, as it may not be suitable for the particular technique you chose. Your mind naturally connects topics, associates information and does its own reviews as you progress. Letting it do so helps the whole memorizing process.

Memletic Techniques lock in knowledge

You mainly use the Memletic Techniques during the reinforcing activity of the Memletic Process. The techniques are the primary methods of reinforcing the knowledge you need to remember for the long term.

You can use many techniques in your learning activities. I've grouped these into six main categories, based on the underlying principles of how the techniques work.

These categories are:

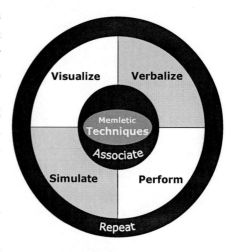

- **Associate.** Associate new knowledge with knowledge that's already in your memory. These techniques are great for facts and procedures.

An Overview of Neurons—Basic Brain Cells

Neurons are the fundamental cells that support memory. The majority of memory is represented via large networks of neurons within the brain, sometimes called neural networks. The neurons connect to other neurons via synapses. Synapses are like a tiny telephone exchange between two or more neurons.

There are four main components of the typical neuron:

- **The dendrites.** These receive signals from other neurons.

- **The cell body.** This manages the overall cell function and maintenance.

- **The axon.** This transmits the signal to another area. This other area may be as close as a hair-width away, or sometimes up to three feet (one meter) away.

- **The pre-synaptic terminal.** This is the bulge at the tip of the axon. It passes the neuron signal on to the dendrites of other neurons.

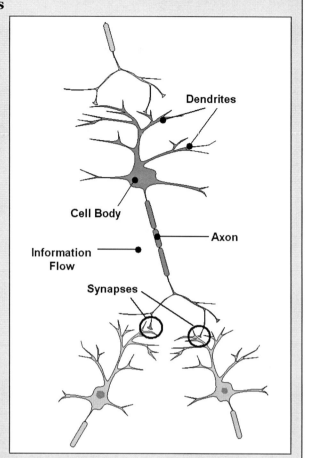

The signals that flow through the neurons and axons are very small changes in the electrical charge of cell components. The changes are achieved via the flow of various molecules and chemical compounds into and out of the cells.

In the synapse, the pre-synaptic terminal of the transmitting neuron and the dendrite of the receiving neuron do not touch. The signal passes from one neuron to another by the release of certain chemicals called neurotransmitters. The amount of neurotransmitter released depends on the strength of the signal received at the pre-synaptic terminal, as well as the number of times it's been triggered recently. Therefore, the overall strength of the signal passed from one neuron to another depends on the strength of the first trigger, moderated by how often the same signal has passed through that synapse.

Now, I've simplified the structure of the neural network to give you an idea of the basics. If you want an idea of how complex the brain is, consider these statistics. Researchers estimate there are up to roughly 10^{11} neurons in your brain alone (not considering the rest of the nervous system). That's perhaps 100,000,000,000, or one hundred billion neurons. If each neuron just stored a 1 or 0 like a computer, you would have around 93 gigabits of storage. But that's not all. Each neuron typically has between 1,000 and 10,000 synapses. The combinations of the synapses control whether a signal is passed on or not. Multiply out those numbers, and you have purely staggering storage and processing abilities all within the space the size of your head.

- **Visualize.** Use your "mind's eye" to recreate sensory abilities, experiences, ideas and views in your mind. Visualization can be creative, for example for experiences that have not happened yet. You can use it to rehearse new procedures and skills, and as well use it to strengthen other techniques.

- **Verbalize.** Your internal self-talk influences your behavior. Using verbal techniques such as assertions (or affirmations), scripting and a "mental firewall" you can alter your internal self-talk to align with your learning objectives.

- **Simulate.** Simulation reinforces a behavior or skill using external tools. Basic simulation can involve just cardboard cutouts or household items, while PC based simulation is becoming more and more advanced. Role-playing is also another form of simulation.

- **Perform.** There are specific techniques to improve skill performance. Some of these techniques involve understanding the theory behind learning and performing skills. Other Perform techniques help change existing behaviors, as well as improve performance of already learned skills.

- **Repeat.** While Memletics aims to reduce rote repetition, rote learning is still a common and sometimes useful technique. Flashcards are also useful, however some newer software can significantly improve the way you learn and retain new material.

I've listed the techniques in each of these categories in the following table:

Associate	General association	Peg events
	First letter mnemonics	Mental journey or story
	Acrostic mnemonics	Roman Rooms
	Linked lists	Chunking
	Peg words	
Visualize	General visualization	Mental rehearsal
	Creative visualization	Strengthening techniques
Verbalize	General verbalization	Mental firewall
	Assertions	Scripting
Simulate	Basic simulation	Advanced simulation
	PC simulation	Role-playing
Perform	Three stage skill learning	Shunt
	Part task training	Anchoring
	Performance variation	Modeling
	Overlearning	
Repeat	Rote learning	Scheduled review
	Flashcards	Programmed repetition

As well as the techniques, I also discuss some common reasons why techniques may not work as well as you expect at the end of the techniques chapter.

Memletic Styles personalize your learning

The Memletic Styles recognize that each of us prefers to learn in different ways. There are many variations on this theme and different ways to describe these preferences, however the Memletic Styles uses the seven shown in the diagram as its basis. These seven Learning Styles are:

- **Visual.** You use pictures, images, visualization, and spatial arrangements.
- **Aural**. You use voice, sounds and music.
- **Verbal.** You use words and writing.
- **Physical.** You use your body, hands, and sense of touch.
- **Logical.** You use logic, reasoning and systems.
- **Social.** You prefer to learn with groups or other people.
- **Solitary.** You prefer to work alone and use self-study.

All of these styles are effective learning styles. Your favored use of particular styles does not make you a more or less effective learner. Current school approaches tend to focus on only two of these. This bias may have influenced how you view your own learning abilities. I'll talk more about this in the Memletic Styles chapter when we discuss learning styles in detail.

Memletic Approach—the path to your goals

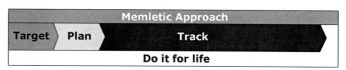

The Memletic Approach is a series of tasks that you can use to approach and manage any learning journey. The time you spend in this activity varies according to the length and importance of your goals.

The four tasks of the Memletic Approach are:

- **Target.** Choose and clarify your goal. Targeting your goal involves understanding your reasons, exploring your goal and setting your objectives.
- **Plan.** Decide your approach. Do prior research, plan your course map, and work out time and cost estimates.
- **Track.** Track your progress. This involves regularly (but not too regularly) checking your progress and adjusting where necessary.
- **Do it.** Enjoy it for life. This one is self-explanatory!

How can you apply Memletics?

I mentioned in the preface that Memletics grew from my flight training experiences. Memletics is now a system you can apply to a wide range of learning activities. In this section I outline my thoughts on some of those activities. I do this for two reasons:

- If you are already do some of these activities, to encourage you to see ways you can apply Memletics to your current goals.
- If you are looking for a new goal, to give you ideas of what activities you may want to try.

Let's look at how you can apply Memletics during major life phases, as well as some specific activities.

Using Memletics during major life phases

Here are a few points on using Memletics during major life phases—early years, formal education, employment and later years.

- **Early years.** Your children can benefit from your understanding and use of Memletics. Children find many of the techniques such as association and visualization easier than adults. This can give them a good head start in their schooling and life education.
- **Formal education.** School, college, and university are great places to apply Memletics. Often applying some structure to study can make a big difference. Understanding and using these techniques can help you learn faster. This could allow you to spend more time increasing the quality of your education through extra study, or allow you to spend more time outside school. Your choice!
- **Employment.** You may not realize just how many opportunities for better learning there are in the workplace. Examples include job hunting skills, learning new roles and skills, and continuing training. You may want to consider using Memletics to help you change your career or learn new skills after redundancy or a layoff. I list some more specific examples below.
- **Later years.** One of the major concerns of older individuals is the onset of age-related mental decline or dementia, and potential diseases such as Alzheimer's disease. Good Memletic fitness helps keep your mind and body active, helping to ward off or reduce the impact of these brain problems. Also, as retirees typically live longer, they have more time available for recreational activities. Memletics can also help here. See further below for examples.

Specific activities

Let's look at more specific examples of where you can apply Memletics. I've listed four types of activities: personal skill development, professional training, recreational activities, and sports. I'm sure there are others out there as well. If you think of more, feel free to post them on the website.

Personal skill development

Regardless of your occupation, you are likely to benefit from improved personal skills. You can apply many of the techniques to develop your skills in areas such as:

- Communication
- Presentation
- Negotiation
- Leadership
- Time management
- Etiquette
- Networking
- Stress, conflict and anger management
- Interviewing
- Learning other languages
- Selling and marketing
- Consulting
- Coaching and mentoring
- Management
- Creativity
- Problem solving
- Training others
- Relationships
- Planning
- Financial Management

If you are looking for a topic to start learning Memletics, these are often good places to start. Even if your work role does not need these skills directly, you can still gain many benefits from developing these skills. Consider selling and consulting. When you are searching for a job, you are selling your time. Or, when taking on an assignment from your boss, consulting skills can help you better understand your assignment and deliver to requirements. This results in you being more valuable, and hopefully more rewarded (if not, use your selling skills to find another buyer of your time)!

Professional training

There are a wide range of professions that can benefit from Memletic training. These include the flight, medical and legal professions.

- **Flight training.** One reason I started flight training was to understand and develop my skills using various memory and learning techniques I'd read about. I've mentioned elsewhere that I believe flying is a great activity in which to develop your Memletic fitness.

- **Medicine.** There are many parallels between the medical and flight professions. The key one is that you are often solely responsible for the lives of others. Whether you are a doctor, nurse, physiotherapist or psychologist, your use of Memletics can help you learn and refine skills and as well help pass on useful knowledge to others. Indeed, some of the research for this book came directly from the medical fields. For example, the effectiveness of various relaxation techniques and the impact on anxiety has been researched for use in many medical contexts. One area is pain control.

- **Law.** While law may not involve the responsibility for a human life, it often involves the responsibility for the livelihood of clients. The win or loss of a case may depend on the good functioning of your memory, the ability to learn key skills such as communication and persuasion, and the ability to resolve challenges quickly (such as managing false assumptions). There are also parallels between flight training and law. For example, I know of an experienced flight training author and ex-accident investigator who helps legal organizations reduce their insurance costs by applying the same principles of pilot error management in a legal context.

Recreational activities

If you are looking for a new activity outside work, why not try some recreational activities. These are another way to learn more about Memletics, while developing your skills at something not directly related to your occupation. Some examples include:

- Photography and Video
- Sailing
- Four wheel driving
- Hiking and Orienteering
- Flying (recreationally)
- Woodwork, metalwork
- Martial arts, yoga, tai chi
- Wine appreciation
- Astronomy
- Fishing, bird-watching
- Travel (the wider the better)
- Creative activities—painting, drawing, writing etc.
- Home renovations and interior design
- Gardening and landscaping
- Cooking
- Dancing, theatre, performance
- Music and singing
- Historical and genealogy studies

These are just a sample. There are more out there. These activities are also conducive to higher motivation as they have direct benefits for you (and potentially your family) rather than your employer!

Sports and competition

Many of the techniques in this book have already been applied in a sporting context. Visualization, relaxation, concentration and modeling can lead to superior sporting performance. Books like "The Inner Game of Tennis" and "The Inner Game of Golf" helped launch visualization into mainstream sports as well as wider use. While you may not be aiming to compete on an international level, sports and other competitive activities are a great way to also develop your Memletic fitness. Here are just a few examples:

- Archery
- Badminton
- Baseball
- Basketball
- Biathlon
- Bowling
- Cricket
- Cycling
- Diving
- Fencing
- Football
- Golf
- Gymnastics
- Hockey
- Netball
- Polo
- Racquetball
- Rowing
- Running
- Rugby
- Shooting
- Skating
- Skiing
- Soccer
- Softball
- Squash
- Surfing
- Swimming
- Table Tennis
- Tennis
- Track & Field
- Triathlon
- Volleyball
- Water Polo
- Water-skiing
- Weight-lifting
- Windsurfing
- Wrestling

Others

Here are a few others applications that don't fit into the categories above.

- **Driving.** You may already know how to drive. Why not try a more advanced driving course. Are you comfortable you could handle a loss of control in wet weather? You may also want to try some of the principles of Memletics while teaching your son, daughter or others to drive.

- **Dating.** Yes, dating. While I haven't specifically tried it myself, I'm sure that many of the principles of Memletics could help you out in the dating game. Keep in mind that just being in Memletic State (healthy, fit, active mind etc.) may be more likely to help you along than learning specific "pickup lines" or other similar techniques.
- **General living.** Whether it's learning to be a better domestic partner, or developing other life skills not mentioned here, Memletics can help you along.

Chapter summary

In this overview you've started to develop an understanding of Memletics. You've seen that Memletic State helps you develop the best condition for learning. You now know the Memletic Process is five steps to faster LEARNing. You've seen the broad categories of the Memletic Techniques. You realize the Memletic Styles adapt how you use Memletics according to your learning styles. You know about the Memletic Approach and that it helps you tackle any learning goal.

As Memletics is a practical system, rather than theory, I've also given you some examples of where you can apply Memletics. We looked at how you can apply Memletics in various life phases. We also looked at specific applications in careers, education, recreation, sport and more.

I've taken you through this overview of Memletics because there are many links between the individual parts of Memletics. Having this broad understanding helps you recognize those links as you start learning Memletics in depth. This is exactly what you are about to do in the next five chapters. We begin with Memletic State.

While Memletics may seem overwhelming at first, you don't need to use every part to have the system start working for you. You can choose the techniques and adapt Memletics to what feels right for you. Later in the book I'll give you some more suggestions on how to start learning Memletics. For now, just read, absorb and enjoy!

Chapter

2 Perform in the Memletic State

You learn faster if your cells, body and mind are in good condition, or good "state." Memletic State describes the best state for learning. This chapter shows you what Memletic State is, and how to achieve it. We look at the benefits of general health and fitness right through to the latest results from brain research. Being in Memletic State doesn't just increase your memory and learning performance. Memletic State is the peak condition for performing well in many human endeavors, from flying a plane to playing football.

Memletic State is when your body and mind are in the best condition for learning. This chapter tells you how to get in that state. Applying the information in this chapter will increase your learning performance without using any of the other techniques in this book. Being in Memletic State also helps improve your health and well-being, with resulting benefits in many other areas of your life.

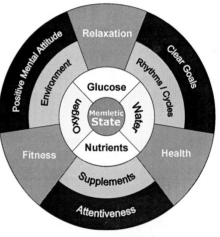

I've grouped the major contributors to Memletic State into three layers. These are the cell, physical and mental state layers. In summary, the elements that make up each of these layers are:

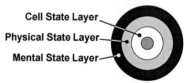

- **Cell State Layer:** Water, Glucose, Oxygen, and Basic Nutrients.
- **Physical State Layer:** Health, Fitness, Relaxation, Environment, Sleep and Body Rhythms, and Supplements.
- **Mental State Layer:** Health, Fitness, Relaxation, Attention and Concentration, Positive Mental Attitude, and Goals.

The learning state diagram below shows these layers and elements. Cell state is fundamental and therefore the innermost layer. You will find it hard to learn without satisfactory functioning of cells. The next layer is the physical state layer. These elements impact how well you breathe, circulate blood, fight off illness and more. The outer layer is the mental state layer. The elements of this layer are within our mind. Notice how cell state layer supports the physical state layer, and the physical state layer supports the next layer out, the mental state layer.

 CAUTION. This chapter includes information on health and fitness. This is not specific advice for your personal situation. Applying the content in this chapter may involve changes to your diet, physical activity levels and other day-to-day behaviors. If you plan to make changes to these areas, you should always consult a medical practitioner or other appropriate specialist. Discuss activities that may affect particular illnesses or conditions you have. This applies in particular to:

- Breathing exercises if you have any lung illness or condition
- Physical exercise if you are unfit or have a heart or lung condition.
- Supplements, especially if you suffer any form of illness or are on any medication.

Cell state—ensure your brain cells are well nourished

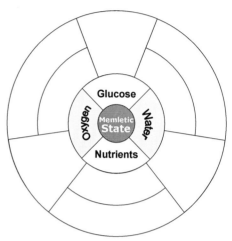

Good cell state ensures an adequate supply of materials that brain cells, primarily neurons, need to work. Like other human cells, Neurons need water, energy and oxygen. Neurons and other cells around them also need certain nutrients to work effectively. The lack of any of these basic materials significantly decreases your ability to learn, even to live. Ensuring your brain has a good supply of all these materials provides a solid base on which the other learning state layers can perform well.

The four materials we examine in cell state are glucose, oxygen, basic nutrients and water.

Glucose

Your brain needs much energy. Nerve transmission, or signals passing from one neuron to another, consumes over half of the energy used by your brain. This can be over ten percent of your body's total energy use. The brain's neurons consume more energy during learning and other mental activities.

Each neuron takes mainly one form of sugar, glucose, and burns it with oxygen to supply its energy needs. Neurons use this energy to fire when triggered, for growing new connections, and for general cell maintenance.

Neurons cannot store glucose. They can only get it, when needed, from the bloodstream. The hippocampus, one particular area in the brain, suffers when it cannot get enough glucose. As the hippocampus helps sort and store key types of memories, any lack of energy in this area results in less effective learning. Low blood glucose directly affects other areas of the brain as well. For example, low blood glucose results in slower processing of visual and auditory information.

Your body gains glucose mainly from the carbohydrates in the foods we eat. The stomach breaks carbohydrates into glucose, which is a simpler carbohydrate. In some foods, the sugar is already glucose and it passes directly into the bloodstream.

So how do you keep up good levels of blood glucose? Eat complex carbohydrates from plant-based foods such as grains, legumes, fruits and vegetables. These provide the best form of carbohydrates because they take time to break down in the stomach. They release their glucose over several hours.

Not all forms of carbohydrates are good for boosting brain performance though. Avoid large injections of sugar such as soft drinks, cakes, chocolate, and other refined sugary foods. While it may seem these should help your brain work well, it's only a temporary effect. With such a large change in blood glucose, your body releases large amounts of insulin, a compound that regulates the levels of sugar in your bloodstream. The presence of insulin signals various parts of the body to take glucose from the blood. The body turns that excess glucose into compounds that store the energy for later use. It turns the glucose into fat.

Because these sugars in these foods are short lived, the body soon finds itself with not enough glucose and too much insulin in the blood. This causes large swings between too much and then too little sugar in the blood. These swings result in you feeling tired or spaced out within a few hours after consuming such a food or drink. If you then consume another high sugar snack, off goes the process again. These swings, over time, can reduce your body's sensitivity to insulin. This can result in diet-induced diabetes.

What is the lesson to take away from this? Eat a diet rich in complex carbohydrates from whole grain foods, vegetables, fruits and nuts. Don't skip breakfast, and don't "load up" on sugary foods before class and especially not before exams. Before a long exam or other mentally intensive activity, eat a good meal with both proteins and complex carbohydrates. Also, if allowed, take in wholesome snacks that you can eat each hour or so, *before you feel hungry.*

A last point about brain energy is that eating a large meal can negatively affect brain performance. Glucose gets to the brain via your bloodstream. After eating a large meal, the body diverts blood to the stomach to digest the incoming food. This diversion of blood takes blood away from the brain. This leaves you feeling tired or sleepy (especially after a big Sunday lunch). Avoid eating a large fat- and protein-rich meal directly before class, training, a performance or an exam if you want your brain performing at its best!

Where is memory located? A short history:

This question has been asked by humans for thousands of years. Through the ages there have been a range of theories.

The ancient Greeks thought that many of the brain's functions were located in the heart. Aristotle thought along similar lines, and that the brain was primarily there to cool the blood. Intelligence, according to this theory, could be measured by the amount of cooling required, hence the size of the human brain.

From around 200 AD to 1400 AD the popular theory was that memory was located in the ventricles, the liquid filled spaces in the brain. Leonardo da Vinci helped dispel this theory.

In the early 1900's a Spaniard determined the basic roles of neurons and synapses. This is the basis of our current view of memory being a complex network of neurons.

Oxygen

As mentioned above in the section on energy, each neuron burns glucose with oxygen to obtain energy. How goes oxygen get from the air outside our body to the cells within our brain? Oxygen enters the bloodstream through our lungs. The oxygen attaches itself to special proteins in the blood. The blood then transports oxygen to the brain via blood vessels, and these vessels break down into smaller and smaller pathways until they become capillaries. Capillaries weave throughout the brain and flow close to each neuron. When needed, oxygen detaches itself from the blood and flows into the neuron.

While your brain is only around three percent of your body mass, it can consume more than twenty percent of your body's oxygen intake. Its consumption increases during mental activities such as learning. Let's look at ways to ensure your oxygen use is ideal for learning. This involves good blood efficiency, good lung efficiency, good pulse rate and strength, and good breathing.

Good blood efficiency

Blood efficiency is how well your blood takes up, transports and releases oxygen. The key nutrient that helps your blood transport oxygen is iron. Be sure to get enough iron in your diet. Good sources include wholegrain cereals and breads, green leafy vegetables, and meat (especially red meat). Vitamin C also helps absorption of iron.

Iron deficiency is common in western diets, especially in women and vegetarians. If you regularly feel tired, have less energy, or look pale, see a medical practitioner to have a blood check. Not all people display symptoms of anemia, so why not ask for a test next time you visit the doctor. Too much iron is not good for you either—another reason to check.

Good lung efficiency

Efficient lungs more easily move oxygen into your blood. They also do a better job at removing carbon dioxide. Here are four ways you can support and improve lung efficiency:

- **Eat your fruits, vegetables and grains.** Anti-oxidants such as vitamins E and C, and beta-carotene can improve how well your lungs work. The best source of these anti-oxidants is from a diet rich in fruit, vegetables and grains.
- **Stay fit.** Aerobic fitness improves your lung efficiency, both during exercise and during rest.
- **Try a lung exerciser.** These are fairly new products on the market that provide variable resistance to breathing. They look similar to an asthma inhaler. Used for a few minutes a day these appear to improve lung efficiency. Brand names include PowerLung™ and PowerBreathe™.
- **Don't smoke.** Smoking drastically reduces lung efficiency.

Good pulse rate and strength

Increasing your pulse rate and strength increases the blood flow into the brain. This increases both oxygen and glucose availability. You can improve your pulse rate during learning as well as over a longer term:

- **During lessons.** Get up occasionally and do some light exercise during lessons. Go for a walk while learning or memorizing some material. Involve some elements of the physical style in your learning, even if it's not one of your strengths.

- **Longer term.** The key is cardiovascular fitness, or fitness of the heart. Normal regular exercise provides a good base. If you want to further improve your heart fitness, try some interval training. Interval training consists of repetitions of a short burst of high-effort exercise, followed by a medium intensity recovery period. Here's an example for when you are already reasonably fit: While jogging, jog or run harder for thirty seconds, and then jog slowly for two minutes while you recover. Then jog hard again for the thirty seconds, and recover for two minutes. Continue for ten repetitions. This is a simple example. You can vary the intensity period, the recovery period and the number of repetitions based on your fitness levels.

Good breathing

Good abdominal breathing improves your lung efficiency. You can find many ways to improve your breathing in various books and on the web. Many of us are lazy when it comes to strong abdominal breathing. Here are some basic points on breathing and learning:

- **Before learning.** Incorporate some breathing exercises into a relaxation exercise before each lesson (coming up).

- **During learning.** Be aware of your breath while you are learning. Avoid shallow breathing, even if you are just sitting at a desk. If you become aware you barely breathed over the past few minutes, take moment to take a few deep breaths. Use a short inhale and a long exhale, at a minimum ratio of 1:4 seconds (for example a two-second inhale, and an eight-second exhale). Also try increasing the pressure in your lungs by occasionally breathing out through pursed or partly closed lips. Don't go too far and get dizzy though!

- **After learning.** Take a few minutes after learning to repeat your breathing exercises.

- **During day-to-day activities.** There are many other benefits from improving your overall breathing during the day. Spending time focusing on your breathing habits is well worthwhile.

Continual deep breathing is not a complete answer to lung efficiency. For some people, better breathing may involve reducing their breathing rate. Some researchers believe that breathing difficulties (such as asthma) may be the result of too much breathing. Again, do more research or talk to the doctor if you want to check or improve your breathing habits.

Basic Nutrients

There are three basic nutrients, besides glucose, that are essential for good learning state. Fatty acids build your brain, amino acids help it communicate, and micronutrients protect it.

Fatty acids build your brain

Each neuron has an outer membrane or skin which defines the cell border. This membrane controls the flow of other materials into and out of the cell. It's a thin double layer of special fats called lipids. These lipids come from fats in your diet.

Not all fats are bad for you! You need to include the *right types* of fat in your diet. There are two types of fat your brain needs, and which your body cannot produce from other sources. These fats must come directly from your food:

- **Alpha-linolenic acid** or ALA, part of the "omega 3" family of fatty acids. This is in flax seeds, chia seeds, walnuts, green leafy vegetables and sea vegetables. Animals that feed on sea vegetables, such as fish, also contain this nutrient.

- **Linoleic acid or LA**, part of the "omega-6" family of fatty acids. This is in expeller cold-pressed sunflower, safflower, corn, and sesame oils.

A good balance of essential omega-3 and omega-6 fatty acids is important. A good ratio of omega-3 to omega-6 fatty acids is 1:1, however many western diets contain ratios like 1:20 or higher. This poor ratio is because western diets typically contain high amounts of meat and dairy products, and other omega-6 fatty acids are in these foods. Vegetable oils, like sunflower oil, are increasingly used in fried foods as well.

Change your meat consumption to sometimes include fish. This will help balance out your omega-3 to omega-6 intake. The best fish are high-fat, cold-water varieties like salmon, mackerel, sardines, and trout. Be aware of possible contaminants in your source of fish, and avoid eating the skin. Also, consider reducing your intake of other meats and food fried in oil.

If you choose to use an omega-3 supplement such as fish oil or flax seed oil, be aware that these are sensitive to light and air oxidation. Buy these products refrigerated and in small quantities. Try to use them quickly.

Amino acids connect your brain

The brain stores longer-term memories in the many connections between neurons. While the electrical signal flows through the neuron, it does not jump directly into the receiving neurons. Rather, the electrical signal stimulates the release of chemicals called neurotransmitters, and these pass (or inhibit) the signal to the receiving neurons. These neurotransmitters are essential to the memory and learning process. Yet again, the food you eat every day influences these important chemicals. This time the important nutrients are proteins.

Like fatty acids, there are many varieties of protein. These are "amino acids." There are eight essential amino acids. The body cannot make these acids and so they must come from your daily food intake. Thankfully though, you don't need to keep track of all eight. What you do need to be aware of are the two forms of protein—complete and incomplete proteins.

- **Complete proteins** contain ample amounts of all eight essential amino acids. Fish, meat, eggs, cheese and yoghurt are examples of complete proteins. If you regularly consume these foods, it's likely you are getting enough essential amino acids.

- **Incomplete Proteins** only contain some of the amino acids. This includes grains, legumes, seeds and nuts. Correct combinations of these foods can result in proper consumption of all these amino acids, and traditional diets may contain these correct combinations (such as rice and beans together). If you are a vegetarian, make sure that you are getting the complete set of amino acids.

Micronutrients protect your brain

The use of oxygen in cells also creates unstable bits of oxygen (and other materials) called "free radicals." Free radicals want to link with other materials to become stable again. Unfortunately, by doing so, they often cause chemical reactions that damage cells. Some theories suggest that ageing is no more than the continuous build-up of damage caused by free radicals.

Above I mentioned the brain uses much oxygen. It can sometimes use more than twenty percent of the body's intake. This high use of oxygen makes the brain more susceptible to free radical damage.

Naturally, the body has a form of defense against these free radicals, and these are anti-oxidants. Anti-oxidants appear more attractive to a free radical than say part of a cell. Anti-oxidants sacrifice themselves to prevent a free radical from damaging your cells. This makes the free radical harmless.

You want to have plenty of anti-oxidants in your body to neutralize these free radicals. Key anti-oxidants include Vitamin E, Vitamin C, glutathione, coenzyme Q10, and lipoic acid.

Again your diet has a big influence on the levels of anti-oxidants in your body. Try to get these from natural foods first. Vegetables and fruit are the best source. You may also want to do more research on anti-oxidant and super-anti-oxidant supplements. This area is receiving much interest at present.

Water

Water is the most plentiful compound in our body. Over sixty percent of our body mass is water. Our blood is mainly water, and our blood transports oxygen, energy and nutrients around the body. Our brain also has a large volume of water inside and around it. It uses water both for transport of various compounds as well as for protection. Water also plays a key role in cell metabolism. Water moves materials into and out of the cell.

Dehydration, or lack of water in the body, has a harmful impact on learning. Typical symptoms of mild dehydration include headaches, sleepiness and dizziness.

You may have heard of the "eight glasses a day" guideline. This guideline however doesn't consider your own body weight or the large amount of water you get from the foods and drinks you consume each day. Let your own body signal how much water you should drink. If you need to visit the bathroom every hour, you may be drinking too much. If your urine is a dark yellow color, you may not be drinking enough. Find a balance where you visit the restroom perhaps four to five times a day, and you don't feel thirsty.

Don't use thirst as the trigger to drink more water though. The thirst sensation triggers only after you have already lost roughly one and half quarts or liters from normal, or around two percent of body mass. When you feel thirsty, you have already lost a reasonable amount of water.

Adjust your water intake based on upcoming events. Increase your intake *before* you exercise, go into a hot or dry environment, or if you are drinking a lot of coffee or alcohol. Note that coffee and alcohol usually take more water out of your system than they put in.

Also be aware that stress can increase the urge to urinate more often. Even in mildly stressful situations, such as before or during exams, the body releases hormones (such as adrenaline) to prime it for physical activity. This can increase the tension in your muscles, including the muscles around your bladder. Your nervous system can misread this tension as a full bladder, causing you feel the urge to go to the bathroom more often than you actually need to. The increased tension in your muscles can also increase the level of waste products in the bloodstream. Your body clears these via your urine. Be aware of the impact of stress and adjust your water intake according to how much you urinate, not by how many visits you make!

Physical state—keep your body systems in good shape

The next learning state layer, the physical layer, deals with critical body and brain systems that support good learning state. Good physical state consists of:

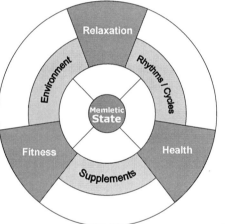

- **General health and nutrition.** The overall health of your body system influences your ability to learn.
- **Physical fitness.** Bodily fitness supports good learning.
- **Physical relaxation.** A relaxed state contributes to good learning.
- **Physical environment.** The physical environment should support your bodily needs.
- **Body and brain rhythms.** Sleep supports learning. Knowledge of other body and brain rhythms also helps your learning.
- **Dietary supplements.** Some dietary supplements may improve learning and brain performance.

General health and nutrition

Your overall health and nutrition has a significant impact on how well you learn and remember. I cover more detail of some specific parts of health and nutrition in other parts of this chapter, however some key points for good health and nutrition include:

- **Eat a varied diet.** Ensure that you get a balanced mix of foods. General advice may be to "eat less meat, animal fat, salt and processed foods" and "eat more fruit, vegetables, and fish." Recent research also suggests using more plant-based oils in your diet. This includes oils such as olive, canola, soy, corn, sunflower, peanut and other vegetable oils☯.

- **Get regular exercise.** Even basic exercise such as a regular walk has many health benefits. Exercise helps control weight, blood sugar and cholesterol levels. It improves cardiovascular fitness and circulation, and helps manage blood pressure. It helps the immune system. It also helps stimulate a sense of well-being and reduces the risk of other mental disorders such as anxiety and depression. With all these benefits, the "apple a day keeps the doctor away" quote should be "a walk a day keeps the doctor away."

- **Relax more, stress less.** Regular relaxation has many positive health benefits. It helps control stress. Excessive stress insidiously affects your physical health in so many ways, and not just mentally. Stress seriously affects your immune system, your endocrine system, your gastrointestinal system, and your cardiovascular system. There are many ways to control stress. See your doctor or web references if you believe you are suffering from excessive stress.

- **Deal with illnesses and injuries quickly.** Many of us avoid visits to the doctor. This is more obvious in men. Most would prefer to wait until their arm falls off before thinking about seeing a doctor. Even seemingly minor injuries can impact you in ways you cannot predict. An example is an airline captain who turned up for work with an injured thumb. The first part of the flight finished easily, however during the second leg they met severe turbulence. The captain found that controlling the aircraft caused extreme pain in his thumb. He had to hand over to the co-pilot. Minor injuries can have unexpected impacts on your overall health and performance, so treat them early.

- **Keep a positive mental attitude and outlook.** Having a positive mental attitude positively influences your overall health. Until recently, the medical field largely treated the body and mind as two separate entities that had little influence over each other. A relatively new branch of medicine, *psychoneuroimmunology*, now studies the links between mental attitudes and bodily health. Keeping a positive mental outlook provides better disease resistance, improves heart health and speeds recovery from illness. Some suggestions that help a positive mental attitude are to laugh more, use assertions, set and achieve goals, and avoid negative people!

- **Take responsibility for your life.** Taking on more responsibility in your life can lead to *better* health, contrary to popular opinion. Many people associate higher responsibility to higher stress, illness and heart attack. There is an interesting paradox in this. Those who have more *sense of control* of the environment around them appear to have better health than those who resign that control to others. For example, the incidence of heart attack is higher in those with low levels of responsibility at work, rather than those in higher executive positions. However, when those executives retire the chance of heart attack *goes up*. It appears that retirement causes these once-powerful individuals to feel a loss of control over their lives.

  Taking responsibility doesn't necessarily mean you should immediately start striving for the boss's job. However, you should begin to accept that where you are today is the result of the choices *you* have made. This is part of personal responsibility. You have either made a choice yourself, or you have chosen to give someone else control over a decision. If you allow others to make choices for you, they often make those choices based on their own self-interest. It's up to you whether you allow that to happen. Those types of decisions have a significant impact on your physical and mental health, so choose wisely!

On the negative side of learning state, alcohol and some other drugs (such as ecstasy and marijuana) have a harmful effect on the general health of the brain. I suggest you:

- **Avoid excessive alcohol consumption.** While small amounts of alcohol appear to aid overall health, excessive alcohol consumption has a definite and observable impact on brain size and construction. Binge drinking (consuming large amounts of alcohol at one time) can cause the most damage.

- **Avoid other psychedelic drugs.** While drugs such as ecstasy and marijuana may appear safe, there are disturbing trends of long-term impacts on brain functions. These include decreased memory and learning capacity. If you want to use these drugs, I suggest you research and understand the full long-term implications. Unlike with cigarettes, in twenty years there won't be any companies to blame (and sue) when we know the full effects.

Physical fitness

We often hear the advice "be fit" these days. Many of us though have become desensitized to the role of physical fitness in good health. Fitness, in particular cardiovascular fitness, influences memory and learning. Let's explore some of the reasons. Improving fitness leads to:

- **Improved blood flow, improved circulation and more blood pumped.** All these provide more blood to the brain, making sure there is enough oxygen and glucose available for the brain's work.

- **More and better quality blood.** Better fitness increases blood production, resulting in more volume and more red blood cells (the oxygen carrying cells).

- **Improved lung efficiency.** Exercise helps increase the surface area in the lungs, resulting in better oxygen uptake and carbon dioxide removal.

- **Better immune and lymphatic systems.** Exercise helps keep your immune and lymphatic systems in shape too. This helps prevent disease and infection, as well as making it less likely you suffer from colds and other minor illnesses. This means illness is less likely to interrupt your learning program.

The basic mechanism for getting and staying fit is easy. Get your heart rate up to sixty to seventy percent of your maximum rate for at least thirty minutes, at least three times a week. A common guideline for your maximum heart rate (in beats per minute, or BPM) is 220 minus your age (in years). This applies to both men and women☺.

Let's assume you are forty years old. Your maximum heart rate would be 220-40 = 180 BPM. Therefore a good exercise range would be 60-70% of 180 BPM, or roughly 108 to 122 BPM.

The difficulty for most people is the will power to start. I hope this information provides you with more reasons for you to get you started on a general fitness program, if you are not already reasonably fit. You can also use some of the goal setting and assertion techniques described later in this book. It doesn't have to be much. A brisk 30-minute walk a few times a week could be a good start. You soon notice the benefits!

> **Example Physical Relaxation Exercise**
>
> Here is an example relaxation exercise that focuses on physical relaxation.
>
> 1. Close your eyes. If you can, lie down (unless you are tired - you may fall asleep. Sit up in a chair if you are tired).
>
> 2. Clench your whole body. Pull taught every muscle you can feel... tightly! Make a face. Strain those arms, legs, shoulders, everywhere. Hold for about ten seconds. Then let go.
>
> 3. Do this again but focus on individual muscle groups one at a time. Start at your toes, then your calves, quads, all the way up to the muscles around your face. Strain and relax each group for around five seconds.
>
> 4. Breathe in for a beat of 1, 2, 3. Then out on a beat of 1, 2, 3, 4, 5, 6. Fill your lungs to capacity. Visualize relaxation flowing into your body through your lungs as you breathe in, and then feel tension and stress flow out of your body as you breathe out.
>
> 5. Repeat the above with beats of 1, 2, 3, 4. Then out on a beat of 1, 2, 3, 4, 5, 6, 7, 8. Your breath out is twice as long breathing out as you do in.
>
> 6. Repeat step 5, breathing in for five, then six beats (ie out on ten, then twelve beats). If you can comfortably go higher, then do so. Don't stretch it though. (If you get light-headed you are probably going too far!)
>
> 7. Then go backwards, starting at six beats in (twelve out), then five in (ten out), down to three in (six out).
>
> That's it. This exercise is a good way to relax before starting any kind of study or work requiring concentration. It's also a good exercise to do when you are feeling stressed, pressured, angry, or upset. It helps you wind down and puts you in a better peace of mind.

As with all changes in lifestyle, be sure to consult a doctor if it has been a while since you last exercised.

Physical relaxation

There has been much publicity about the role relaxation plays in learning. Examples include the SuperLearning system and variations such as "The Mozart Effect." Authors claim these systems provide incredibly high learning performance in a relaxed state. Unfortunately there have not been clear clinical studies that support the theory that relaxation induced by music provides greatly increased learning performance.

There are particular reasons though why you should incorporate relaxation (both physical and mental) into your learning state.

- **Relaxation exercises improve concentration.** Basic relaxation exercises before study can help clear the mind of distractions and concerns.

- **Relaxation exercises reduce stress.** Stress has a direct impact on memory. While short-term stress doesn't always degrade learning new information, it does degrade recall of previously learned information. Long-term excessive stress can also irreparably damage parts of the brain used in learning new information.

If you feel stressed before or during a study period, you may want to spend a few minutes doing a relaxation exercise. You can also use these relaxation exercises to increase the effectiveness of study breaks. Contrary to popular opinion though, doing specific relaxation exercises if you already feel relaxed won't significantly increase your learning performance.

Relaxation exercises appear more useful in lowering long-term stress. Consider making relaxation exercises part of your daily routine, even if only for twenty minutes. Relaxation exercises can also help you get to sleep faster.

Note that the exercises in this section focus on physical relaxation. In the next section on mental learning state, more exercises focus on mental relaxation. They support each other though. Combine them and you get a better result. Let's look at some types of physical relaxation exercises:

- **Deep breathing.** Deep breathing involves abdominal breathing for 10-20 minutes. You take shorter breaths in and longer breaths out. If you start to feel light-headed or get a tingling sensation, you may be doing the cycle too fast. See the text box on page 33 for an example.

- **Progressive Muscular Relaxation (PMR).** PMR involves progressively tensing and relaxing groups of muscles. The principle is that if you tense a muscle and then let it go, it should be in a more relaxed state. It is also easier to relax muscles this way instead of trying to detect tense muscles and release them. The relaxation exercise example in the text box on page 33 also includes a basic version of PMR.

- **Autogenics.** Autogenics is a relaxation skill that takes some time to learn (roughly three months), but provides better and faster relaxation once mastered. It first involves learning to produce a sense of limpness, heaviness and warmth in your body, and then involves explicitly slowing your breathing and heart rate. The result is you can deeply relax in only a few minutes, whenever you need it.

- **Sensory deprivation, for example float tanks.** Rather than being a passing fad, float tanks do have a significant amount of controlled research backing up their marketed benefits. They greatly assist relaxation. They also improve general health and performance. These tanks work by removing as much physical stimulation as possible. They are usually lightproof and soundproof, the temperature is typically at skin temperature, and you float on a buoyant solution of water and Epsom salts. These conditions can induce a deeper relaxation response than is possible using standard relaxation techniques, although you can't always use float tanks when you want to! Float tanks can also provide you with a guide to what deep relaxation can be like. This can improve your relaxation exercises outside the tank.

- **Massage.** Massage can also induce the relaxation response in many individuals, however it may not always suit your study timing as it typically involves another person.

- **Biofeedback.** Biofeedback is a technology that has only become readily available to consumers over the past few years. It involves using electronic equipment to provide you with various biological statistics, such as heart rate, blood pressure, skin temperature or muscle tension. Using this technology, you can train yourself to understand how well your body is performing. Using this information you can then influence body systems previously thought to be unconscious. This technology is only just starting to become useful to the general population. Expect to see more in the future.

Physical environment

Your physical environment influences your learning performance. Correct temperature, fresh clean air, good light, supportive furniture, and nearby services (rest rooms, break areas, etc.) all contribute to good learning. Let's look at these in more detail.

Correct temperature

Your body works well in a reasonably limited temperature range. The best temperature for learning is around 73°F or 23°C. Even small variations from this temperature have a noticeable impact on learning. For example, a temperature of 78°F or 26°C decreases learning performance.

Fresh clean air

The key purpose of fresh air is not so much to replace oxygen, but rather to remove carbon dioxide. In confined unventilated spaces, the build-up of carbon dioxide affects you first, long before the oxygen levels drop far enough to cause any issues. Carbon dioxide can negatively affect your learning state even before you feel the effects.

It's rather startling to see how fast carbon dioxide builds up in a confined space. Let's use a small tutorial-style classroom as an example. Take four students (sitting) and one teacher (standing) in a small closed room approx 10.5 X 12 X 8 feet, or 3.2 X 3.7 X 2.8 metres. These people create enough carbon dioxide to cause increased breathing rates and headaches in some people after forty minutes, and significant symptoms after ninety minutes. The same can happen in larger rooms with lots of people sitting closely together.

Carbon dioxide more quickly affects some individuals depending on their location in the room, their health, and whether they smoke. For example, it more quickly affects a teacher who is standing up. Carbon dioxide rich air is usually warmer from being in the lungs of those in the room. If the room temperature is not too hot, this warmer air rises to the upper part of the room. The teacher, standing up, is the first to breathe this air containing more carbon dioxide.

Be aware of ventilation and fresh air in any enclosed building. Even with ventilation, carbon dioxide levels may rise and affect you without you being aware. Be doubly careful in colder climates where heating (especially from naked flame heaters) can significantly add to carbon dioxide levels. Also, you may have heard of "sick buildings." A lack of ventilation from the outside sometimes causes more than average health issues for the building's occupants. Sometimes the building designers may be at fault, however building owners or operators sometimes cause this problem when they close fresh air vents to save on heating costs.

Good light

Common sense usually tells you if you have enough light for learning. For reading and writing work, light should be reasonably bright. Dim lighting is important when viewing video or projection based presentations (eg overheads or computer projectors). Dim light can also be helpful during relaxation exercises. Avoid dim lighting in the afternoon though, especially just after lunchtime, as it is likely to encourage drowsiness with negative impacts on learning.

On a related point, there is little reliable proof to suggest that "full spectrum lighting" has any direct effect on learning. Full spectrum light includes sunlight. Some manufacturers now make artificial lights that supposedly give lighting that is more balanced. In my view, your *beliefs* about lighting affect your learning performance far more than sunlight or full spectrum lighting.

Supportive furniture

The furniture you use directly affects your posture, which in turn affects your learning potential. Muscular tension caused by poor furniture, or poor use of furniture, uses up blood and energy. This can draw blood and energy away from the brain, resulting in less efficient learning.

Use correct furniture and use furniture correctly! Also, avoid introducing tension. For example, sit somewhere in class where you direct face the instructor or teacher, rather than having to turn your body or head significantly to look at them.

Nearby services

If you are responsible for selecting a learning location, be sure to address easy access to restrooms, break areas, food and water, and other services such as phones. Good access to these services usually helps students concentrate more.

Body and brain rhythms

Your body runs to many cycles and rhythms. Two important cycles have a direct impact on your ability to learn efficiently. One is the circadian rhythm, familiar to us as the daily pattern of waking and sleeping. Circadian means once a day. The second less-known rhythm runs to a rough ninety-minute cycle. This is an *ultradian rhythm*. Ultradian means more than once a day. Both of these rhythms have an important role in learning. As well as these overall rhythms, there is also a brain characteristic I've called "Brain Drain" that you should also consider when planning breaks. Let's look at these now.

The circadian rhythm

The circadian rhythm wakes us up in the morning and makes us sleepy late in the evening. Set by daylight and darkness, the circadian rhythm is powerful. It drives the release of various substances in the brain at different times of the day to induce sleep or to wake you up. It does this because the body usually can't work properly for more than twenty-four hours without sleep.

Researchers are yet to identify the exact workings of sleep, however much is already known sleep and learning performance. Sleep affects memory and learning both before and after a lesson:

- **Before your lesson.** Without enough sleep, it's harder to concentrate and focus on the material you are learning. The easiest way to forget something is to not pay attention when you are learning it! By making sure you have had enough sleep in the days before lessons, you are more likely to learn efficiently. This also goes for exams. Last-minute late-night cramming may cost you more because a lack of sleep makes it harder to remember what you do know during the exam!

- **After your lesson.** Some evidence suggests the quality of sleep after a lesson may influence how well you recall what you learned. There is still much debate on this particular topic, however it's clear that sleep is an integral part of good learning performance.

The circadian rhythm also has a large impact on your learning effectiveness through the day. The following graph gives a general indication of alertness during the day. The alertness curve reflects the effect that the circadian rhythm, and other rhythms, has on your body and brain. At the bottom of the graph there are examples of activities best suited to that time of day.

Note that this curve assumes reasonably standard hours of daylight and darkness, and a normal working day. Those in more extreme climates, or on different work schedules, may have a different alertness graph.

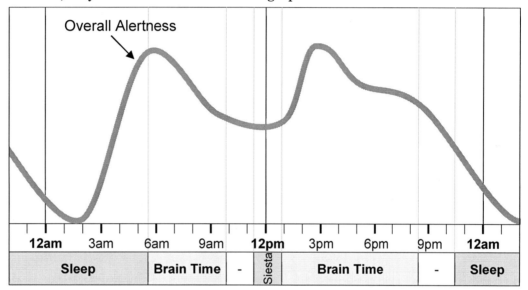

Of particular interest:

- **The morning brainwork period.** The body and brain is usually more alert and creative earlier in the morning. This is usually the best time for brain work. If you think you are the opposite, pay attention to my comments further on about the "lark-owl" myth.

- **Lunchtime siesta.** Around lunchtime, your body naturally wants a short sleep, typically between 11am and 1pm. Some cultures have given up the afternoon siesta for continued work, often with a loss of productivity and safety. Work accident statistics show for example that workplace accidents are more likely to occur during and after this time. If possible, a brief 30-minute nap during this time can bring you many benefits, including better concentration and alertness for the rest of the afternoon. If a nap in the office cubicle or classroom is not possible, know that you probably won't be at peak performance for a while. This may help you schedule your activities to make the most of this down time.

- **The afternoon power period.** After this siesta time, the afternoon is usually good for productive brainwork, however it's also during this time your body is also primed for physical achievements.

- **The evening wind-down.** As the evening progresses, your body prepares for sleep. Your body temperature drops, and sleep hormones increase. You still feel reasonably alert during this time though because of another body cycle. Your body has an inbuilt system that usually prevents you from falling into deep sleep fewer than fifteen to nineteen hours since you last slept. Once you pass this period though, it's usually a steep descent into sleepiness.

Lastly, let's put to rest a common myth about sleeping patterns. The "lark-owl" myth, although popular, is essentially unfounded. The myth is that you are either a morning person (lark) or evening person (owl). In truth, you can switch from one to the other within a few days simply by going to sleep thirty to forty-five minutes earlier or later each day. Given the body's natural brainpower period earlier in the morning, there may be benefits in switching to be a lark if you are currently an owl.

The ninety-minute ultradian rhythm

Although you may not have heard of it, the ninety-minute ultradian rhythm also affects your learning performance. Essentially the brain works on a ninety-minute cycle of alertness and rest. You feel alert for about seventy minutes, and then your alertness drops for about twenty minutes. This natural cycle helps your brain take a break. Consider taking a short break when you feel the first wave of tiredness wash over you, for example at the first time your eyelids drop. Perhaps do a relaxation exercise. Also, try to keep lessons or continued mental activity to within 70-80 minute periods.

In the early afternoon, you are especially susceptible to tiredness when the sleepiness of the circadian rhythm and a dip of the ultradian rhythm coincide. Add the effects of a big lunch and you get a triple-dose of sleep inducing agents. Again, it's better to try to work with this natural schedule rather than trying to work through it.

Brain drain

Prolonged mental activity without breaks can literally *drain your brain* of two key materials needed for learning and recall. These materials are neurotransmitters and glucose. "Brain Drain" is in this section of the book because it's a cycle of use and replenishment of these key materials. You need to take this cycle into account when planning breaks during study.

- **Neurotransmitters.** The brain only has limited levels of neurotransmitters available at any one time. It takes time to create more as the brain uses them up, especially during learning. Prolonged mental activity without breaks can reduce neurotransmitter levels in key areas responsible for learning, making it harder to learn effectively.

- **Glucose.** In addition, prolonged mental activity can also drain certain parts of the brain of glucose, the key nutrient the brain uses for energy. This may be more pronounced as you get older. In addition, study that involves sitting inanimate at a desk or in front of a computer lowers your heart rate. Lower heart rate means less blood delivered to the brain, which then means less available glucose for your neurons.

While there is still more research needed in this area, these points further support the case for regular breaks during learning. There is an interesting twist here though - the ultradian rhythm prefers a more relaxing break, however light exercise would likely best resolve "Brain Drain" described here. Personally I try to alternate between these two types of breaks.

* * *

So what's the best pattern to use when studying or learning? In summary:

- Get enough good sleep, both before and after study.
- Get up earlier in the morning, and do more study in the morning period (if possible)
- Don't study intensively for more than forty to forty-five minutes at a time
- Alternate breaks between light exercise and relaxation. Try to time the relaxation break to your ultradian rhythm.

Dietary supplements

A healthy and balanced diet is the most important nutritional contributor to well functioning memory. Over the years though there has been hundreds of memory and brainpower improvement supplements advertised. Unfortunately, most of these are ineffective and some are dangerous.

There are certain drugs and substances that do improve memory and learning though. I'll discuss some of these in this section. A huge number of supplements on the market, though, don't have satisfactory testing. We don't know if they work as marketed, nor do we know the *contraindications*. Contraindications describe when you shouldn't use the supplement because you have an existing condition or you taking other drugs. You may want to avoid any supplement that doesn't have independent medical research to provide such information.

You can use the Internet to research information on drugs and their effects. *Pubmed* ⊕, on the Internet, is a good place to start. It's a publicly available database based on *MEDLINE*, the reference source for medical research information. If Pubmed doesn't mention a drug, or if it contains citations linking a drug to negative research, that's usually a good sign to stay away.

Be mindful of other sites you visit on the Internet. If a site describes the benefits of a particular supplement, and also sells it, you may want to look elsewhere for independent information.

In this section I share with you the results of some of the latest research on dietary supplements that can aid memory and learning. Before I do so, there are three important points to keep in mind.

- **These supplements only alter basic brain functions.** For example, it's unlikely they can directly change your attitudes towards learning. If you believe you are a bad learner, a supplement may help you remember more reasons to support that belief! Your beliefs about your learning ability have far more impact on your learning effectiveness than any dietary supplement. Once you do have the right beliefs about learning, these supplements may then improve your overall learning performance.
- **If you are going to use a supplement, buy from a large reputable manufacturer.** The quality and safety of products from large manufacturers is likely to be higher because they usually aim to preserve their reputation.
- **If you are a pilot, surgeon or other similar professional, you should only try dietary supplements after a discussion with your flight surgeon or medical practitioner.** While I've only included supplements with a

reasonable body of research, there may still be contraindications for your particular conditions and activities. Until you have discussed a supplement with your medical practitioner, avoid using it for at least twenty-four hours before critical activities.

I present the safer supplements in two groups: Those that appear to have good overall memory effects and those that have partial memory effects. I've also included some information about unproven, ineffective or unsafe supplements.

NOTE: The US Food and Drug Administration (FDA) and similar government agencies in other countries have not tested nor approved many of the supplements below. The information presented here is for informational purposes only. These supplements are not intended to diagnose, treat, cure or prevent any disease or condition. See the notes at the start of this chapter about getting proper advice for your personal situation.

Good overall memory effects

After much research there are only three supplements I believe have good overall memory and learning improvement effects, while being safe. These are B-group vitamins, Ginkgo Biloba and Brahmi.

- **Vitamins B1, B3 and B6.** Ensuring your daily intake of Thiamine (B1), Niacin (B3), and Pyridoxine (B6) at least meets the recommended daily allowance, or RDA. These three vitamins have significant brain benefits, with little risk, at these levels. You can usually meet the RDA through a normal diet. You may want to consider a supplement if you suspect your intake is below the RDA. You can typically find RDAs on government sites on the Internet. 🜚

  Not only do these vitamins keep your brain functioning properly, they can also have positive cognitive and memory improvements when taken in larger doses. For example, Niacin studies show that it can improve brain processing and working memory of young to middle-aged people. Tests used dosages five to ten times the RDA without ill effect, however these tests are usually for short periods. If you are considering these larger doses, it's wise to first discuss this with your medical practitioner.

- **Ginkgo Biloba Extract (GBE).** Ginkgo Biloba is an ancient Chinese tree (another name is the Maidenhair Tree). Ginkgo Biloba extract comes from the leaves of the tree. The extract improves memory and cognitive abilities in healthy younger (eighteen to forty year old) individuals. It improves blood circulation, and this means more oxygen, energy and nutrient enriched blood reaches more parts of the brain. Contrary to earlier research though, recent studies suggest it's not as effective in older healthy individuals.

  The general daily dosage of *standardized GBE* is 120mg to 240mg a day. Standardized GBE (typically available in health food stores) contains twenty-four percent of the key active ingredient, ginkgo-flavone glycosides. Therefore, a typical daily intake of 160mg provides 38mg of glycosides. Note that some products give the potency of preparations as the equivalent dry leaf weight. It takes about 8,000mg of dry leaf to make 160mg of GBE, or a 50:1 ratio. The sidebar has an example to help you understand these calculations.

Many preparations contain low levels of extract for their price, so check the strength before you buy. Typically the higher strength products are better value for money. Also, buy a reputable brand.

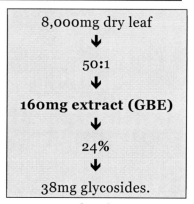

As GBE has partial blood thinning properties, those with blood related issues should not use it. If you have clotting disorders, are taking anticoagulants, aspirin or other blood thinning medications you should consult a medical practitioner before taking GBE. If you are to undergo surgery, let the surgeon know you use it.

- **Brahmi (Bacopa Monnieri).** Similar to Ginkgo, Brahmi also appears to improve memory and learning performance. Clinical studies on healthy adults suggest that Brahmi reduces forgetting of newly learned information. It also appears to improve visual information processing, learning rate and memory consolidation. Best effects appear after twelve weeks of daily use.

  Western research has not yet determined why Brahmi works. It may improve blood circulation in the brain or it may be an anti-oxidant. It may also directly affect brain functioning, for example in the hippocampus.

  Daily dosage recommendations vary. Literature suggests a dosage of 45mg to 135mg of the primary active ingredients, "Bacosides A & B" a day. This equals 2g to 6g of the whole plant using a standardized extract. Some providers suggest a double dosage for the first twelve weeks. Be sure to check the manufacturer's recommendation and use this as the primary guide.

  There are few side effects or warnings for Brahmi. Various materials suggest you should avoid Brahmi if you are pregnant or suffer from an infectious illness. It may also have a sedative effect in some individuals.

  One last point on Brahmi: Don't confuse Brahmi, or Bacopa Monnieri, with Gotu Kola, or Centella asiatica. Gotu Kola is also sometimes called Brahmi. There is less clinical research on the effectiveness and side effects of Gotu Kola.

Some memory effects

Two further supplements appear to have some effects on memory and learning. These are caffeine and Acetyl-L-Carnitine.

- **Caffeine.** Caffeine may be the most widely used psychoactive drug in western society. It improves alertness, reaction times and information processing. This indirectly helps you learn and remember new information. Caffeine is also helpful in creative tasks, such as writing and free association. This aids techniques described later such as association and visualization.

  Caffeine is helpful in these activities as well as simple and repetitive tasks. However, caffeine can interfere as tasks get more complex. It can degrade our ability to pick out important information in a high workload environment, keep that information in working memory, and solve complex problems. As the load on working memory increases, the effect of caffeine changes from good to bad. You may want to keep this in mind if you are performing complex activities.

Like other drugs, it's essential to know when to use caffeine. Indeed, it appears that some of the negative side effects of caffeine only appear if you abuse it. Here are some points to keep in mind:

- Use it after sleep. Use caffeine in the morning to speed the transition from sleep to full mental alertness. It's also useful after a lunchtime siesta. Some researchers believe the only "right" time to use caffeine is after sleep or rest.
- Use it for creative activities. Such as writing, visualization and association activities.
- Avoid it before bed. Caffeine has a half-life in the body of 6 hours. Use of caffeine before bedtime negatively influences sleep patterns. This may then mean you want more caffeine the next day!
- Don't use it as a substitute for sleep. You should not use caffeine to battle circadian sleepiness. This is where people abuse caffeine the most, and also where most side effects appear. These side effects can include irritability, depression and overwhelming tiredness.
- Minimal use during flying and other complex high-workload activities. Discuss with your flight surgeon or medical practitioner if you need to work at times that conflict with your circadian rhythm.

Safe dosages range between 200 to 400mg a day. Rough amounts of caffeine in typical drinks are: coffee - 100mg a cup, tea - 50mg a cup, cola soft drink - 40mg a can.

- **Acetyl-L-Carnitine.** This is an amino acid typically available over the counter. Some studies show it to have cognitive benefit to older people suffering from Alzheimer's disease. It may be effective in reducing the effects of age-related cognitive or memory decline. It does not appear useful to younger healthy adults.

General dosages are in the 1g to 1.5g a day range. There are no reported warnings. Note that this supplement is functionally different to a similarly named compound called DL-carnitine. DL-carnitine can negatively interfere with brain and muscle cells.

Potentially Dangerous Supplements

Here are some examples of supplements that highlight the need for careful research before use:

Fipexide (also known as Visilor, Attentil, and BP662) may have some positive memory effects but it could also cause liver damage.

Inderel, often sold over the Internet, has some cognitive effect but can cause problems in those with heart, lung, diabetic, liver, or kidney problems. In addition, it could fatally interact with some prescription drugs.

Vincamine, often marketed as safe, could cause severe heart problems if used over a long term. These could be fatal.

Vasopressin, also known as Ditressin, Syntopressin, and Diapid, could induce life-threatening problems in healthy individuals and could be fatal to those with certain diseases. It's also sold over the Internet.

Ineffective, unsafe or unknown

There are many other supplements marketed as having worthwhile effects on memory and brainpower. Some of these may fall into one of the following three categories:

- **No effect.** The effect on memory and learning has proven minimal in some research.

- **Dangerous.** The supplement has serious contraindications. Some possible contraindications even include cardiac and cancer complications, so don't take this warning lightly!

- **Unknown.** There is no known reliable research on either the benefits or the contraindications, or research is still contradictory. No reliable research may mean there are serious contraindications we don't know about yet.

See the textbox above for some examples.

ⓘ *Be sure to do plenty of research before trying or continuing to use any supplement as a memory aid!*

On the website there are references to materials that contain more information on commonly available supplements. One book alone lists more than twenty-five supplements that appear to have little effect, may be dangerous or are unproven🌐.

Mental state—get your mind ready for learning

The last learning state layer, mental state, deals with the mind. The inner state layers (cell and physical) influence the mind and its workings, however this layer is also influenced by our own thoughts. Six key contributors to good mental state are:

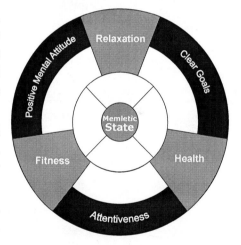

- **General mental health.** Good mental health supports learning performance. Stress and Depression are prevalent today and have a harmful effect.

- **Mental fitness.** Like physical fitness, mental fitness benefits the whole brain. You can develop mental fitness through mental exercises and other activities.

- **Mental relaxation.** Mental relaxation also plays a role in supporting good mental performance.

- **Attention and concentration.** If you concentrate and pay attention when you learn, your content has a much better chance of making it into your long-term memory.

- **Positive mental attitude.** Your self-image influences your memory and learning performance. You can alter your self-image through self-talk.

- **Clear, desirable and achievable goals.** If you don't believe in the direction your learning is taking you, it's unlikely you can sustain good learning performance.

General mental health

Like good physical health, good mental health contributes to good learning performance. There are many ways you can improve and maintain your overall mental health. Some examples include:

- **Take time out.** Take time out from a busy schedule occasionally. There are many ways to do this. Start a hobby, go for a walk, get some exercise, spend time with friends, take up art, singing, or music, keep a journal, or paint the fence. These kinds of activities can give your brain a welcome mental break and help preserve good mental health.

- **Make positive choices.** Two people may react to an event in two different ways. Let's take an example of changing jobs. One person may see this change as a time of excitement and opportunity. The other may see it as a negative and stressful experience. This choice has a significant physical effect on the brain. In the one who makes the positive choice to see the change as an exciting opportunity, the brain releases more neurotransmitters that support that good mood (such as dopamine). In the one who sees the change as stressful, the brain releases more cortisol, a stress hormone. Cortisol damages the brain. The only difference between these two outcomes (one keeping the brain healthy, one killing brain cells) is the mental choice that each of these individuals made.

  You always have a choice in how you react to the events that life presents you. Reacting to events in a negative way is still a choice in itself. Believing you have no choice is just mental laziness.

Good mental health also needs the absence (or control) of a wide range of possible mental illnesses. These can include disorders such as anxiety disorders, Attention Deficit disorders, Borderline Personality Disorders, Obsessive-Compulsive disorders, Panic Disorders, Post-Traumatic Stress Disorders, Schizophrenia, and Phobias. The two most prevalent mental health issues in the western world today though are excessive stress and depression. These are the two I talk about here.

Seven of the top ten causes of death in the USA associate stress as a primary contributor. This includes heart disease, the top killer. Depression is the top ranked disability in the world for those aged fifteen to forty-four years old. Both of these health issues negatively affect learning and memory:

- **Stress.** Both mental and physical stress causes the body to release cortisol. Cortisol has both an immediate and a long-term negative effect on memory and cognitive performance. Long-term excessive stress can irreparably damage how the body regulates cortisol levels. This can lead to shrinkage in the hippocampus, resulting in irreversible memory performance decline. Stress can also increase the occurrence of depression in those more susceptible to the illness.

- **Depression.** Researchers link long-term depression to lower levels of serotonin, a key neurotransmitter needed for learning. Depression also negatively affects energy levels, attention and concentration. Both of these side-effects of depression result in decreased learning performance.

If you suffer from either of these two issues, or any of the others listed above, you should seek assistance from a suitable medical practitioner. These are serious illnesses.

Mental fitness

You can improve your memory and learning performance if you improve your overall mental fitness. There are many likenesses between physical and mental fitness. Let's explore some:

- You can build up your mental fitness over time using various exercises and activities.
- You should not expect immediate results. Good results come with time.
- Good mental fitness impacts many other areas of brain performance, not just those directly involved in the exercises.
- Don't try to do too much at once. Start slowly and find exercises you enjoy and could do regularly.
- Good mental fitness protects the brain and helps it stay healthy for longer.

As I mentioned, various exercises and activities can increase your mental fitness. I've listed some examples below:

- **Try Neurobics.** Neurobics is a relatively new term for a style of brain exercises. Neurobic exercises involve at least one of three features: "They involve one or more of your senses in a novel way, they engage your attention, and they break up a routine activity in an unexpected, novel way." Examples from a book called "Keep Your Brain Alive" (by Lawrence Katz) include:
  - Changing the hand you write or brush your teeth with.
  - Taking a different route, or means of transport, to work.
  - Finding your way around a room with your eyes closed.
  - Interacting with others without talking.
  - Turning pictures or a clock on your desk upside-down.
  - Tasting food with your eyes closed.
  - ...and more - the book contains eighty-three examples!

- **Learn music or singing.** Learning a musical instrument or learning to sing at any age does not just develop your aural skills. It also exercises your memory and concentration skills, and positively influences your visual and spatial reasoning abilities.

- **Games and puzzles.** Many games and puzzles exercise various mental skills - from the basic "Concentration" card game through to whole books of puzzles that challenge various parts of the brain. Many of these are available free on the web. (I talk more about the Concentration game on page 49).

- **Try some software.** You can exercise your brain and memory with the help of some specialist software. Some examples include IQ Builder, Brain Builder and MindGym and various packages based on the "Concentration" card game. Be wary of anything that has an excessive price or that promotes it can improve mental performance without any effort on your part. Examples include only listening to sounds or music, or watching light patterns, or "altering brainwaves."

- **Travel.** Travel, especially international travel, exercises a wide range of brain abilities. Finding your way around with a map, running into unexpected problems, being aware of your surroundings, planning and getting lost are some examples. More include currency conversions, breaking your usual routines, developing your understanding of history and other cultures and trying to communicate with others without a common language. All these activities are great for exercising your brain and are the perfect excuse for an overseas holiday!

These are just a start. There are so many other ways to exercise your brain. Here are some quick thoughts: Learn another language, develop your social networks, do volunteer work, read more widely, or try a new hobby. More include: Get creative and learn to write, draw, or paint; learn photography, change careers, or learn to fly! All of these contribute to good mental fitness, so long as you keep a positive mental attitude while doing them.

Mental relaxation

Earlier in this chapter I discussed physical relaxation and the effect that has on the body-mind system. In this section, I focus on mental relaxation and some of the techniques you can use.

The primary purpose of mental relaxation, for learning, is to control stress. We are all subject to mental stress in our daily lives. Work is typically the highest cause of stress. Use these exercises regularly in your daily cycle to help manage the impact of stress on your mind.

As I mentioned in physical relaxation though, there is little reliable evidence to suggest that relaxation directly before or during a learning activity significantly improves learning performance. Specific relaxation exercises before or during a learning activity appears useful if you feel stressed or lacking in concentration. Use the exercises to get into a better state of mind for learning.

Let's look at some common mental relaxation exercises:

- **Meditation.** Meditation is a healthy modern activity. You don't need to submit to the traditional religious or spiritual dogma once associated with its practice, and it does not need to be complex. The basic exercise of sitting calmly and focusing on the breath is often the most effective form and provides many of the benefits ascribed to meditation. This includes good relaxation and better overall concentration. Find a good reference (you can learn it from a book) or attend a class if that suits you better.

- **Guided imagery.** Guided imagery involves concentrating on a scene or script that helps you relax. An example of a simple script may involve walking along a beach and then swimming in the surf. Another example could be walking through a warm forest, coming across a waterfall, stripping off your clothes and swimming under the falling water.

  You can use many methods to guide you through the visualization. You may choose to write basic points of the script first, and then rely on your memory to take you through the scene. You could record your own voice and play it back, or you could try a commercial recording. In my view you are better off recording your own script.

  The main point is to stay focused on the imagery. Concentrate on experiencing as many of the senses as possible. Feel the wind on the beach, smell the thick air of the rainforest, and feel the cool water as you are swimming. If you find your concentration wandering onto another topic, simply bring it back to where you where in your script and continue.

- **Music.** There is a widespread misrepresentation that music offers huge gains in learning performance. In many controlled studies music alone has not performed much better than silence in improving learning and memory. Music does have a role to play in heightening relaxation though. Many clinical studies show that certain types of music increase relaxation—some types more than others. When combined with other relaxation techniques, music can further increase relaxation. For example, using music with Progressive Muscle Relaxation (PMR) increases relaxation more than just doing PMR alone. Personally, I also find music useful for relaxation and concentration when there is some distracting noise in the background.

  Let's look at some points to keep in mind if you want to try music for relaxation. First, *choose music and volume that feels relaxing to you*. Don't worry too much about the supposed effectiveness of the different types of music (except rock and rap music, as this increases stress in many individuals). Second, try music with a slower beat. Lastly, if you are studying or relaxing you may want to avoid music with singing or voices as these can distract you.

- **Anchoring.** Try creating some anchors for specific times where you feel the most relaxed (I describe anchors in the Memletic Techniques chapter). Later, when you want to take a moment to relax, use your anchor to quickly bring back the relaxation response you experienced during the exercise.

You don't necessarily need complex relaxation exercises. The simplest exercises often work best because you think about them less. Most of the mental relaxation exercises simply aim to train the mind to avoid unwanted thoughts for a while. Use whatever method you find works best for you.

You may want to combine these mental relaxation techniques with physical relaxation exercises (from the physical state layer) to achieve the maximum benefit for the time spent.

Control stress and fear with relaxation

I've already mentioned that when under stress the body releases a hormone called cortisol. Cortisol can inhibit memory recall. After a stressful incident cortisol may reach a level that impacts your memory performance after thirty minutes. It then takes a few hours for the effect to wear off.

This is why staying relaxed before and during an exam or test is important, as is how you react to incidents during that time. If you make a mistake at the start of an exam, take a moment to relax and ensure you don't let your stress response go too far. If you let that mistake start to stress you further, your cortisone rises and thirty minutes later, you will find it harder to remember what you already know.

Fear and nervousness are also harmful to good learning state. Often you can overcome nervousness by simply relaxing and getting your breathing back in control. Later in the book, in the Challenges section, I provide you with specific strategies for dealing with risks, fears and nervousness, as well as some other common challenges.

Attention and concentration

Attention and concentration are fundamental to learning and memorizing. If you don't pay attention when you first encounter a particular fact, it's unlikely it even makes it into your memory. If it isn't in there, you don't have much chance of recalling it.

Nearly all the other good state principles influence your attention and concentration. For example, a distracting environment affects your concentration. Not eating well or failing to follow natural body rhythms also negatively impacts concentration. You may also find it hard to concentrate if you don't believe the material you are studying contributes to your overall goals.

If you find your concentration wandering or staying attentive is difficult, scan through all the state layers and see if there is an obvious problem somewhere.

You may also want to try some specific concentration techniques during study, or try some longer-term exercises to improve your overall concentration. Let's look at these two in more detail.

Concentration techniques during study

Some specific techniques can help you stay focused on your material. These include:

- **"Be here now."** Every time you find yourself distracted, say "Be Here Now." Say it aloud if possible, otherwise just repeat it in your mind. Then bring your attention back to your task. In the beginning, you may find that you do this a lot. Over time, you gain more focus and your mind stays where you want it.

- **The spider approach.** If you hold a vibrating tuning fork next to a spider web, the spider usually comes to see what's happening, thinking it may be an insect. Do it a few times and the spider eventually chooses to ignore the distraction. You too can train yourself to ignore distractions. The sensations from your ears and eyes are simply sensations you can choose whether to react to or not.

- **Paragraph marking.** If you are reading a book or article, tick each paragraph as you read it. Use a pencil in case you want to re-read parts of it later.

- **Keep a distraction log**. Every time you find yourself distracted, draw a tick or write the current time on a separate piece of paper. This is your *distraction log*. Initially the number of distractions may surprise you. By highlighting your distractions, you can begin to control and reduce them.

- **Write down distractions.** If something important comes up as a distraction, simply write it down so you can deal with it later. Better yet, set a *distraction time*. Agree with yourself to take a break and deal with those distractions at that time.

- **Switch topics.** Rather than spending a long time on one particular topic, switch between various unrelated topics if possible. The brain loves variety and rewards you with better concentration.

- **Make it interactive.** If studying with others, plan some time to get together and discuss the material you are learning. Even if you are not at the same stage in the course, simply agree to spend ten minutes listening to one another talk about their current study topic.

Longer-term improvement of concentration

The previous techniques are good for keeping up concentration while you study. Some longer-term techniques can improve your overall concentration as well. These include:

- **Games.** The old card game of "Concentration" is still effective in improving concentration. If you have not come across it, the basic idea is to lay down a set of playing cards in a grid, all face-down. You then turn over a pair of cards. If they match number and color (if using playing cards), then you take them out of the grid. If they don't match, you place them back face down and pick another pair. Better concentration, through practice, results in a shorter time to clear the grid. You can also play with a friend for competition. The one with the most pairs at the end of the game wins!

  Many expensive software packages claiming to improve concentration still use this principle in many guises, often with pictures instead of playing cards. There are also free computer games, based on Concentration, available on the Internet. Using these and some notes in a spreadsheet to track progress can be just as effective as the more expensive packages. ☯

- **Meditation.** Meditation is an effective way of improving your concentration. See my comments in "Mental Relaxation" for more comments on meditation.

- **Other exercises.** Many other exercises can help you increase your concentration. From simply staring at a fixed point or candle, to martial arts, these can all help improve your overall concentration.

Environment and concentration

When possible, choose a place for learning that is relatively free from external distractions. This helps attention and concentration. Let family, friends, or colleagues know that you are studying and would prefer no interruptions for a while. Use a *do not disturb* sign—but don't overuse it!

Be aware of unwanted noise in your environment, including noise from overhead lights or electrical equipment. Consider using light background music to mask this noise if you are unable to control it.

Also, be aware of visual distractions, even if they are only in your peripheral vision. For example, while in a library sit facing a wall in a secluded area, rather than near a passageway or door.

Even in the best-planned environment, you may still have interruptions. Train yourself to pause for a moment before responding to an interruption. During that pause make a note, mentally or on paper, of where you are. It's then easier to regain your concentration when you return. How do you train yourself? An idea is to ask someone to help you. Role-play the interruption and your action!

Positive Mental Attitude (PMA)

Our beliefs significantly influence how well we learn and remember. Let's see an example. Yesterday someone told you a phone number, and today asked you whether you can remember it. Your ability to remember it largely depends on whether you *believe* you can remember it. If your first thought is "Of course I can remember, it's ..." then you are far more likely to recall the number. If your first thought is "There is no way I can remember that number. I didn't write it down" then it's a lot less likely you can remember it.

If you believe you have a good memory, your brain builds neural networks that support that belief. If you believe you have a bad memory, your brain builds neural networks that block recall of material that otherwise might be available. You consistently act in a manner that matches your self-image.

Self-image interacts with two other parts our mental attitude—Self-Talk and Self-Esteem. How is your self-image related to self-talk and self-esteem? The diagram on the right provides a basic summary. What you say to yourself (your automatic thoughts) guides how you see yourself, and this guides how you feel about yourself. The cycle can run the other way as well.

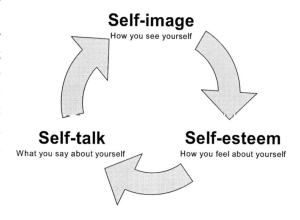

Self-image
How you see yourself

Self-talk
What you say about yourself

Self-esteem
How you feel about yourself

The good news is that you can change those neural networks that support your self-image. It's not difficult! You can use some of the techniques you learn later in this book to challenge and change negative self-talk. As you change your self-talk, it then starts to change your self-image, and from there your self-esteem. As those positive experiences build, it's easier to make more changes to what you think, feel, and say about yourself.

This is a fundamental way you can improve your mental attitude. "Quick Fix" techniques are unlikely to work in the long term if you don't address a faulty self-image.

Next is a basic outline on how you could use three techniques, assertions, mental firewall and anchoring, to help change your self-talk. I cover these techniques in the Memletic Techniques chapter.

Assertions

In summary, an assertion is a short positive phrase that asserts some behavior or outcome as if you have already achieved it, regardless of whether you have or not. Review the assertions below, and make up a few personal ones along similar lines. Write these down so that before each study or learning period, you can briefly review these assertions.

- I am a fast learner
- I pursue my objectives with determination
- I finish what I start
- I reward my achievements along the way
- I have an open mind to new information
- I am a learning adventurer

Mental firewall

Use the mental firewall technique to filter out negative and self-defeating self-talk. If you find yourself continually criticizing yourself, this is a good way to help change the habit. Replace those self-defeating thoughts with positive assertions and your self-image and self-esteem change to match.

Anchoring

Often you can look back over your life you and find some positive learning experiences. It may be a particular topic at school, or an activity such as music or sport. You can use the anchoring technique to recall similar positive feelings when you need them, for example at the start of a study period or during a difficult test.

* * *

Many issues can affect your positive mental attitude. If you feel your mental attitude is suffering, there is more information in the "Deal with Challenges" part of this book. This part deals with fear, motivation and other learning-related issues. Tackle and resolve these issues, if they arise, to stay in Memletic State.

Clear, desirable and achievable goals

A clear, desirable and achievable goal is important for good learning state. This provides the underlying motivation to start out the adventure, get through the tough times, and keep going until completion. If you don't believe in the direction your learning is taking you, you may not achieve anywhere near your full learning potential.

There are three key ingredients though that I find compelling and I recommend. Written objectives help clarify and keep your goal in your mind. Set various rewards for yourself along the path to celebrate each step of the way. Lastly, collect a set of images to help you visualize what success looks like.

Objectives

In the Memletic Approach chapter, I discuss in more detail how to create and use a written set of objectives. Review these objectives regularly to help your good learning state. Written goal scripts are also good to review occasionally.

Rewards

As you start each major learning activity, write down some rewards you can give yourself at different points along the way. These may be at various stages through your training, as well as once you have achieved your overall goal. Some may simply be to reward yourself for being on the journey anyway, not just at specific checkpoints. Examples might include going out for dinner to a great restaurant, buying a new piece of equipment, or simply taking a break away from training. The size of the reward does not have to reflect the scale of what you have achieved. Rewards may simply be symbolic of your achievement.

Build the enthusiasm of those around you, such as family members, by involving them in your rewards. Perhaps a weekend away with the family is a good way to help them feel more involved with your achievements, especially if you haven't paid them much attention recently.

Lastly, visualize (and write down) a certain activity you would like to do once you have completed your training. If you are learning to sail, perhaps it is to hire a yacht and sail to a particular location. If you are learning to fly, think about a particular flight you want to do as your "reward flight." Perhaps it's to fly up into the mountains and stay overnight at a remote airstrip. Perhaps fly cross-country to your home town or parent's home. If you are learning to dance, perhaps it's spending a night "out on the town" and staying at a luxury hotel.

Images

Start a collection of images, such as photographs, that are symbolic of your objective. If you are learning to sail and you have a particular yacht you would one day like to sail, try to get some photographs of it. If you are learning to fly, what about a location you would like to fly to once you have your pilot's license? If you are learning how to present or speak in public, have someone take a photo of you looking like you are presenting, even if you are not in front of an audience. You look calm and confident.

Use clear and provocative images that give you a sense of excitement when you see them. You may also want to write a script or short story that involves you and that particular picture, as if you have already achieved your goal. Think of the story each time you see the image.

Place these images in locations so you can see them before or during a lesson. Perhaps place them on the wall of your study or in the front of your folder or notebook. Another idea is to use the desktop or screensaver on your computer.

* * *

No doubt your path will change and obstacles will arise while you pursue your goals, however this is normal for any goal worth achieving. Keep these objectives, rewards and images close by as you start and progress. Refer to them often.

Chapter summary

Being in Memletic State means you are in peak condition for learning. It also helps you perform well in many other areas of your life.

You've seen how to make sure your cells get the materials they need to work correctly. Glucose is your brain's energy source. Your cells use oxygen to create energy from glucose. Water is important for transporting materials as well as protection. Basic nutrients help run the brain and protect it.

Good physical state comes from keeping your body systems in good condition. We've discussed general health, nutrition and fitness. You've seen the role relaxation plays in learning, and you know that the physical environment has a large influence on physical state. You now understand how important sleep is to learning, and how body and mind state change throughout the day. You've seen which supplements can improve brain performance, and you now understand the need for caution with all supplements.

Mental health, fitness and relaxation are three key contributors to good mental state. You now have some ways to keep up your attention and concentration during learning. You've seen how a positive mental attitude influences your mental state, as do clear, desirable and achievable goals.

You may already have a good idea of which parts of Memletic State you already have under control, as well as which parts may need more work. I covered Memletic State so you could start working on Memletic State while you read the rest of the book. In the next chapter on Memletic Process, we look at the steps you follow for fast learning and long-term recall.

LEARN with the Memletic Process

The Memletic Process is five core steps that help you learn faster and remember more. It uses much of what we know about strong learning performance. Each step provides you with new insights into learning well. All the steps together deliver a powerful and repeatable method for achieving many learning goals. Let's explore the Memletic Process...

The Memletic Process is five steps to follow while learning any new topic or skill. These steps are Locate, Explore, Arrange, Reinforce, and eNquire. The following diagram outlines these steps:

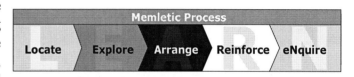

As you can see above, the first letters (or sounds) of these steps create the mnemonic LEARN. Here's a summary of each of these five steps:

- **Locate.** Find content for your course. This may involve using standard books and manuals, however it could also involve getting material from lectures, one-on-one tutoring sessions, the Internet and other references.

- **Explore.** Work through and understand your content. There are some general principles to follow, such as learning content using the *deeper, wider, higher* principle. You may also want to try some exploration techniques specific to your personal learning styles.

- **Arrange.** Prepare your content for memorization, where needed. In this step you select suitable techniques to reinforce the content you've explored, and then prepare content to use with those techniques

- **Reinforce.** In this step, you use the various techniques to reinforce knowledge, skills and behaviors. This book has many different techniques you can apply to various forms of content.

- **eNquire.** eNquire on your overall progress. Review both the content you've learned, as well as the effectiveness of the techniques and processes you've used along the way.

This chapter looks at each of these steps in more detail. Two quick points before we begin though. Firstly, you may find that you already use a similar approach when you are learning. That's fine. The Memletic Process makes each step clear. This helps you understand how the other parts of Memletics fit into your overall learning strategy. It also allows you to compare your current practices and discover if you're missing any key steps or activities.

Secondly, don't consider these steps as rigid or prescriptive. You may find that you move back and forward between the steps. In addition, you may not need to do all the steps for every learning objective.

For example, when you explore some material you may find you need more information on a particular topic, and so you go back to the Locate step to find it. Alternatively, when you start to reinforce (and practice) what you've learned, you may find you need to explore it further to understand it fully. Lastly, a simple learning objective may allow you to skip the explore step.

Locate—find content for learning

The locate step involves gathering the content you need for learning. Sometimes this may be easy. The course

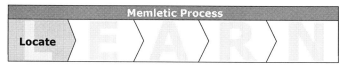

may prescribe texts and materials for you. At other times you may be learning something that few others have, so you have to forge your own way. You may be somewhere in the middle, with some texts prescribed for you and some further research to do.

Let's look at some typical content sources, as well as some general tips for locating content.

Content sources

There are many sources of content for learning. You may find some materials already well organized, for example well-written books or course manuals. You may also find unstructured content. For example, content may inside someone else's head. It's your job to locate this content and prepare it for the next stage of the learning process.

Some common sources for content include:

- **Books, texts and manuals.** Books are still the most common source for content. Look beyond the standard references though. What other references may be useful? Where can you get them? Which should you buy yourself, versus which should you borrow? I recommend you buy at least the core set of texts or references. You should then have no hesitation to write notes or highlight text in them.

- **Instructors or lecturers.** Often you gain content from a knowledgeable person. You may have one-to-one access to an instructor. For other courses, you may need to spend time in lectures. Either way, make sure your note taking skills are good and you have a system for organizing and referencing them later (some tips are on page 57).

- **The Internet.** Over the past decade, the Internet has made more and more information available to us. Often you can find further information related to your training topics. Be mindful of the source though. Not everything you find is legitimate.

- **Computer-Based Training.** Computer-based training courses, or CBTs, have become more popular recently. However, many are ineffective. Sitting in front of the computer doing a CBT is not usually enough to learn the content well. You still need to go through the process of exploring, arranging, reinforcing and reviewing. After doing many CBTs myself, I recommend using them mainly as a source of content. Treat them like a lecture or book, and write your own notes. After completing the CBT, continue with the Memletic Process to explore, reinforce and memorize the content. It's also easier to refer to your notes later, rather than trying to restart the course to find what you are looking for.

- **Other students.** Often you can gain good content by talking to other students. They may have helpful references you haven't come across. They also have tips and techniques they've learned from different sources. Share some of your own experiences as well.

- **Others already in the field.** Those who've already learned what you are learning often have useful information. Don't just limit yourself to those immediately around you either. Biographies of famous people from your field may also hold many lessons. Some of these stay in your mind longer because of the emotional content.

- **Video.** The prevalence and availability of domestic video cameras and PC editing software make it easy to capture your own learning content on video. It's a great way to help you visualize and review the skills you are learning.

- **Other references.** Be sure to have a good dictionary so you can quickly check unfamiliar terms. An encyclopedia can also provide related or extra information on a topic not covered well in your training material.

What to look for while searching for content

Later in this chapter, I introduce you to two ways to classify content by the way you use it. Once you understand these two ways, you start to realize that many books and courses out there contain little practical content. This is especially true of many self-help and business books. They contain supporting facts, ideas and principles, rather than practical content. Of the ones that do, even fewer contain specific steps or ideas on how to learn that content.

I want to give you a feel for what information you may find while gathering content for training purposes. I'm going to give you some examples of the content you may find in a book on presentation skills, specifically on making eye contact during a presentation. In some of these books, you may find this information:

Example A: The *why it's important* book

Good eye contact with the audience is important. It helps the presenter connect with the audience. It also helps the presenter gauge the audience's reaction to the material. The presenter appears more confident and "in control."

That's interesting information. What does good eye contact mean though? It doesn't tell you! I've read some books that go on for pages about why some particular skill is important, citing many examples and research. A better presentation book gives you specific details about what good eye contact means:

Example B: The *here's how to do it* book

To develop good eye contact, you first have to stop reading your presentations word for word. It's difficult to keep good eye contact while you are reading directly from notes. See [some other part of the book] to learn how to do this.

Once you have your notes under control, you then need to get your eyes up and looking at the audience. It's not just a matter of looking at the back of the room. You need to search out individuals and make eye contact with them.

Hold their attention for two to three seconds, and then move to someone else or back to your notes for the next point. Spread your attention to various parts of the audience. Be sure not to focus in one part of the room, or on one individual, for too long either. This alienates others or makes the individual feel uncomfortable.

If you are presenting to a much larger audience, sometimes it's difficult to make eye contact with a single individual. The audience may seem more of a blur, especially up the back and in low light conditions. Don't avoid these areas, as there are still people there. Hold your focus in a particular area for a few seconds, before moving to another.

Can you see the difference between these two examples? Example A doesn't tell you much about what the skill is, whereas example B does. I'd have even more respect for a presentation book that then went further with information like this:

Example C: The *here's how to learn it* book.

Here are some suggestions on how you can learn to make eye contact in your own presentations:

Practice reading a point from your notes and then physically looking up. Put together some meaningless points, and then stand up in your kitchen or other room and practice. Put a mark at the end of each line, for example an up arrow like ↑, to remind you to look up. When you do look up, look at different parts of the room. If you are in the kitchen, visualize the microwave, stove, sink and refrigerator as members of your audience. Make your point directly to one of these audience members, and then move on to the next point.

Better yet, if you have access to computer image projection equipment, get a picture of an audience from the speaker's perspective and project it on the wall. Stand facing the screen and practice making eye contact with your captive audience.

Before your next presentation, ask a friend or colleague who will be in the audience to help you out. Have them stand behind the audience and give you gestures to remind you to look around. They may also give you signals to slow down your speaking, stop fidgeting, or to relax your posture. Also, ask them to give you some comments and suggestions after the presentation.

Consider whether the content you find is more like example A, B or C above. Are you getting the "why it's important," "here's how to do it," or "here's how to learn it"? This doesn't just apply to books either. Some training courses and presentations also focus on "why it is important," rather than covering practical and useful information you can use to build your skills. Memorizing ten points about why good eye contact is important doesn't necessarily help you improve your own eye contact.

Keep these three examples in mind while you locate content for learning. If the content you find is like example A, you need to find more information to understand what "making eye contact" involves. If it's example B, that's fine. You then use Memletics to learn the material. If it's example C, they are giving you a shortcut!

Specific content collection tips

Two important skills to use during the locate step are note taking and highlighting. Often people have trouble with these skills, so let's look at some specific tips on how to do these well. In addition, you should organize what you collect to make it easier to use in the next steps of the process.

Intelligent note taking

Intelligent note taking may range from writing comments in textbooks or review notes after lessons, right through to heavy-duty note taking during fast-paced lectures. Here are a few points on how to take intelligent notes:

- **Don't write everything down.** Listen for the main points and summarize where possible. While listening to a lecturer, listen for changes in tone, inflection and other cues to decide what's important. This can also suggest when the topic changes. If you are learning with an instructor or with a smaller group of people, ask the instructor or lecturer to outline the lesson first. This helps your context during the lesson.
- **Leave white space.** Leave space to fill in more notes later, especially in the margin. One note taking system (Cornell) involves writing summary points in the margin for each paragraph of notes. This is a good way to organize and review your notes.
- **Scribble in your own books.** Write, mark and highlight key points in your own textbooks and references. Some people feel you should not write in or mark printed books. If you are one of these people, I suggest you buy a cheap book and scribble all over and through it. Do what you need to do to break this limiting belief. If writing or highlighting sections in a book makes it easier to learn, go right ahead!
- **Use alternative formats.** Alternative formats include Mind Maps and diagrams. I cover mind maps in more detail in the next section. Use diagrams if you can draw them quickly enough.

Intelligent highlighting and marking

Many people mistake highlighting for learning. Some study guides recommend you don't do it all, because so many people do it poorly and it can give a false sense of accomplishment.

I believe highlighting is an important and useful skill. Treat it as a content collection technique though. Collect the key points, ideas and definitions for use in the next steps—exploring and learning what you've collected.

Here are some specific tips for intelligent highlighting:

- **Only mark the key points.** You can usually find these at the start or end of a paragraph, but not always. Even when marking a key point, only mark at maximum three or four words within that point (if possible).
- **Highlight after you read.** Make sure you read the entire paragraph, or even page, before you go back and highlight the key points.
- **Only highlight the defined word, not the whole sentence.** Use a normal pen and put brackets around the word's definition if you would like to separate them.
- **Mark unusual, uncommon or questionable items.** Perhaps use a different color. Make a point somewhere to come back to it if needed.
- **Try different colors.** Try using different color highlighters for different points. This may work for some people and not others. Don't go too far though. Use a maximum of three colors! If you plan to photocopy or scan notes later, only use a light-colored highlighter. Yellow appears the best. Other colors can come out black!
- **Still write notes.** When you are highlighting, keep a normal pen handy as well. For example, write some notes in the margins on why you've highlighted particular points.
- **Transfer to other notes or a mind map.** If a point is important, don't just highlight it. Transfer it to your main notes or to a mind map (described soon) for your topic. One of my study techniques involves highlighting while I read the material, then transferring the main points to a mind map afterwards.

Use highlighting sparingly otherwise the unmarked text may stand out more. Take care that you don't finish with a book full of colored paper! I know of one flight instructor who hands out a summary of her lessons on bright yellow paper. This saves those with questionable highlighting skills the trouble of creating the notes themselves.

Just to reiterate. Highlighting is a content collection exercise. Don't mistake highlighting for learning.

Organizing content

I believe it's better to have more information available than the minimum you need to complete your course. To make this work, you need to organize your content well.

While you locate and collect information, keep a summary or index of the material you find, where you found it, and when. Also, *rate* the quality and relevance of the content. Use the A, B, and C categories from above if this helps. This extra information helps you when you explore the topics in the next step.

Occasionally check your summary against an overall training plan, and look for areas where you have weaknesses or gaps. If you find yourself chasing some curious reference that probably won't add much value to your training, take a step back. It's better to have all topics covered to a good level, rather than spending significant amounts of time looking for too much detail in one particular topic.

Explore—understand content

The next step in the learning process is to *explore* your topic and the material you've collected. Your goal is to

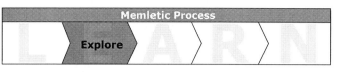

understand the topic, rather than just rote learn it. A fundamental learning principle underlies exploration. If you learn something in more depth up front, you remember it for longer.

Learning material by rote sometimes appears easier. You *could* learn some topics faster by rote compared to trying to understand the details behind the topic. However, this typically results in slower overall learning for two reasons.

Firstly, if you forget part of the topic learned by rote, you have little to help you recall it. If you understand the underlying ideas, it's more likely you can rebuild parts of the topic in your mind. Consider a mathematical formula. If you only rote learn it, you may forget whether to add or subtract some item in the formula. If you understand the theory behind the formula, it's more likely you can work out whether to add or subtract.

Secondly, it's less likely you can apply a topic in a slightly different way if you only rote learn it. If you learn the details behind a topic, you have more opportunity to work out what you need to change to apply the topic differently. For example, understanding some details behind aircraft navigation makes it easier to apply the same knowledge to maritime navigation.

You can explore at many levels. When you first start your training, you explore the overall course content and understand how each lower level module contributes to the overall objectives. As you progress, you then explore each part in more detail. Both the high and low-level details form part of your understanding of a topic.

Many techniques and tools can help you explore your content. In this section, we first look at some general techniques you can apply to any exploration activity. Then I present more techniques grouped (roughly) into the most relevant Memletic Style. We are yet to cover these styles in detail, so you may want to review the basics of each style in the Overview chapter. In summary, the styles are Visual, Aural, Verbal, Physical, Logical, Social and Solitary learning styles.

Here is a summary of the exploration techniques described in this section:

General exploration
- High altitude view
- Deeper level
- Branch wider
- Abstractions
- Bottom up
- Questions[3]

Visual exploration
- Diagrams, graphs, and sketches
- Mind maps
- Systems diagrams
- Visualization

Physical exploration
- Walk about
- Get hands-on
- Role-playing
- Index cards & Post-It notes
- Tick it off

Logical exploration
- Logic analysis—OSAID
- Logic trees
- Play with numbers

Social exploration
- Group learning

Aural exploration
- Sound focus
- Record sounds

Verbal exploration
- Lectures and discussions
- Dramatic reading
- Express and summarize aloud
- Write and rewrite
- Write articles
- Write summaries
- Record

- Study buddy
- Opposite view
- Role-play
- Involve others

Solitary exploration
- Reaction notes
- Learning journal or log
- People exploration
- Make up your own mind

How far should you go when exploring your material? It depends on your objectives. If you want to know a particular topic well, you may want to explore it in more detail than a course mandates. Don't go too far though. If you find yourself analyzing the behavior of electrons in water molecules, and how that contributes to a landscape photograph, you have probably gone too far!

General exploration techniques

I use a topic pyramid to help me understand general exploration techniques. Let me expand on this idea. Think of the knowledge you need for your course or topic as a pyramid, with the goal at the top. Branching down and out from there are major topics, subtopics, sub-sub-topics (and so on) that you need to know. Look at the example in this diagram:

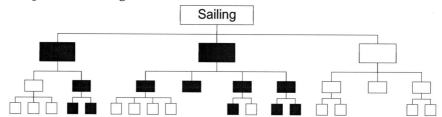

Each of the dark boxes shows a compulsory topic for a beginners sailing course. The white boxes show topics that you don't need to know to complete that sailing course. You can imagine each of the lower level boxes continuing to break down into more and more detail. This pyramid goes right down to basic chunks of knowledge, such as individual facts, skills and behaviors. We'll use this example as we go through the general exploration techniques.

General techniques that can help you explore a wide range of content include high-level views, going a level deeper, going wider, abstracting, and a bottom up approach. In addition, you can use the Five Ws technique to help you with these techniques. Let's look at these in more detail.

Get a high altitude view

Before you start a topic or lesson, begin by getting a high-level view of where it fits into your current learning objective. This is "getting the big picture" or the "forty thousand foot view." Using the topic pyramid above, this technique involves looking at the whole pyramid from a high level. Also, look at the topic of focus for your current lesson. This helps you decide what to concentrate on during the lesson, and it helps you discard what you don't need to know.

You can get this view before beginning a book or training manual. Flip through the major sections. Review the chapter titles. Read each chapter's introduction. Think about which chapters are more relevant, and which chapters contain secondary information. If your course lacks this organization, you may want to consider creating your own topic pyramid.

Go a level deeper

At some point down each branch of the pyramid, imagine a line drawn across. This marks the minimum needed knowledge for your course or topic. I suggest you go one pyramid level lower than this line. For example, understand and learn a few key points underneath a compulsory topic, even if these are not compulsory.

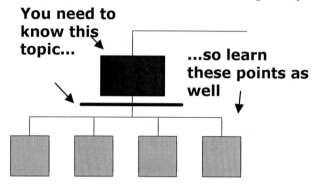

Let's look at our pyramid example. The black box is a compulsory topic. The shaded boxes are topics you don't *need* to know. If you learn the key points from these grey boxes, you will remember the compulsory topic better.

While this may initially take longer, it usually needs less overall time and results in better recall. For example, you could spend thirty minutes trying to rote-learn a particular topic or chunk of content. Alternatively, you could spend fifteen minutes finding a few key points underneath that topic, and ten minutes summarizing those. Not only do you improve your understanding, you also remember it better as well. Over the following weeks you would likely spend less time reviewing that topic, compared to if you just tried to rote learn it.

Go one branch wider

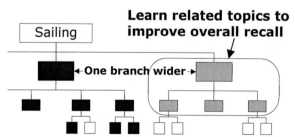

Continuing the pyramid analogy above, widen out your pyramid by understanding topics related to your course but not compulsory. Looking again at our pyramid example, we see the main branch to the right of the core sailing topics is not compulsory. If you spend some time learning some key points from this branch, you will likely improve your overall understanding and retention of the compulsory topics.

For example, one particular branch may be the history of your topic. What impact has your topic of focus had on society? Who were some of the early pioneers, and what did they contribute to where you are today? You could also look up related jobs or industries.

While this information may not be compulsory to complete a course, it aids your learning and understanding of core topics.

Understand higher level abstractions

Abstraction involves looking at some facts or ideas and drawing out some higher-level observations from those. You may note that you can apply a particular technique or approach in a different context or area. For example, you could abstract the general principle of asking questions while selling, and then apply those same principles to increase your persuasion in other areas.

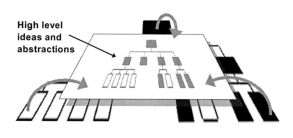

At the end of each lesson, see if you can abstract the top three ideas from that lesson. See if you can apply those ideas to other subjects or topics.

Bottom up approach

Sometimes a particular idea is difficult to grasp fully until you understand the lower level details. You need to learn those lower level details first, before bringing together that understanding into a coherent picture.

Some people may prefer this bottom up approach rather than top down. Issues can arise when an instructor or author teaches one way while you prefer the other. If this is the case, you may need to restructure your material to suit your preference. Alternatively, you could try accepting that both ways can be effective in learning a topic. If you typically prefer a top down approach, try resisting that preference and start at the bottom. If you prefer a bottom up approach, make an effort to understand the high-level organization first.

Questions questions questions—how to expand your pyramid

If you are not sure how to expand your pyramid, try the Five Ws technique. Later in this chapter I discuss the Five Whys technique. This involves asking "why" five times in a row to help discover underlying causes of problems. The Five W's technique uses a similar approach to help you expand your pyramid.

To use the technique, state a fact, idea or principle from your topic. Now ask a question about that statement beginning with one of the W words. The five W words are Who, What, Why, Where and When. If you know the answer, keep going with more questions. When you hit questions you don't know the answer to, write them down for further research. Ask another question starting with 'W', and repeat this until you have at least five new questions you can research.

For example, pilots study meteorology as part of their training. Five questions you could ask about weather forecasting are: "Who does the forecasts?" "Why are they sometimes wrong?" "What do they do to prepare forecasts?" "Where do they do it?" "When (how often) do they do it?" Answering these questions broadens your understanding of the forecast. You may then understand, for example, why the forecast is sometimes different to the weather on the day.

A way to remember these words is the phrase "A hen wearing a hat said 'Hi-di-ho I'm here!' " Add a W to the front of each of the words starting with H and you get the five W's.

Visual style exploration

Most learning materials rely on printed text to provide information. As a visual learner, find ways to represent information visually. Here are some ways you can do this:

- **Use diagrams, graphs and sketches.** If you can't find good diagrams, graphs and sketches that represent the key messages in your topics, create them yourself. Just start drawing, even if you don't think you draw well. In addition, easily accessible spreadsheet programs now allow you to create graphs for all kinds of data.

- **Use Mind Maps®.** Organize topics and ideas using a drawing technique called mind mapping. This helps you visualize and understand the hierarchy and linkages between topics. Tony Buzan, in some of his books, describes this technique in detail. In addition, some software programs can help you easily create mind maps. The software I use is "Mind Manager" from MindJet☺. Rather than describe mind maps in detail, I'll let my mind map below do it for me.

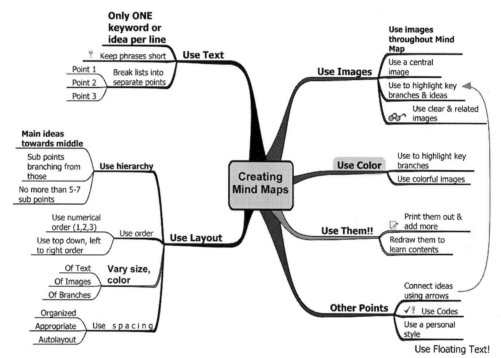

- **Use systems diagrams.** Systems diagrams are another diagramming technique you can use to help understand a dynamic system, such as an engine, body, yacht or network. The traditional way of dissecting something into separate parts, to understand their roles, often makes it harder to understand the system. For example, it's hard to understand the workings of the human body by simply looking at the individual parts. Similarly, understanding how a yacht stays in equilibrium under full sail is hard if you only look at the sail, rudder, keel and hull individually.

The linkages between multiple parts are usually what make these dynamic systems work. These linkages may not be visible when the system is lying in bits on the floor, or in separate topics in your mind. Systems diagrams help show and explain those linkages. The diagram below is an example of a systems diagram. It shows how various parts of an aircraft engine work together.

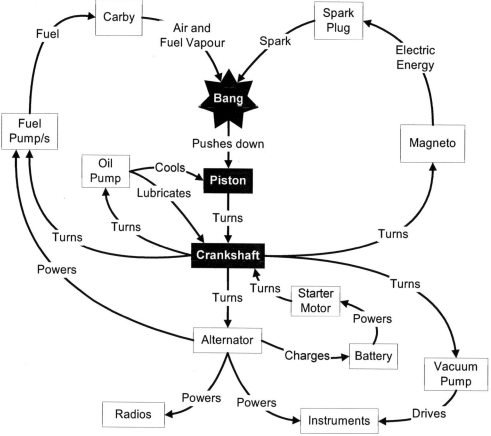

- **Use visualization.** Use the visualization techniques outlined in the Memletic Techniques chapter to help understand various topics. If you can visualize a topic clearly and precisely, you should have a good understanding of it. If some areas appear grey or fuzzy, this suggests you still have some further work to do to understand it fully.

Aural style exploration

Aural exploration involves exploring the sounds and rhythms present in your learning topic. Unless you're studying a music-based topic, there may not be many musical or rhythmic areas to explore. Here are a few ideas though:

- **Focus on sound.** Pay particular attention to sounds in your environment. In an aircraft, examples may include the engine, gyros, wind sound (more at higher speeds, and lack of it at lower speeds). On a yacht, examples may include the sound of wind in the rigging, the hum of the tension in the shrouds, the sound of the water gurgling past. All these can give you extra perspectives in your training.

- **Record sounds on to a tape or computer.** If it's possible, try to record sounds from your topic on to a tape or computer. Make use of these recordings when you use techniques such as visualization and simulation.

Verbal style exploration

Exploration using the verbal style involves using spoken and written words. This could be via attending lectures, engaging in discussion, writing articles, rewriting topics, talking and summarizing aloud, and more. Let's look at some more details:

- **Attend lectures or engage in discussions.** Find ways to involve more listening in you content collection and exploration. Attend a class, lecture, or study group. If possible, engage in discussion with your lecturer or instructor, and ask them to explain topics in more detail.

- **Read dramatically.** When reading important material, try reading it out loud and dramatically. Act as if you were on stage in a play or similar production. Say the important points with volume and strength. Skip over less important information more quickly and quietly.

- **Talk yourself through material and summarize aloud.** As you read, pause after each paragraph and read aloud the key points from that paragraph. Also, summarize each lesson aloud.

- **Reword and rewrite learning material.** Rewrite important sections of your training material. Think about how you would write that section if you were writing your own instruction book or manual.

- **Write an article.** A powerful way to learn a topic is to write an article on it. Do some further research, think about your audience, look through your content and then express the core ideas in your own words. Why not send it to a related magazine as a "student's view on topic X?"

- **Write summaries.** Write your own summaries of each lesson or topic. Review them periodically as you progress, and keep them for future reference.

- **Record notes on to a tape or computer.** Record lectures, discussions or readings on to tape or on to a computer (for example via an MP3 player or recorder). Copy important parts and put them together into a summary recording.

Physical style exploration

Exploring with the physical style involves finding ways to incorporate movement and touch into your training. Get up and move around while learning. Try walking around while reading or listening. Go further and get your hands on physical expressions of the topics you are learning. Use role-playing. Try using index cards to arrange topics physically, or tick off items as you read them. Here are those points in more depth:

- **Walk about while reading or listening.** If possible, get up and walk around while reading or listening to content. Stop and pause on important points, and keep walking when reading less important material. Another idea is to simulate procedures while walking around a room. For example, for flight training try "flying" circuits, forced landings, instrument approaches and other procedures by walking around your living room. If you are learning to sail, perhaps try tacking and docking in a similar way. Have your notes with you and read out what you are doing at the time.

- **Get hands on.** If you are learning about physical objects or topics, find ways to get your hands on them. For example, if you are learning about how an engine works, get outside and open the front of a car or aircraft. Touch each of the parts. Some schools also have old parts around so you can see the internal workings, so ask around. If you have an old engine, for example from a worn-out lawn mower or chain-saw, pull it apart. Note likenesses and differences between that engine and the engine you are studying.

Another example: If you are learning about the weather, keep your own weather station for a while. Observe and write down rainfall, cloud, wind, temperature, and barometric pressure daily.

- **Use role-playing.** If you are in a group, why not try some role-playing exercises that involve physical activity. Instead of reading about the rules controlling right of way when approaching another aircraft or boat, for example, get up and do a few examples with other students.

- **Use index cards & Post-it notes.** Write the key facts and ideas on index cards, and then physically sort them in different ways. Alternatively, write snippets of information on post-it notes and stick them to a wall according to relationships with other ideas. This is almost like physically building a mind map on the wall.

- **Tick it off.** While you read, tick off or mark each paragraph as you read and understand it. This helps you concentrate as well as involves movement.

Logical style exploration

You can explore content from a logical perspective by using the OSAID model to analyze logic further. You can visualize logic using a logic tree, and you may want to look in more detail at the mathematics behind your topics. Let's explore these further:

- **Analyze the logic.** Look at the logic within your learning material. Don't always accept that your material is correct. Much material is still only the expressed beliefs of the author. Use the following OSAID model to probe the author's logic, as well as your own logic. OSAID is a mnemonic for:

  - **Objective reasoning.** Does the author base an argument on facts? Questions: How do you know they are facts? Could they be opinions or assumptions?

  - **Subjective reasoning.** Does the author base an argument on personal opinions or the opinions of others? Questions: Do you believe the source? How reliable is it?

  - **Assumptive reasoning.** Does the author base an argument on assumptions? Questions: Whose assumptions? What if these are wrong?

  - **Inductive reasoning.** Does the author provide a reasonable conclusion by noting some specific cases? Questions: Can you think of cases that disprove the conclusion?

  - **Deductive reasoning.** Does the author provide a specific conclusion based on principles accepted to be true? Questions: Are the principles correct? Is it a logical step from the principles to the conclusion?

  These questions can help you test the underlying logic of your learning material, rather than just accepting everything at "face value."

- **Create a logic tree.** A logic tree is a diagram that starts with a key statement, and then branches out with further logic or points that support that statement. If you want to go further with this, find more information on using deductive or inductive reasoning. Find why it's important that each branch is MECE (mutually exclusive and collectively exhaustive). See the diagram below for an example of a logic tree.

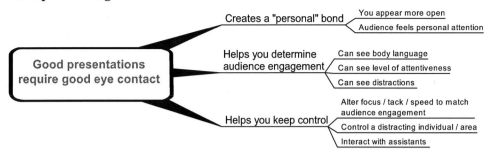

- **Play with numbers.** If you are more mathematically minded, explore some topics by numbers. For example, use a spreadsheet program to graph mathematical formulas or information from your training.

Social style exploration

Social style exploration techniques involve learning with other people. The discussion, debate and agreement helps you better understand a particular topic. Here are some ideas:

- **Learn with a group.** This is the basic technique of learning socially. Join a class or study group for your topic of study. If none exists, consider creating one. Suggest class discussions or debates on particular topics of interest.

- **Work with a *study buddy*.** If you can't find or create a group, try to find someone at a similar point in their training. Work together through material and exercises, comparing and contrasting answers and viewpoints.

- **Play the opposite view.** In a group or "study buddy" setting, try taking the opposite viewpoint or opinion on various topics. Play the "devils advocate." Let the others know you are going to challenge them with an opposing view, and ask them to do the same at other times. This challenges yourself and others to defend the topic of focus, leading to better understanding.

- **Role-play.** I've already discussed role-playing with a physical activity focus, however you can also use role-playing as a social learning technique. Role-playing in this way works well for activities that involve communication between two or more people.

- **Involve others.** Find ways to involve those around you in your learning. If you live at home with your parents, involve them by asking them their opinions on various topics. Try explaining to them some of the ideas you've learned. If you have children, how can you involve them in your training and learning? Sometimes children have a way of revealing your lack of understanding in a particular area by their own technique—the barrage of "why" questions.

Solitary style exploration

Solitary style exploration involves learning mainly on your own. Solitary exploration also involves understanding your own views and emotions on particular topics. You can extend this to try to understand other people's motivation behind their work. Here are some techniques to try:

- **Note your own reactions.** Keep track of your own reactions, opinions and emotions as you progress through your course. Do you find it interesting, exciting, boring or dull? How do you feel when something finally makes sense, versus when you are struggling to understand an idea? Emotions play a big role in understanding and remembering material, so don't ignore this valuable part of learning.

- **Keep a journal or learning log.** While you are studying, keep a journal or log of your activities. Take particular attention to your reactions to various topics as outlined above. Through history, some of the greatest contributors to society and science wrote down their inner thoughts, emotions, hopes and ambitions. They used diaries, journals, letters, poems, essays and articles to capture and explore their lives. These include people such as Newton, Jefferson, Bach, Edison, da Vinci, and more. Some researchers believe their scribbling and writing helped them achieve their success.

- **Explore the people.** Ask your instructor or lecturer what motivates them to teach what they do. Explore the people behind your topics, both current and past. What can you find out about their lives, motivation, concerns and other achievements? Try reading biographies or do some research on the Internet.

- **Make up your own mind.** Much of what you read is an expression of beliefs of other people. Those people are not always right. Try keeping an attitude of "I choose to believe that for now." Keep an open and independent mind.

Arrange—prepare for retention

Once you've explored your material, you then need to work out how you are going to memorize what you've

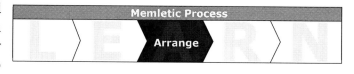

learned. As you can see in the text box on page 69, long-term learning needs to change your brain. Consider this step as preparing your material to help you change your brain.

Arranging involves three basic steps. The first is to analyze your content to understand the type of knowledge it is. This then helps you with the second step— choosing the techniques to use to reinforce and memorize that knowledge. Thirdly, you then prepare the content to suit the techniques you've selected.

This section describes these three steps—analyze, choose, and prepare. Like many other parts of Memletics, you can choose how much time to spend on arranging. Simpler learning objectives may not need much arranging. For important or complex learning objectives, you may need to understand this Arrange step in more detail.

Analyze content

Before we start, let's better understand my definitions of knowledge. There are several differing definitions of knowledge, so knowing my views will help you better understand this step. I use two definitions or "knowledge types" in this book. These are:

Learning changes the structure of your brain

Once we are adults, the neurons in our brain don't move that much. When we learn though, the networks between the neurons change and expand. How does the brain achieve this? The networks change and expand through a process called "Synaptic Change." Synapses are like muscles, in that repetition is needed to make the change that embeds learning. Continuing exercise is needed to maintain the learning. These similarities between muscles and synapses partly led me to use athletics in the "Mem*letics*" name.

The way the networks change depends on whether it's a short duration memory or a long-term memory:

- **For short duration memories** (from a few seconds to a few hours): These memories change the strength of the signals between neurons. The sending neuron changes the signal strength, the receiving neuron changes its sensitivity, or both.

- **For longer term memories** (from a day to a lifetime): These memories change the number of connections between one neuron and another, or change which neurons a particular neuron connects to, or both.

What interests us is how short duration memories move to long term memories. The basic steps of this process are:

1. The brain places the memory into an area called "working memory" first. The memory only changes the signaling strength between neurons.

2. At various times, these memories move to longer-term memory structures throughout the brain. The hippocampus, a small region in the lower middle of the brain, plays a key role for many memories. It organizes and then distributes parts of those memories to the proper places in the brain. Neurons in these locations start to grow and change connections.

3. Repeated exposures to the experiences, and our recall of those, reinforce those memories we wish to memorize. More neuron connections grow and change.

- **Knowledge as stored.** The brain stores and works with facts, principles, skills, procedures and other knowledge in different ways. This influences how you learn each of these knowledge types.

- **Knowledge as used.** Knowledge is also the ability to express or use information through action. This ability may range from unconscious use, such as an automatic skill, through to finding and using some information in a book or reference manual.

Analyzing content involves breaking down your material into chunks you can classify according to these two definitions. Once you've done this, the task of choosing techniques becomes easier. Let's first understand these two knowledge types separately, and then combine them to gain a clear picture of how you analyze your content for long-term memorizing.

Understand the knowledge storage types

I use a scheme of five basic storage types that are easy to understand. These are facts, concepts and principles, sensory-motor skills, procedures, and higher-order skills. When you analyze content, you assign each chunk to one of these five types.

- **Facts.** Facts at a basic level are associations between two (or more) things. Examples include capitals of states and countries, the names of animals, and the names of the parts of an aircraft. You display competence by being able to state the fact.

- **Concepts and principles.** Concepts are a way of grouping, classifying or defining the features of objects, behaviors, or events. Principles are relationships between concepts. Don't get too caught up in the differences between these two definitions. Just recognize the knowledge types that fall in this area. Examples of concepts include symmetry, equilibrium, force, conifer and justice. Examples of principles include the relationship between force, mass and acceleration, or that lift is a result of airflow, airfoil shape and angle of attack. You show understanding of concepts and principles by being able to classify or group related facts, provide examples, or explain how or why a particular behavior or event occurs.

- **Sensory-motor skills.** Sensory-motor skills involve some co-ordination of physical movement using sensory perception. Examples of this knowledge type include many sports, keeping a car on the road, and physical control of an aircraft. You display competence in this knowledge type by performance of the skill within satisfactory bounds.

- **Procedures.** Procedures involve carrying out a series of ordered steps, usually with some decisions at different points. Examples include starting a car, providing first aid, or landing an aircraft. Competency in this knowledge type involves correct execution of the procedure.

- **Higher order (cognitive) skills.** These skills involve higher cognitive activity. These skills include problem solving, decision-making and judgment, self-monitoring and assessment, critical thinking, reflection, communication, collaboration and creativity.

Understand knowledge usage types

You next consider how you use the information you are learning. The question to ask is "do I need to recall from memory, partially or fully, how to use this information?" Three categories help me think about how I use information:

- **Automatic knowledge.** I must be able to recall or use this information from memory, with little or no external prompting.

- **Working knowledge.** I need to know how to apply the information, however I may use external references to help me do so.

- **Supporting knowledge.** This information is useful to know, however I just need to know how to find it later.

Here are some examples of these usage types for both presentation and aviation training. First are some presentation training examples:

Usage Type	Examples
Automatic	Posture, gestures, reading or recalling notes, eye contact, using equipment and controlling nervousness.
Working	Planning and writing the presentation, principles of effective presentation, preparation of materials and setup of equipment.
Supporting	Good quotes, anecdotes and persuasive words.

Here are some aviation training examples:

Usage Type	Examples
Automatic	Control of the aircraft, airspeeds, radio calls, circuit procedures and critical checklists.
Working	Preflight planning, some checklists, finding and using radio frequencies and correct oil temperature and pressures.
Supporting	Principles of lift and drag, how weather works, the internal workings of an engine and the history of aviation.

Use the knowledge types to analyze your content

Now that you understand the two key knowledge types (as stored and as used), let's see how you can apply them. Break down your training material into chunks, and assign each chunk a storage and usage type. The following table can help this step:

Knowledge types table		Storage types				
		Facts	**Concepts and principles**	**Motor-sensory skills**	**Procedures**	**Higher-order Skills**
Usage types	**Automatic**	FC-A	CP-A	MS-A	PD-A	HO-A
	Working	FC-W	CP-W	MS-W	PD-W	HO-W
	Supporting	FC-S	CP-S		PD-S	

Draw your own version of this table on a large sheet, and sort the major chunks of your topic into the cells. Alternatively, label your material using the abbreviations shown in the cells above.

If you find you want to assign a chunk of knowledge into two or more categories, try to break the chunk down further. Nearly all human activities use one or more of these five storage types.

You can use these knowledge types to help you plan and rank what you need to memorize versus when you can use an external reference. This approach can also help you decide when to use longer-

What do the abbreviations in the table mean?

The first two letters of the abbreviation is the storage type, the third letter is the usage type. So for example, FC-W marks a chunk of knowledge as a fact, for which you need a working usage.

Why are some boxes in the table shaded?

These storage types rely on memorized skills. If you use an aid, you are practicing less of a skill and more of a procedure.

term repetition techniques.

You may need to change your rankings because you temporarily need higher recall. For example, you need to pass an exam or test at the end of a course, without the use of external aids. Keep in mind, though, your goal is to perform an activity for the long term, not necessarily to pass an arbitrary exam at the end of the course. You may want to consider altering your rankings after you finish the course.

Choose your retention approach

Once you have analyzed your content using the knowledge type table above, you can then look at how you can reinforce that content. Decide what you need to memorize, and then choose suitable techniques for initial learning as well as reinforcing. Be sure to combine techniques for ideal learning. It's also helpful to use the principles of part task training. Let's look in more detail at these activities.

Choose what to memorize

Do you need to memorize the details of how to set up an audio system for a presentation, when you can simply refer to notes while doing so? Do you need to memorize a flight-planning checklist if you can have the checklist next to you while you plan? Often when first given new set of memory techniques, students want to memorize everything they can. Avoid falling victim to the proverb: "When you have a hammer, everything looks like nail."

You do not need to memorize everything! Choose what you do need to memorize. If you can use an external reference or aid for some content, be sure to do so. If you decide you can use an external reference, design it now so you can consider its use while choosing other techniques to learn a particular topic.

The following table is a guide you to help you choose how much memorization you need. The fully shaded circles show a strong need, an empty circle shows little need.

Usage Type	Level of Memorization	Need for Repetition	Use of External Aids
Automatic Usage	●	●	◔
Working Usage	◑	◕	◑
Supporting Usage	◔	◔	●

Developing automatic knowledge needs memorization and repetition. Supporting knowledge relies heavily on external aids, and doesn't need as much memorization or repetition.

Choose techniques

Once you have decided what you need to memorize, choose the Memletic Techniques that best help you reinforce each chunk of content. Use the Technique Selection Matrix table below as a guide to the techniques that are effective for the various knowledge storage types. A fully shaded circle tells you the technique is useful. A half-filled circle tells you the technique may be useful, or is partially useful.

This table is just a starting point for you to get an idea of which techniques may be suitable. You may want to start building your own version based on your experiences.

Here are some further tips for choosing techniques:

- **Vary your choices for initial learning versus reinforcing.** Some techniques are better for initial learning, whereas others are better for reinforcing material once you have a good understanding. These vary depending on the content, so keep this principle in mind as you choose and use techniques.

- **Combine techniques.** Often you need to combine techniques to memorize material well. For example, learning a checklist can involve techniques from all the categories—associate, visualize, verbalize, simulate, perform and repeat. Don't look for just one "silver bullet" technique perfectly suited to a chunk of content.

- **Use part task training and recombination techniques.** You may need to split some tasks and activities up into smaller parts. You then learn these smaller parts before bringing the tasks back together. This is "part task training" and recombination. I cover these techniques in the Memletic Techniques chapter. Use these principles when deciding how to memorize topics that are more complex.

Prepare for application

Once you have determined the approach for keeping knowledge, you then prepare the content for your

Technique Selection Matrix	Type				
	Facts	Concepts/Princ.	Sensory-Motor	Procedures	Higher Order
Associate Techniques					
General Association	●	◑	◑	◑	◑
Basic Mnemonics	●	◑		◑	
Linked Lists	●			●	
Peg Words	●	◑		◑	
Peg Events				◑	◑
Mental Journey/Story	●	◑		●	
Roman Rooms	●	◑		◑	
Chunking	●	◑	◑	◑	
Visualise Techniques					
General Visualisation	◑	●	●	●	◑
Creative Visualisation	◑				◑
Mental Rehearsal		◑	●	●	◑
Strengthen Others	◑	◑	◑	◑	◑
Verbalise Techniques					
General Verbalise	◑	◑	◑	◑	◑
Affirmations		◑	◑	◑	●
Mental Firewall				◑	◑
Scripting		◑	◑	●	◑
Simulate Techniques					
General Simulation		◑	●	●	●
Basic Simulation		◑	●	●	◑
PC Simulation		◑	●	●	●
Role-Playing				●	◑
Perform Techniques					
3 Stage Acquisition			●	●	●
Part Task Training		◑	●	●	●
Performance Variation		◑	●	●	●
Overlearning	◑	●	●	●	◑
Shunt		◑	◑	◑	◑
Anchoring			◑	◑	◑
Modelling			◑	◑	◑
Repeat Techniques					
General Repetition	●	●	●	●	●
Rote Learning	◑	◑		◑	
Flash Cards	◑	◑		◑	
Planned Review	◑	◑		◑	◑
SuperMemo	●	◑		◑	◑

chosen techniques. Review the techniques you are about to use and decide the best way to organize the content. Some examples from each category of Memletics techniques are:

- **Associate.** Organize content into sequential lists for peg word or linked list techniques.
- **Visualize.** Invent a visualization scenario to include key points from your content.
- **Verbalize.** Work out key points to write into a script.
- **Simulate.** Design a scenario to run in a simulator to include key learning points
- **Perform.** Split a complex task into parts for part task training, or work out variation and interference scenarios.
- **Repeat.** Organize content for flashcards, or extract question-answer pairs for SuperMemo (a software program discussed soon).

Once you have your material ready for application, move on to the next stage to use the techniques.

Reinforce—build brain networks for the long term

The reinforce step involves applying the techniques you have selected and prepared for during the previous

Arrange step. The previous arrange step prepared material for your brain. This step is where you change your brain for long term memorization.

The reinforce step involves three activities. These are applying the techniques, using repetition, and then continuing with refresh reviews. The following diagram outlines these stages. This is an example timeframe. Your individual course may vary in length and timing.

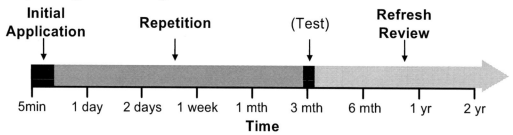

Think of repetition as building your brain networks, and refresh reviews as preserving them for the long term. Usually you will have an exam or test to complete as part of a course, so this may be a good point to split these tasks. You may choose any point you like.

In this section, I cover these tasks in more detail. I also discuss some points on effective repetition, including some information on helpful software.

Apply the techniques

When it comes to using the techniques, there isn't too much to say here. It's a matter of applying them and noting the outcomes.

Before you do so, make sure you are in good learning state. Depending on which techniques you use, you may also want a quiet isolated environment for the first time. Sometimes this is not possible.

Keep an open mind while trying out the techniques for the first time. Don't let previous judgments or beliefs sway your opinion on their effectiveness. All the techniques are in this book because they work for many people.

Certain techniques may not work as you expect though. Sometimes it will take some time for the techniques to work, so don't give up too early. Review the instructions again, or review the section at the end of the techniques chapter for help on common problems. You may also try looking for some further help on the website. If you still have difficulties, relax and try out some of the other techniques.

Regardless of how you go, be sure to write down some basic notes on your application of the techniques. If you have some suggestions or improvements, feel free to contribute them to the website.

Use repetition to reinforce your knowledge

An objective of many of the techniques in this book is to reduce the reliance on rote repetition as a primary learning technique. However, repetition is still a fundamental part of learning any new material.

The key to *effective* repetition though is *spaced repetition*. Let's look at why. Look at the first graph below. It shows three ways you could learn a simple skill through repetition. These three ways are to spread sixty repetitions across one session a day, one session a week or one session a fortnight. The graph is over a four-week period.

> **How does frequency and timing influence retention?**
>
> An experiment on a simple nervous system found that forty exposures (frequency) to an experience in a single session (timing) resulted in a memory that lasted only ten to fifteen minutes. Any more than ten exposures in that single session had little impact in the overall recall.
>
> In contrast, forty exposures spread over four days resulted in a memory that lasted three weeks. That's a two thousand-fold increase in the length of retention!
>
> Use this principle in your own training. Five repetitions spread over a week are usually better than fifty repetitions on one day.

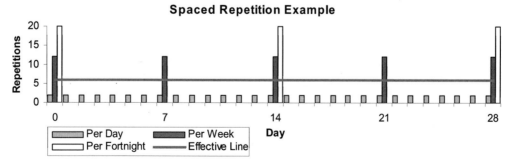

Spaced Repetition Example

For the "one session a week" and "one session a fortnight" approaches, you have something working against you. Review the text box on page 75 and you will see what it is. If you exceed a certain number of repetitions in a single learning session, the extra repetitions have little effect on overall recall. The shaded line across the middle of the graph marks this trait of memory. Any more repetitions above this line in a single session are not effective.

The next graph shows the overall effect of this trait. It shows the total effective repetitions over the four weeks.

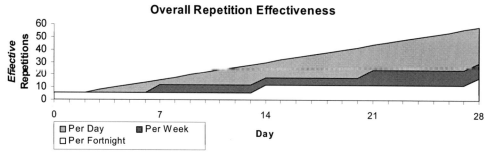

This graph shows the overall effectiveness of each of the three approaches—one session a day, a week and a fortnight. As you can see (for this example), doing one session a day is twice as effective as one session a week. One session a day is more than *three times* as effective as one session a fortnight. Keep in mind the overall number of repetitions over the four weeks is the same—sixty repetitions. While this is a simple example, it provides strong support for spreading repetitions over time.

One item to note from this example is the number of possible effective repetitions in a day depends on many factors. These include the complexity of your activities, the time for each repetition, the type of knowledge you are learning, and others.

Let's look at how you can apply this principle in your own learning. Three tips are to spread repetition, use the Memletic Techniques to support repetition, and to reduce repetition over time.

Spread repetitions

As you can see, short periods of repetition each day can significantly improve your overall retention. In addition, this example does not consider the impact of forgetting on the "once a week" and "once a fortnight" examples. You'll see more on this in a moment when we discuss refresh reviews.

Doing ten minutes of a learning activity once a day is often better than doing an hour a week. An hour a week though is better than doing a four-hour session once a month, or an all-night cramming session right before an exam.

Spread repetition to be as frequent as practical. Looking at the first graph above, doing repetitions every two or three days should be just as effective as every day (for this example). This is because you are not going above the effective repetition line.

Use the Memletic Techniques to support repetition

Find ways to do repetitions using suitable Memletic Techniques. If for example you do flying training once a week, you can still benefit from using a simulator or visualization for short periods during the week. The same applies in a wide range of other training topics.

You can also use general performance techniques outlined in the "Perform" section of the Memletic Techniques chapter. Two specific examples include:

- **Introduce variety and interference.** Use the Task Variation technique and the Task Interference technique during your repetitions. These not only improve your retention and skill level, they also help reduce the monotony of repetitions.
- **Use overlearning.** Go beyond the standard number of repetitions to keep knowledge for longer. Spread these out over time though. If you do too many at once they may not be effective.

Reduce repetition over time

As time progresses (and your knowledge increases), you can lessen the frequency of repetition. For example, for the week after learning new material you might repeat a learning technique each day. For the second week, you might do two or three sessions with one or two repetitions in each session. In the third week, you may incorporate the material into a review session in which you only perform the repetition once. At the fifth week, you do a review session once a week for a few weeks, before then falling back to once a month. You are now into the "refresh review" area (covered soon), and so you may now review your material once a quarter, and eventually even less than that. By this time, the knowledge should be firmly in your long-term memory.

This repetition approach assumes you are not using what you've learned in regular activities. For example, you may not need to repeat an exercise to improve your eye contact with an audience, if you are presenting regularly and using that skill.

This amount of repetition may seem excessive. The various techniques in this book, as well as future advances, can help reduce our reliance on repetition. However, it's the primary way we commit information to long-term memory. Use the techniques in this book for more effective repetition, and your learning performance will improve enormously.

Use refresh reviews to keep your knowledge for the long term

I've discussed using regular repetition to improve your learning. Now let's look at the impact of forgetting. How much do we forget after a single lesson? Look at the graph below.

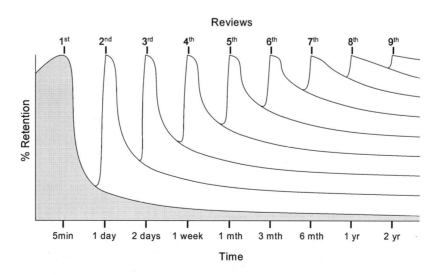

Look at the shaded area to the left of the graph. It shows that we typically forget *eighty percent* of new information within the first twenty-four hours of the first lesson. With repetition and review though, we can eventually achieve significant recall. Regularly reviewing your material improves your overall recall of material as time progresses. Alternatively, if you do not *use* what you have learned, you will start to *lose* it.

Many of our current training approaches do not recognize the need for refresh reviews. This I believe is a fundamental flaw and reflects the view that passing an exam or test is the main objective of the course. You should judge the success of a training course on the use and retention of the training material after six, twelve and twenty-four months. The refresh review is a key strategy to help you achieve long-term retention.

Refreshing reviews don't have to take long. They may take a few minutes a week or a few hours a month. You can vary the time depending on how important the knowledge is and how often you use it. Review your content, redo some techniques, perhaps run a few visualizations or jump in the simulator. This helps restore and strengthen the links your mind has made and ensures those links do not wither away with time.

Regular reviews mean you don't have to start from scratch in twelve months when you realize you cannot remember the links and mnemonics you created during your training.

Let's now consider what to review, when to review and how deep you should go.

What to review

When I introduced the knowledge storage types (facts, principles, skills, procedures etc.), I mentioned the brain stores these in different ways in the brain. Because of these differences, you also forget these types of knowledge at different rates.

Automatic skills need less refresh. For example, once you have learned to ride a bike, you will likely remember for the rest of your life. You will typically forget facts, concepts and principles before you forget automatic skills. Procedural memories also weaken fast, especially when there is no cuing or prompting by the environment. This is why pilots and other similar professionals have to practice complex procedures to stay current.

Let's use an emergency flight procedure, a forced landing sequence, as an example. A pilot doesn't use this procedure often, so it's likely they will forget parts of it. When it's time to use it though, in a real emergency, the pilot may not remember all of it. This is especially true while under pressure. The pilot could help prevent this by spending some time every three months on a PC-based simulator, and practicing the routine in an aircraft at least once a year.

Similarly, if you have recently done a course on public speaking, you may want to spend a few minutes each month reviewing what you learned. Stand up and practice a few techniques. This is important if you don't get many opportunities to present for a while after the course.

In summary, use this as a guide to decide what to review and how often:
- **Review more often:** Facts, concepts, principles and procedures.
- **Review less often:** Automatic motor skills and higher-level cognitive skills.

When to review

When you are learning new material, you need review it often. This is mainly the role of repetition (as we've just discussed) as you build your knowledge. At some point, usually after an exam or at the end of a course, you need to adopt a refresh review schedule that helps you keep your knowledge.

You may want to start with a review session once a month, and then move it to longer or shorter periods, as you feel necessary to keep your knowledge. Set aside some time in your calendar, and keep to your schedule.

Some tools (such as SuperMemo, discussed soon) can help manage your reviews. These allow you to do daily reviews, but without a large time commitment.

Using what you've learned lessens the need for scheduled reviews. Alternatively, keeping up a regular review during long stints away from an activity can reduce the time it takes to "get back into it" when you return. Adapt your review schedule to match how often you are using what you've learned.

Depth of Review

You do not need to review everything to a deep level each time you perform a refresh review. Simply reading some material is sometimes enough to invigorate those facts and principles again. You can step through procedures, for example, using visualization or a simulator. You don't need to use the real equipment every time.

If you are not using what you've learned regularly, you may want to aim to cover all the content from your course over a two to three month period. You can vary this cycle based on how important or complex the material is, and how long you've been reviewing it.

You may also want to reassess your material to check what needs to be automatic, working and supporting knowledge. Often these needs change after you have completed the course or exam. If you no longer need to memorize some content, set up a system or reference that allows you to find it when you need it. You can also adapt what you cover in your reviews to match these needs.

Effective repetition tips

As one of the objectives of Memletics is to reduce reliance on rote repetition, I suggest you adopt practices that help you manage repetition both during and after your training:

- **During training.** Manage repetition by regularly reviewing your progress. Keep track of when you perform well, when you have difficulties, and what you do to correct those difficulties. These reviews help you apply repetition more effectively by adapting your training to what works best for you. We discuss reviews next.

  You may also want to try using the Programmed Repetition technique during your training as well.

- **After training.** Use the Scheduled Review technique, or continue using the Programmed Repetition technique. These techniques can help keep your review activities to a minimum, while still keeping the knowledge you have learned for the long term.

I cover the Programmed Repetition technique in more detail in the Memletic Techniques chapter, however I feel it's worth a mention here as well. You can now get specific software tools that help you manage repetition. An example of this software is "SuperMemo." Software like SuperMemo I believe is an important step forward for effective learning programs.

The software allows you to capture question-answer type content while you study. You then spend a few minutes on the software each day. How much time you spend depends on how much new material you are learning, and how well you remember it. The software decides what questions to ask you by analyzing how well you remember the answers. If you remember something well, it doesn't test you often (it may eventually ask you once every six or twelve months, if not longer). If you continue to forget the item though, it asks you more often until you do remember the answer.

This approach makes standard review methods look ancient in comparison. While there is still more work needed in this area, it's a great step forward for those who want to keep what they learn while making effective use of their time.

eNquire—review your learning effectiveness

The last step of the Memletic Process is eNquire. Enquire involves reviewing the effectiveness of your learning efforts. In this section, I first

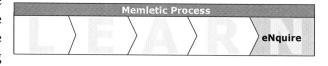

discuss creating and using a review log. I then describe four types of review:

- **Immediate review.** Receive immediate feedback and correction while learning (but not too much).
- **Lesson review.** Review the effectiveness of the previous steps when learning new material.
- **Formal review.** Use tests or examinations to measure your recall of information.
- **System review.** Review your overall use of Memletics.

The enquire step of the Memletics Process helps you improve your training and learning. It's not just a record of what you did wrong. Making mistakes helps you learn, so don't be afraid to make them (see the Challenges chapter for more thoughts on mistakes). Do be diligent in recognizing them and correcting them though. Using reviews is a key part of this diligence, and this in turn accelerates your overall learning.

Create your review log

Your first activity is to create your review log, or logs. I suggest you have two. I call these the detailed review log and the summary review log.

In the detailed review log, you record the details of each lesson, session, presentation, game or other activity. In the summary review log, you collect key learning points, action points and assertions from your detailed reviews.

It doesn't matter that much if you use a computer or if you hand write your reviews. I use a standard paper notebook (Legal/A4 format) because I can take it anywhere and I don't have to worry about flat batteries! In the front part, I do the detailed reviews. I do the summary review lists in the back of the same notebook.

You can improve your overall confidence using this technique. You know you can detect issues, analyze them and take action to resolve them. This is a strong deterrent to "fear of failure" that many people suffer. In addition, your coach, instructor or even employer sees that you are flexible and can deal successfully with challenges and mistakes.

Here are four tips for review logs. I suggest you phrase your review comments in a positive way, you use an assertions list in your summary review log, and you consider memorizing that list. A review log is also useful after finishing your training or course. Let's look at these points.

Use positive phrasing

Phrase the outcomes from your reviews in a positive way. This includes even the mistakes or problems you had. Use the same rules as for assertions. This helps you focus on the outcome you want, rather than the issue you had. For example, instead of writing:

- Forgot to make an inbound radio call at Bendigo, or
- Forget to keep eye contact with the audience

Write instead:

- I make inbound radio calls on time at all locations (including Bendigo), or
- I keep good eye contact with the audience.

Create an assertions list in your summary review logs

Collect key assertions from your detailed review logs, and create a summary assertions list for major areas of your training. Keep them in your summary review log.

I used assertions throughout my flight training, and I continue to use them to keep up my flying standard. My list of assertions reflected both specific issues I had in training, as well as issues that cause problems for other pilots. I reviewed this list often during training. At the end of training, that list was eighty items long. Below is an example of some of those training assertions:

1 I use the map with the largest scale.

2 I remember to include "AMENDED" in a clearance when needed.

3 I complete CLEARA checks before and after changes in height, heading, and every 5-10 minutes.

4 I make correct and early radio calls when climbing or descending into new airspaces.

5 I make correct and early radio calls before entering a new airspace (laterally).

6 … etc.

Some of these are mistakes I made during training, while many are just potential errors I know can be easy to make. I want to reduce the likelihood of these outcomes happening. If I read about a mistake another pilot has made (for example from an accident report), I also add an assertion to this list. The list also includes assertions of behavior that simply contribute to a good flying standard.

Review your assertions regularly during your training, the more often the better. As you review each assertion, briefly pause and visualize yourself in a scenario that uses that assertion. It only needs a few seconds. Lastly, don't be too concerned if your assertions are in random order, as this helps add variety to your reviews.

Make your assertions list even more powerful—peg it!

If you want to make the assertions review list even more powerful, try combining it with peg words (see side box). Notice how I've numbered each assertion in the example above. I memorized each assertion by associating it with a peg word. I didn't know eighty peg words at the time, so this gave me a reason to learn them.

> **What are peg words?**
> I introduce peg words in the Techniques chapter. Peg words allow you to memorize any number of items in a list.

What's the benefit of doing this? It means you can recite your assertions more often, adding to their effectiveness. I recited them while traveling to work, in the car on the way to the airfield, even while swimming laps in the pool. You don't need anything with you.

Use during training as well as afterwards

Detailed and summary reviews are not just useful during training. You may also want to consider using a cut down version each time you do what you have learned after training. For example, consider every flight, cruise, presentation, or other performance as a learning experience, and take the time to complete a review after those activities. These reviews don't have to be as comprehensive as a training review. Regularly reviewing your activities for potential areas of concern is a good habit to have.

After finishing my flight license, I've since expanded my assertions review list with points that have come up in following flights, and it is now over 200 items. Nowadays I have those assertions in SuperMemo, so I can review them effectively.

Get immediate feedback, but not too much

One of the key reasons one-on-one instruction is effective is that it provides you with instant feedback while you learn. The right instruction when first starting helps considerably. Without this, you might have to relearn something. Unlearning wrong knowledge, and replacing it with new knowledge, is a lot harder (and more time consuming) than learning the correct way the first time.

While immediate feedback helps when you are first learning a task or skill, continual feedback can have a negative effect. To understand this, let's look at an example. In the early stages of flight training, you want an instructor there to give you immediate feedback and avoid danger. However, it can be dangerous if your instructor continues to prompt you every time you start getting too low or slow, for example.

How can it be dangerous? You don't get the opportunity to recognize and correct the error yourself, as you have to do when your instructor is not there. At some point, you need to fly alone, and without the feedback you previously received from the instructor, you may get yourself into trouble.

The name for this feedback is *augmented feedback*. You may not always receive this extra feedback during the task. While continual augmented feedback may help you perform well during training, you must also train without it. If you don't train without it, you are less likely to perform well longer term.

Most good instructors reduce feedback over time. Some do this more effectively than others. For example, in flight training one instructor may correct a flight plan miscalculation for you. Another may let you fly with the mistake. As a result, you become lost during your flight. This is a great learning opportunity! You'd miss this opportunity if your instructor simply corrected mistakes for you every time.

While your training performance may be lower for that particular flight, the exercise does have a worthwhile long-term positive effect. You are more likely to handle similar circumstances well if they happen sometime after you finish your training. Why? Because reduced feedback often leads to task variety and task interference—both good for learning. In this example, the reduced feedback results in an increase in the variety and interference in the following flight. You get a variation in navigation training by having to find your location after getting lost. You also get interference from the likely stress you put yourself under when you realize you are not sure of your location.

It's good for you to understand this principle so you can seek more or less feedback as you feel you need. You can often use the principle yourself. For example, navigation aids such as a compass and GPS provide augmented feedback. Ensure you do some training without these aids.

Do lesson reviews

You naturally review your progress as you move through the other steps of the process above. For example, during a flying lesson you may find you cannot recall a few items on the checklist. You are already reviewing your learning performance. It's now up to you to decide why you could not remember those items, and go back to the steps that need work.

I recommend taking the review process one step further and *formalize your lesson reviews*. What do I mean by this? At the end of each lesson, within a few hours, write down all the areas that you feel you did well, and why. This is positive reinforcement. In addition, write down all the areas you feel need further work. This is a key use of the detailed review log we discussed above.

Once you've done this, you can then decide why these areas need work. Which step (or steps) of the Memletic Process do you need more time in? Do you need to try a new technique? Do you just need more reinforcing and repetition?

If possible, ask your instructor, coach or teacher what you do well, as well as what areas you may need to work on. This feedback improves your review. By formalizing the review process, you get much more value from each lesson.

Let's now look at some specific points on formalizing your reviews. We cover when to do a review, what to include, how to mark and analyze issues, and how to turn issues to actions. Feel free to vary the depth you go to in your reviews, so don't worry if this appears excessive for some training activities. Just pick up what you think is useful to you.

When to write your review

Write your review as soon as possible after you finish your lesson. If it's relevant, write down as many points as you can while you debrief with your coach, trainer or instructor. If they don't spend the time with you immediately after your lesson, consider finding another who will.

If you do make a mistake or error during a lesson, immediately take any actions to correct the mistake as needed. If it's possible though, also make a note on something you can look at later. This helps you remember the mistake so you can add it to the review process. Use a particular symbol, for example '⟡', to mark items you want to review (target) later. If you do something well, also make a note of this so you can capture and expand it later.

Another idea is to ask your coach, trainer or instructor to write down notes while you are training. You should be able to cover most review points between the both of you. Alternatively, you may want to ask someone else to make some notes. For example, if you are doing presentation training, ask a friend in the audience to take notes while you present. Give them some points to think about, such as speech rate, volume, pauses and pitch.

Lastly, if you use or keep notes as part of a task or activity, review those afterwards to trigger more items to consider or improve. Examples of these notes might include meeting notes, flight plans, score sheets, and plans.

What to include in your review

I organize my reviews into two sections. One section is an overview, the other is a description of the outcomes. Let's look at what I used during flight training as an example.

The overview summarizes the lesson. For example, it may include:

- The date and time of the lesson.
- The particular aircraft I flew and any issues with it.
- The basic lesson plan - including the flight route and the learning objectives for this lesson.
- Whether my instructor or any passengers were onboard.
- The weather, including wind, clouds, visibility and rain.
- How I felt at the time. Was I alert, tired, excited, bored, challenged or overworked? Were there any significant changes before, during or after the flight?

The outcomes consist of:

- Reinforcement of what I did well.
- New techniques I tried and whether they worked well.
- Assertions of what I'd like to do better next time.

Mark and analyze issues

Once you have written all the points you can recall, go back over each one. Grade each issue according to its severity or its ability to affect your progress. For example, for activities involving some risk you might mark each one as follows:

- **C. Critical issue.** The issue could have led to a loss, failure or safety problem if not corrected. Note that it doesn't have to have happened, however it could have led to one of these types of problems.

- **P. Procedural issue.** The issue may not have been critical, however you didn't follow the correct procedure.
- **G. General issue.** This is not a critical or procedural issue. This item could improve your overall competence if done correctly.

Once you have done the first marking, go through at least the critical items on your list and review what led to the issue. Try to understand the underlying causes.

A good technique to help you discover underlying causes is the Five Whys technique. Ask "why did that happen" at least five times in a row, and write down the result. For example, if you were doing flight training and you accidentally taxied across an active runway without permission, the exercise could go like this:

> **Issue:** "I taxied across an active runway without permission."
>
> **Why?** I forgot to ask for permission.
>
> **Why did you forget?** Maybe because I was at the end of a long flight and I was just glad to get on the ground.
>
> **Why were you glad to get on the ground?** The flight was busy and was stressful. I probably just relaxed too early.
>
> **Why was the flight stressful?** I probably didn't do enough planning, and I was tired.
>
> **Why didn't you plan enough?** I stayed out late the night before, and then slept in. I had to rush my plan.
>
> **Why were you tired?** Same reason. I stayed out late the night before.

Feel free to keep going as long as you need to. Go back to previous answers to explore more. For example, you could start at "Why was the flight stressful" and look at other issues that arose.

Critical issues typically do not happen alone. They are the result of several related issues. The Five Whys technique is a simple way to help elicit some of those related issues.

Turn issues into actions

Once you have analyzed your issues, you have some solid material to help prevent these issues from reoccurring. You can decide on the actions to take. Continuing from the example above, for critical issues consider perhaps five actions. For procedural issues try three. For general issues, one to two might be enough.

Be creative when coming up with potential actions. Again, in the example above, it would be easy to jump to the conclusion "don't go out the night before." Instead, look at all the points that came out of your "why" questions. There could be several actions from this example, such as:

- Add some assertions to your review list to practice a conscious trigger every time you are about to taxi across a runway.
- Add a mnemonic letter at the end of a post-landing checklist to "plan" the path back to the hanger, including any active runways.
- Add an assertion that you are alert and aware until you have handed the keys in at the flying school (and you have extra alertness after a long flight).
- Add an entry to your planning checklist to plan via easier routes.

- Add an entry to your planning checklist to check if you have done enough planning.
- Add an assertion that if you are going out the night before, you fly later the following day or do your planning before you go out.
- Do a swish exercise (described in the Memletic Techniques chapter) where your "low point" is seeing yourself having a bad flight because you stayed out later than you should. Contrast this to a "high point" of having a great flight because you left when you planned to. This may help you leave when you intend to.

Keep your "five whys" and "five actions" with your flight review notes for later reference. Capture these points into your detailed review log, and then move the important ones across to your summary log.

Do formal reviews to confirm your understanding

Formal reviews include tests, examinations, orals and other methods to test your knowledge. See these as another positive opportunity to progress towards your learning objective. I talk more about specific exam techniques later in the book.

Exams don't always accurately measure your understanding though. Sometimes examiners may set them as too difficult or too easy. These may fail to measure your understanding. A low score does not necessarily mean low understanding. Alternatively, a higher score does not always suggest good understanding. If you feel there may be a misalignment, find ways to compare your understanding and experience with other candidates. Be especially aware of this when sitting newly written exams.

Use exams as milestones and review points as you progress. After each exam, also consider doing a detailed review, similar to a lesson review. Use this to understand where you did well, as well as potential areas of improvement.

Use system reviews to improve your use of Memletics

Occasionally review your overall use of Memletics. It takes time to understand and use the processes and techniques well. By reviewing your use, you can identify areas you use well, as well as areas that may need more work.

Some questions to ask yourself during this review might include:

- **State.** Are you in Memletic State when you are learning and performing? Which parts are you avoiding? Some of the parts of state are short term and some are long term. Are you working towards good overall learning state?
- **Process.** Are you following the process? If you are skipping areas, why is that?
- **Techniques.** What are your favorite techniques? Which haven't you tried? Which techniques work well for you, which don't?
- **Styles.** Which styles are you predominately using? Which can you use more?
- **Approach.** Did you plan adequately? Are you tracking your progress?

These are just high-level examples of the areas of Memletics you can review. Review each heading in a chapter to trigger further points, and reread sections that you have difficulties with.

You may want go into further detail for certain topics depending on what you find during your review. If you want to know more, don't just rely on what I've written. Right through this book, I've only provided a certain depth of information (to keep the book to a reasonable length). There is still much more information available beyond what's here. If you want to find more, jump on the Internet or go to the library and do some further research. Remember, two of the principles of the Explore step are to go wider and deeper. This increases your understanding of a particular topic. Apply the same principle when using Memletics.

Chapter summary

You've now seen the five core steps of the Memletic Process. Together these steps help you learn faster, and help you remember what you've learned for as long as you wish. You can easily remember the five steps via the LEARN acronym.

The Locate step gave you tips for finding the content you need to learn. You saw three examples of what content you may find in books and courses. We also discussed note taking, highlighting and organizing skills.

The Explore step provides you with over thirty ways to explore content. Some are general techniques, while many are specific to various learning styles.

In the Arrange step, you saw how to prepare content for long-term retention. We looked at how to analyze content, choose your retention approach and prepare content for the next step.

The Reinforce step is where you apply the Memletic Techniques. We discussed how to use repetition effectively, and how to refresh material after you've learned it.

In the last step, eNquire, we considered the many different ways you can review your learning. This includes immediate reviews, lesson reviews, formal reviews and system reviews.

Now you understand the process to follow to learn effectively. In the next chapter we look at the Memletic Techniques.

4 Apply the Memletic Techniques

In this chapter you will discover over thirty techniques dedicated to memorizing information and skills. These techniques will change the way you learn and remember. Some give you immediate results. Others take time to master but also deliver bigger benefits. Either way, you can be confident the time you spend with these techniques will improve your memory and help you learn faster.

While there are many techniques spread throughout all parts of Memletics, this chapter focuses on techniques you use to memorize information and skills. You use these techniques mainly during the reinforce step of the Memletic Process.

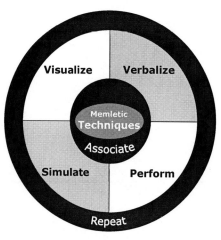

These techniques reduce the overall amount of time you spend on learning and memorizing material. By using them, you reduce your dependence on "rote learning"—simply reading material over and over until it (hopefully) sinks in. The techniques may take some effort to learn, however they pay dividends later. They help by reducing your overall study time and improving how well you remember what have learned.

Some of the techniques I describe have been around since ancient Greek times. Many I've adapted from recently written references. A few are the result of my own work and I'm publishing them here for the first time.

To make it easier to understand and remember these techniques, I've grouped them into six categories. These are:

- **Associate.** Use basic characteristics of memory to learn new material.
- **Visualize.** Use mental imagery to support goals, rehearse skills and reinforce other techniques.
- **Verbalize.** Use words and writing to learn faster.
- **Simulate.** Simulate real-life performances using basic or advanced tools.
- **Perform.** Use specific techniques to learn skills and behaviors.
- **Repeat.** Use repetition techniques to help you lock in what you've learned.

The rest of this chapter covers each of these categories and associated techniques in detail. Here is a summary of all the techniques I describe in this chapter:

Associate	General association	Peg events
	First letter mnemonics	Mental journey or story
	Acrostic mnemonics	Roman Rooms
	Linked lists	Chunking
	Peg words	
Visualize	General visualization	Mental rehearsal
	Creative visualization	Strengthening techniques
Verbalize	General verbalization	Mental firewall
	Assertions	Scripting
Simulate	Basic simulation	Advanced simulation
	PC simulation	Role-playing
Perform	Three stage skill learning	Shunt
	Part task training	Anchoring
	Performance variation	Modeling
	Overlearning	
Repeat	Rote learning	Scheduled review
	Flashcards	Programmed Repetition

As you can see, there are many techniques in this chapter. You may find some of them useful, others you may not. This chapter is not a "prescription" you must follow to the letter. Feel free to choose and use the techniques that feel comfortable. Adapt them to your current learning activities.

Associate—link with what you already know

Before we start, here is a simple exercise. Imagine for a moment a green cat, the size of a car, rollerblading over the Golden Gate Bridge. Seriously. Stop reading, close your eyes, and see that image in your mind's eye. Do this for thirty seconds. We'll come back to this exercise in a moment.

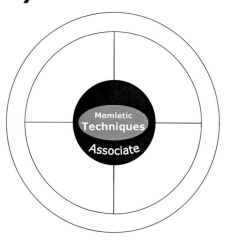

Previously you saw that memory is a network of neurons. The brain learns by associating new information with existing information. It adds new networks to existing networks of neurons. We can use this knowledge to our advantage via "association" techniques. Let's look at another exercise to highlight this.

> **Do the creative association exercise in the appendix.**

If you have just tried the exercise, you may notice it's easier to remember the list of fifteen items when we tied them together in a story. We associated each item in the list with the previous one. We also associated each item with some activities we are already familiar with, even if they don't always make sense.

This is a simple example of association at work. Association helps you quickly memorize a wide range of information, including lists, checklists, procedures, facts, formulas, numerical data and more. While it may sometimes take some effort to create the association, the benefit is longer retention.

In this section I discuss association techniques. We start out by covering some general principles of association, as well as some basic association techniques you may already be familiar with. We then cover linked lists, peg words and peg events. Lastly, we discuss two *Method of Loci* techniques.

Many of the heavily marketed, and expensive, memory systems use association. If you are considering buying one of these courses, check to see they are not just the same techniques in different packaging.

General association principles

What color would a rollerblading cat be? How big would it be? Where would it be rollerblading? If you answered green, about the size of a car, and over the Golden Gate Bridge, then you have just seen another example of how association works. The image is creative and unusual, so it sticks better in your memory. We use this feature of memory in various techniques to improve your retention.

Good associations include senses, emotions, situations, categorization, exaggeration and combinations. There are also some basic steps to follow when creating associations. Next I talk about these two points and provide some thoughts on practicing association. I also discuss the principle of chunking.

Features of good associations

There are six key features that help create powerful associations. The following diagram and points describe these features:

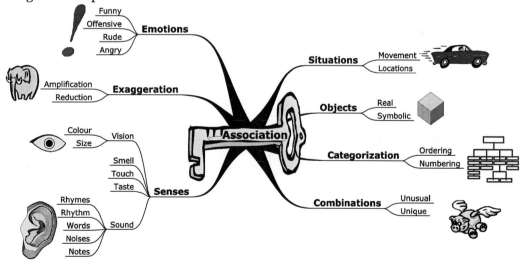

- **Use the senses.** Use many of the senses. Try to include vision, sound, smell, touch and taste. With vision, think about color, size and shapes. For sound, think about rhythm and rhyme in words, noises objects might make, and potentially use music as well.

- **Use emotions.** Emotions also help you recall associations. Using humor is powerful, as is using offensive, rude, or sexual content! Be aware though that your subconscious may block some negative emotions (sadness and anger for example) if they are close to personal experiences.

Association and the Brain's Neural Networks

Recall that the brain works by creating and changing networks of neurons. This holds three important lessons for us.

Firstly, the brain learns new information by expanding existing networks. It does not usually create a completely new network that is isolated from the rest of our experience base. We learn faster by relating new experiences and information back to what we already know. This builds on existing neural networks.

Secondly, the brain learns such information by creating relationships, associations, and other structures such as categories and hierarchies. We remember more accurately when we spend more time creating relationships and associations between existing and new content, and within new content.

Lastly, the brain loves novel, unique and exaggerated relationships and associations between content. Remembering a cat next to a pair of rollerblades is later recalled a lot less accurately than remembering a huge cat rollerblading across the harbor bridge. The same rule applies to learning serious content. The concepts may be serious but we can remember it far more easily if we create unique and exaggerated relationships with them.

- **Use situations.** When you associate two or more objects, imagine them in situations or scenarios. Use movement or relative locations to each other. Examples include crashing objects together, placing objects inside or on top of each other, combining them to form some other object, and more.

- **Use categorization.** Before you memorize multiple pieces of information, try to categories them. You more easily recall four groups of four items than one list of sixteen items. When you number or order items, try to work out a reason for ordering them in the way you have, even if it's simply alphabetical. It's even better if you can find a creative way of ordering the items.

- **Use exaggeration.** For some reason, the mind loves exaggeration. Exaggerate everything you can about each association. Exaggerate the senses by using bright colors, or making objects huge or tiny. Exaggerate situations by using unique or unusual circumstances. Exaggerate emotions by making the objects themselves part of the emotion. For example, an object laughing at the situation it has found itself in.

- **Use objects.** Use tangible, real objects in your associations, as these are easier to visualize. Instead of using *love* for example, perhaps see an object with a big pumping heart. It's pumping fast because it's in love with some other object.

- **Use combinations.** Combine as many of these features as possible, in unique and unusual ways. You more easily recall an association that is bright, colorful, loud, and using a crazy situation, compared with one that relies on visual uniqueness only.

A good way to remember these seven features is to think of association as EESSOCCiation. Each of the first seven letters stands for one of these features— Emotions, Exaggeration, Senses, Situations, Objects, Categorization and Combinations.

Steps to create an association, with an example

The steps to create associations may seem complicated at first. Stay with it. After you have done a few associations it becomes easier. Read the steps below. I've also

---

included an example—how to memorize that one of the roles of engine oil is to cool the engine.

1. **Choose the known key image.** Choose an image that links to the item you wish to remember. This is typically an image that a) is an object, and b) links to information you already know.

   Example: Our known key word is *oil*, however we want to choose an image that we see when we think of oil. Let's use an image of oil in the sump (bottom) of the engine.

2. **Create the target key image.** Think of an image that reminds you of the piece of information you want to link to.

   Example: Our target piece of information we want to remember is "cools the engine," however it's hard to create an image from that fact. So we choose an image that's related to cooling. The first one I thought of was a "Polar Bear." If I think of oil, and then polar bear, that triggers the thought "cools the engine."

3. **Consider both the known and target key images.** Visualize both of them and see if there are any obvious comparisons you can exploit.

   Example: There are many comparisons! Oil is black (usually), polar bears are white. A bear is usually much bigger than an engine. A polar bear uses oil in its hair to keep it warm.

4. **Create the primary link.** Choose one of the association features (senses, emotions, situations, categorization, exaggeration, objects and combinations) to link from the first to the second. Consider some of the comparisons you made, and then perhaps take the opposite of those (the most obvious links don't always work the best, so use creativity). This is your primary link. Make this link stand out on the known image, so it's the first link you think of when you think of the known key word.

   Example: I chose situation as my primary link. I see thousands of tiny polar bears swimming in the oil of the engine.

5. **Create supporting links.** Depending on how critical the knowledge is that you are learning, you can then create more links to support the primary link. If this is an important association, work through the association features and create more links.

   Example: More links could include: For senses, see a visual of a white bear swimming in black oil. For emotions, see the bears having a great time sliding down the metal surfaces of the engine, cooling it as they go. For exaggeration, we've already exaggerated both the size of the bears (tiny) as well as their number (thousands).

6. **Test it out.** Clear your mind for a moment, and then think of the known key word and the image it creates in your mind. Is your attention first drawn to the primary link, which then triggers the second target image? If not, spend some more time focusing on *enriching* the primary link so it stands out the most when you think of the object.

   Example: Try out the visualization. Think of the oil sump. Visualize thousands of polar bears swimming in the engine sump. Imagine seeing the oil on the end of the dip stick. Look closely. What do you see?

Those are the basic steps to create an association. Like I said above, it may seem complicated at first but it does get easier.

As well as these features and steps, here are two further tips for creating good associations:

- **Preserve purity.** Only use objects and features involved in the association you are creating. Involving other unrelated objects can distract you.
- **Keep it simple.** If you find you have to create elaborate stories to link two simple images, you may want to try to find simpler links. The best associations are those that stand out in the mind without needing mental gymnastics to get to the target key word!

Association needs practice

Association is an essential memory skill that takes some time to understand and do well. It does work though. Association is the primary method that memory champions use to win international memory competitions.

You can shorten the time to learn association by using it regularly, as well as by doing some simple exercises. Try spending ten minutes a day for a week doing simple associations. Choose two unrelated objects, and go through all the key association features above. Think of many ways to associate those objects. Try to create the most outrageous and illogical links between them.

You can get better at association by practice as well as using it for real learning work. You can learn some of the following techniques while using them to remember content. For example, I learned peg words twenty to one hundred while memorizing a list of one hundred review points. These review points were from training flights leading up to my pilot's license. As I recalled the list, it also helped strengthen those peg words I had only just learned! Indeed, one author named a memory system the "Self-Enhancing Matrix" because while you use the system you also strengthen your ability to use it.

Chunking and the magical number seven

One trait of *working memory* (a part of overall memory) is that it can work with up to seven pieces of information at any one time. George A. Miller, a psychologist, called this trait the "magical number seven, plus or minus two."

When you are creating associations (or indeed, working with any number of items), try to group or *chunk* larger numbers of items into groups of no more than seven items. It's usually easier to remember a group of three lists of five items than it is to remember a single list of fifteen items.

Let's look at a specific example for presentation training. On the left is an unstructured list of points to remember for good presentations. On the right is the same list "chunked" into four groups.

• Organize the presentation into Intro, Body, and Summary.	**Prepare material** • Think about your audience and what they want to hear.
• Analyze what you did well and not so well afterwards.	• Do your research on the topic. Know it well.
• Understand your lead-in and who follows you.	• Organize the presentation into Intro, Body, and Summary.
• Breathe normally when presenting.	**Prepare on the day**
• Get to the location early and check out facilities.	• Get to the location early and check out facilities.
• Do your research on the topic. Know it well.	• Make sure you have water available.
• Keep your posture relaxed when presenting.	• Understand your lead-in and who follows you.
• Make eye contact with the audience when presenting.	• Ask someone to make notes on how well you perform.
• Ask someone to make notes on how well you perform.	**Present**
• Make sure you have water available when presenting.	• Keep your posture relaxed
• Ask someone to take notes, and follow up with them after the presentation.	• Breathe normally. • Make eye contact with the audience.
• Think about your audience and what they want to hear.	**Review** • Follow up with the person you asked to take notes. • Analyze what you did well and not so well.

Sometimes information is easy to group like this. Other times you may just have to choose arbitrary dividing lines. You can use the principles of association though to decide those dividing lines, the more creative the better!

Basic mnemonics—simple association

Let me first clarify the word *mnemonic*. A mnemonic is any aid or technique that helps you remember something. You could consider all the techniques in this book as mnemonics. When people refer to mnemonics they usually mean these basic mnemonic techniques though.

There are two basic mnemonic techniques you may have already heard of or used. The first is first letter or acronym mnemonics. The second is acrostic mnemonics. You can combine these two techniques as well. In this section, I discuss these techniques, as well as provide some tips on using them.

First letter mnemonics

First letter, or acronym, mnemonics are a proven way to commit sequential lists to memory. Pilots use these extensively. You can easily use these in many areas. Let's see some examples. Here is a checklist a pilot might use before lining up on the runway:

- Flaps Set, Fuel Pump On.
- Instruments Checked and Set.
- Switches set.
- Transponder set to ALT.

Another example is a mnemonic for good photographs: FC-FD-FL-SS

- Film. Use the correct film (quality and speed), or think about the film you have in the camera now.
- Composition. Compose the photo. Don't crop subjects.
- Focus. Make sure focus is good. Where is the main focal point?
- Depth. Think about the depth of field you want in the photo and adjust.
- Flash. Use the flash properly.
- Light. Make sure there's good light on the subject of your photo.
- Surroundings. Capture some of the surroundings. Think about moving around to get the right angle.
- Still. Make sure you remain still when you take the photo. Use a tripod or lean on something.

You could also rearrange these letters into FFF-CDLS and turn this into a phrase like "Three Film CanDLeSS." Visualize three film canisters burning like candles, with emphasis on the 'S' to make it a double S.

Turning checklists into this format makes them easy to remember. Combine this with other techniques, such as visualization, and this technique becomes even more effective.

Acrostic mnemonics

Acrostic mnemonics are similar to first letter mnemonics except they use an easily remembered phrase, rather than a word. One of the first ones I learned (far before I knew these were acrostics), was "Every Good Boy Deserves Fruit." This represents the notes on a music stave (treble clef). These are E G B D F. Another one, "My Very Educated Mother Just Served Us Nine Pizzas," represents the (then) nine planets of the Solar System.

Combinations

Lastly, feel free to combine first letter and acrostic mnemonics. An example again from aviation is from engine failure training: "It's Fuel, MOST of the time." The overall phrase is an acrostic to help you remember "Fuel" and "MOST." MOST stands for "Mixture Oil Switches Throttle." These are the next four checks after checking that fuel is not the problem.

Combining the words and phrases with rhyme and rhythm can also make them more memorable.

Using basic mnemonics

One of the features of basic mnemonics is that they are only useful if you already have some knowledge of what you are memorizing. They remind you of material you already understand.

For example, in the FIST check above, the 'S' simply is a reminder for you to check you've set the switches as needed. You still have to know which switches you have to set, and whether they need to be on or off.

Here is a basic example of how to memorize a checklist:

1. Say the mnemonics while reviewing the checklist, so you can firstly recall each item (not necessarily each item's setting)

2. Read out each check item, noting in your mind if (say) the switch is on or off. Think for a moment why you set it that way. For example, in an aircraft we turn off all the radios before starting the engine. This is because the starting process can cause electrical interference which can damage the radios.

3. Hide each item with a sheet of paper and *test* whether you know it is on or off.

Linked lists and topics—sequential association

A linked list uses association to link from one item to the next. The exercise in the appendix where you linked a list of fifteen items is an example of a linked list. You might want to review the exercise to see how a linked list works.

You can also use this process to link several related points around a particular topic. Above in the association example we looked at using a polar bear to remind us that a role of oil is to keep the engine cool. The other five main roles of oil are shock absorption, protection, cleaning, sealing and lubrication. To create a linked list for this topic, you would then link the polar bear to an image related to the next item, shock absorption. Perhaps the polar bears have shock absorbers in place of their legs. You would then link those shock absorbers with an image that reminds you of protection, and so on until you have memorized the list.

An issue with this technique is you can "break the chain" if you forget one of the items. It's then difficult to remember the next item. The next technique, peg words, does not have this issue.

Peg words—remember lists and numbers

Peg words help you remember numerical and list-type data with ease. Using peg words involves learning a set of words that represent numbers. You then can link items to these words using association. Recalling the items simply involves remembering the peg word and then the association for the item.

Peg words are great for:

- Lists of items or topics
- Numerical Data
- PIN numbers
- Telephone numbers
- Specifications
- Assertion lists
- And more...

Peg words are powerful, however it does take some time to learn how to use them. They also seem cumbersome in the beginning as well. Once mastered though, you have a technique that allows you to recall a wide variety of information with great accuracy.

What are peg words?

Peg words represent numbers. Each peg word contains individual sounds based on the digits in the number. Here are those sounds:

0. s or soft c	5. l
1. d or t	6. sh, ch or j
2. n	7. k, hard g or hard c
3. m	8. v or f
4. r	9. b or p

Say the sounds for each number and you hear they are similar. You use your mouth the same way to form each sound.

Vowels (a, e, i, o, and u) and the remaining letters (h, w, and y) do not represent any number. They just help us create the peg words.

From these sounds, you select words to represent each number. Usually the words are nouns or objects as these are easier to associate with other items. The peg words I use to represent the numbers zero to nine are:

0. Sea	5. Law
1. Tie	6. Shoe
2. Noah	7. Key
3. Ma	8. Ivy
4. Ray	9. Bee

Note that you could select any word with the 't' or 'd' sound for the number '1.' It's easier though if only one object represents each number.

Using peg words for lists

How do you use peg words? Here is an example of one use. If you had to remember a list of ten items, you would associate each of the items with one of these words. Using the association exercise you did previously (in the appendix), you would associate as follows, starting at number 1:

1. **Pencil.** Associate Tie (the peg word for 1) with Pencil. See a large tie walking around wearing its own tie. It's a pencil tie.

2. **Microwave.** See Noah (peg word for 2) on the Ark cooking a hot meal in a Microwave.

3. **Lamp.** See your mother (Ma, peg word for 3) sitting in the corner of a room with a lampshade on her head and her hand in the power socket.

4. **Chair.** Look up and feel a ray (peg word for 4) of light coming from the sun. Then a chair hits you on the head. Where did that come from?

5. **...** and so on

When you want to recall your list, start at number 1 and recall the peg word for 1 is Tie. Your association triggers that "Pencil" is the first item on the list. For 2, recall Noah, and your association triggers an image of him getting his dinner out of the Microwave.

There are two advantages of peg words over "linked lists." First, if you have a linked list of ten items but you forget item number five, it's difficult to keep going through the rest of the list. Peg words don't have this problem. If you forget number five, just go on to item number six. Secondly, you can access any item in the list by its number. If someone asked you what item number seven was in a linked list, you would have to start from item one and count your way through. Using peg words, you just recall the peg word for seven, and then your association with it.

Using peg words to remember numbers

You can also use peg words to remember long numbers. If, for example, your credit card has a numerical password of 384957, here's a way to remember it.

1. Break the number up into two-digit numbers: 38, 49 and 57. Starting at 38, this number has the digits 3 and 8. The sound for 3 is m, and for 8 is f or v. What is a word that just has the sounds m and f/v in it? Move? Mouth? Movie? Keep those in mind. Now for 49, the sounds are r for 4 and p/b for 9. Rope? Robe? Rub? Lastly, for 57 the sounds are l for 5 and k/c/g for 7. Leg? Lock? Lug?

2. Now, associate one of those words for each number together. You could use a linked list approach, and link Mouth (38), Robe (49) and Leg (57) together in a linked list. Another idea is to make a scenario from those words. For example, a "Movie about a Rope Lock."

> Software that can help you learn peg words includes:
> - Total Recall
> - SuperMemo (enter your own words)

3. When you next go to the automatic teller machine, imagine you are getting some money out to go and see a Movie about a Rope Lock. This Rope Lock was feeling upset because all the metal locks were stronger, but in the end it saved the day (somehow).

As you can see, for numbers greater than nine you can make up peg words using the sound of each digit. To reinforce:

- You create a peg word for number 10 by looking at the sounds of its two digits. For 1, it's 't' or 'd'. For 0, it's 's'. You could use toes or dice as the peg word for 10.
- You create a peg word for 91 from the sound of 'b' or 'p' (for 9) and 't' or 'd' (for 1). You could use bat, pad, pod, bid, pit, boat, peat or others to represent 91.

Break down longer numbers into two- or three-digit numbers, come up with the peg words for those numbers, and then link them to remember the larger number.

Here's another example for memorizing a telephone number. Like the numerical password example, break the telephone number up into groups of two or three digits, create a peg word for each group, and then link them. For example, your friend Peter's number might be 613-945-4969. You could represent this number by the peg words chain-ma-pearl-rope-ship. You could then associate this with an image of Peter tying a big chain around his ma, which crushes her pearls. She starts yelling at Peter, and he gets upset. He ties an even bigger rope to the pearls, and ties the other end to a big ship leaving the harbor. In the two minutes I took to create that phrase, I've committed Peter's number to memory.

Peg words for numbers ten onwards

You've seen that you can use the basic set of peg words, zero to nine, in different ways. What happens if you have a list of more than ten items? In addition, doesn't it seem like it would take a long time to work out words each time you needed to remember a longer number?

While you could make up a word each time you needed one for a number greater than ten, other people have made the job easier. They've come up with a predefined set of peg words for the numbers ten to one hundred. Here are the peg words for ten to twenty:

10. Toes	11. Toad	12. Tin	13. Dam	14. Tire
15. Doll	16. Dish	17. Dog	18. Dove	19. Tap

20. Nose.

I've included a full set of peg words for twenty to one hundred in the text box on page 101.

Memorizing more of the standard peg words helps you use them more efficiently. I believe that knowing the peg word for the numbers one to one hundred is a good standard to achieve. That way you have a good range to use without having to think of a key word that matches the numbers every time.

You don't have to memorize these larger numbers to make use of them though. You could also just refer to the list when you need the peg word. Once you have associated the peg word, it's easy to recall the number just by thinking of the individual sounds and working out the number from those.

Tips for using peg words

Here are three tips for using peg words:

- Use tangible things or objects for each peg word. Objects are typically easier to associate other items to.
- Don't use similar peg words for different numbers.
- Keep a small reference of the full list of peg words close by (for example in your wallet or purse).

A party trick, with an important point

The "Total Recall" software includes ideas on how to use peg words to improve your card game ☺. There are also some great party tricks to try.

One of those party tricks also provides an extra technique you can use with peg words. Let's look at the trick first. You can try this with a friend once you have learned more than ten peg words:

1. Have them write down on a piece of paper the numbers one to the highest number for which you can comfortably remember the peg word. If you know the peg words one to twenty, have them write down all the numbers from one to twenty.
2. Have them circle a few of the numbers, without you seeing them.
3. Have them read out the numbers without circles in random order. They cross out the numbers as they read them out.
4. They continue until only the circled numbers remain.

Peg Words 21 to 100

If you are keen, see if you can memorize this entire list. If you are not so keen, you can try the first twenty or forty and make up your own peg words for other numbers when you need them. No-one says you have to use RoPe for number 49, you could also use RoBe. You may also notice differences in the words used by different authors.

The main advantage of using these words is that it takes less time to recall a peg word you already know.

21. Net	22. Nun	23. Gnome	24. Nero	25. Nail
26. Notch	27. Neck	28. Knife	29. Knob	30. Mouse
31. Mat	32. Moon	33. Mummy	34. Mower	35. Mole
36. Match	37. Mug	38. Movie	39. Map	40. Rose
41. Rat	42. Rain	43. Ram	44. Roar	45. Reel
46. Rash	47. Rock	48. Roof	49. Rope	50. Lace
51. Lad	52. Lane	53. Lamb	54. Lair	55. Lolly
56. Leech	57. Leg	58. Loaf	59. Lip	60. Cheese
61. Sheet	62. Chain	63. Jam	64. Jar	65. Jail
66. Judge	67. Shack	68. Chef	69. Ship	70. Goose
71. Cat	72. Coin	73. Comb	74. Car	75. Coal
76. Cage	77. Cake	78. Cave	79. Cab	80. Vase
81. Fat	82. Phone	83. Foam	84. Fire	85. File
86. Fish	87. Fog	88. Fife	89. Fob	90. Bus
91. Bat	92. Bone	93. Bomb	94. Bar	95. Ball
96. Beach	97. Pig	98. Puff	99. Pipe	100. Daisies

5. When they finish, you read back to them the numbers they circled.

Here is how to do it. As they read out each number, *destroy* the image of that peg word in your mind. If the number was 6, visualize ripping a shoe into tiny shreds. If it was 10, visualize obliterating a toe (with blood going everywhere). When they have finished reading out the numbers, start from one and recall each peg word. You can easily see the peg words you didn't destroy. Those are the numbers they circled!

Obviously, this trick is more impressive when you can remember a larger set of peg words.

The extra technique to take from this example is *destroying peg words*. When you no longer need to use a peg word for a particular association, "destroy" it. This is an effective way to make sure you know you've finished with it.

Peg events—remember events

Peg events are similar to peg words. Instead of representing numbers, a peg event represents a point in time. Some peg events you might start with are:

- Waking up in the morning
- Before going to bed
- Arriving at or leaving home
- Arriving at or leaving work

- Arriving at the supermarket
- Seeing specific people
- Getting into or out of the car
- Meeting someone for the first time

Training specific:

- Arriving at or leaving the school or training facility

- Starting or finishing your activity, such as leaving or docking in a yacht

Let's look at how you set up and use peg events.

Setting up peg events

The first step is to choose an object that you can associate with each event. It may be a physical object, for example a garden gnome in your front garden could trigger a peg event for arriving at home. Alternatively, you could use an imagined object each time you experience that event.

Once you have chosen the object you want to use, reinforce the peg event via repetition. For example, leave the house and walk back in, noting or visualizing the peg event and its object. Leave a message on your PC at work to remind you of the peg event when you arrive and leave.

Using peg events

When you want to remember an item later, associate the item with the object you have set for the peg event. If, for example, you want to remember to tell your wife about a future business trip when you arrive home, associate the gnome with a business trip. See the gnome traveling in first class in an aircraft, lapping up the luxury and slurping the champagne.

If you need to associate a few items to a peg event, set up ten pegs using peg words. This helps ensure you don't miss items. Start each peg event at a different number. Associate each new item with both the object and the next available peg word. "Destroy" the peg word in your mind once you don't need it any more.

For example, let's say you associate peg words 20-29 with the garden gnome, 30-39 with some other peg event. When you want to associate the business trip with peg number 22, associate the gnome in first class, traveling next to a nun (the peg word for 22).

Sometimes you may forget to recall the peg event when it occurs. When you realize you did forget, close your eyes and visualize yourself recalling the peg event. Note what may have caused you to forget. In your replay, see yourself in the same circumstances, but this time you easily recall the peg event.

Method of Loci—location-based association

The method of loci is a technique from ancient Greek times. Orators, philosophers and others had to rely on memory for memorizing speeches and knowledge in general, as the printed book only came into use roughly two thousand years later. They devised various memory techniques, one of which is this one.

The method of loci involves associating information you want to remember with specific locations, or loci. These locations may be points along a journey or objects in a room. Usually the journey or room would be one familiar to you, however sometimes you might create the journey or room for a topic. Indeed, the ancient users of this technique didn't create just rooms, but entire palaces and cities to remember much information.

In this section I first look at the general principles of this method. Then I outline two common techniques. These are the mental journey or story technique, and the Roman Rooms technique.

General principles

The principles for associating objects to locations are essentially the same as the general association principles. The term *location* refers to a placeholder. It may be a stop in a journey or an object in a room. There are a few guidelines for selecting locations:

- Each location is specific and distinctive, not easily confused with other locations.
- Don't use a single room for more than one topic.
- Locations should be of intermediate or similar size.
- Locations should be bright and well-lit.
- Keep distracting detail to a minimum.
- Try to make the locations active. Have an item interact with the location in some way. An example may be to pick up an object in the room and see something about it that triggers the association.

The information you memorize should already be familiar to you, for example through the explore step of the Memletic Process. If, for example, you are associating names of famous painters through history, you should have already explored those painters otherwise the location may not trigger the association.

Mental journey or story

The mental journey or story technique involves associating information with locations along a specific path. As a result, this technique is good for recalling information in a certain order.

The path may be a journey that is familiar to you. For example, the stops along a particular train route or the towns along a particular drive. You could also invent a path, however this needs some extra mental effort.

Here are the steps:

1. Select the path you wish to use. It should have about the same number of locations as the number of chunks in the information you wish to memorize.
2. Go through the path in your mind. Make sure each location follows the general principles above. You should be able to recall the specific order of the locations without trouble.
3. Associate. Link the new information with each location using association.
4. Test your associations. Run through the locations and ensure they trigger the association clearly in your mind.

Here's an example of how to use this technique. You want to memorize the key points in a sales presentation on your particular product. The key points are:

- It delivers significant savings to their business.

- It improves their product quality.
- It addresses staff concerns.
- It reduces wastage.
- It only takes four weeks to install.

Let's go through each step of the process together:

1. **Select a path.** For this example, consider the rooms you go through as you get ready for work in the morning. These may be bedroom (getting out of bed), bathroom (shower), bedroom (getting dressed), kitchen (eating breakfast), and bathroom (brushing teeth). You then walk out the front door.

2. **Check the locations.** Yes, these locations should be familiar and the order is easy to remember

3. **Associate the new information.** The table below outlines some possible associations:

Delivers Savings *and* Bedroom, get out of bed	As you get out of bed, you realize it was full of coins. There are round red impressions all over your body.
Improves Quality *and* Bathroom, taking a shower	You don't have an ordinary shower. The water you are using is high quality filtered water. There is a tank of that high quality water right above the shower, with five stars on it. It cost you a fortune!
Addresses staff Concerns *and* Bedroom, getting dressed	When you open your wardrobe, there are twenty staff people hiding in there. They want to thank you for addressing their concerns. You feel embarrassed as you are only wearing a towel.
Reduces wastage *and* Kitchen, eating breakfast	As you prepare your breakfast, use not just the food, but also the packaging. Your aim is to eat the packaging so you can reduce wastage. That cardboard tastes horrible though!
Take four weeks to install *and* Bathroom, brushing teeth	Because you are going to be busy for four weeks, you choose to brush your teeth once to cover the whole four weeks. Twenty days times two minutes a day means you need to brush for forty minutes. Your arm starts to get sore!

4. **Test your associations.** Try running through the example and see how well you remember the points.

Roman Rooms

The Roman Rooms technique is similar to the mental journey or story technique. The difference is the locations are objects in a room. The name comes from the Romans using this technique nearly two thousand years ago.

You can use this technique for both ordered and unordered lists. For an ordered list, follow a specific path around the room. Even for unordered lists, still follow a specific path to ensure you recall each item.

The "room" does not need to be a single room. It may be a series of rooms within a house or building. As I mentioned above in the mental journey technique, the original users of these techniques built palaces and cities to remember the information they wanted. You may choose to use your own house, work building, school, or other familiar buildings. Each room represents a topic, and the items in that room represent individual pieces of information.

You normally choose rooms and buildings you are already familiar with. However, you may choose to create your own. This takes added effort to first create and then fix the locations in your mind, before you start associating your content to those locations. This does have the benefit though that you can create the locations based on the content you wish to memorize. You can make the links more obvious, and you can expand your rooms and buildings without limits!

Another variation on this technique is to create your own *learning campus*. Create a place in your mind that you go to when doing any form of mental work. Create different buildings and rooms for each topic, and then associate specific information with items in those rooms. You can also create an entranceway with which you associate the elements of Memletic State. The entranceway reminds you of those elements as you begin each learning session.

Use the same steps for Roman Rooms as for the mental journey technique above. Select the room or building, create and fix the locations, associate the content, and test the results.

* * *

The underlying lesson for good association is to *use your imagination*. It may take you some time to allow your mind to create the creative, illogical and absurd associations that help you remember more. It comes with practice. And there are some good side effects from letting loose your imagination, such as higher creativity and problem solving skills. All this comes from thinking like a child again.

Visualize—see your lessons in your mind's eye

What your mind sees, it believes! There are many books dedicated solely to visualization and mental imagery. You can use visualization for improving memory, restoring health, reducing stress, increasing relaxation and motivation, improving sport performances, and more. Three main uses of visualization we discuss here include:

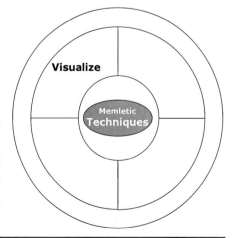

- **Motivation.** Creative visualization is a great way to see a possible future and move yourself towards it.

- **Mental practice or rehearsal.** Mental practice or mental rehearsal is complementary to real practice. Mental practice can also be cost-effective and safer.

- **Reinforcing other techniques.** Visualization is a powerful way to strengthen other techniques, such as association and scripting.

Visualization works because certain areas of the mind cannot distinguish between what you see with your eyes and what you see in your mind. You can manipulate your mind and body to believe what you are visualizing is real. Want a simple example? Read the following script then close your eyes and visualize it.

> You are in a garden somewhere, with a lemon tree, a table and a knife. Relax and breathe in the fresh country air. See through your own eyes as you walk over to the lemon tree. You pick the biggest lemon you can find.
>
> Bring the lemon back to the table, and then use the knife to cut it into quarters. Take one of the quarters, and bring it up to your nose. Smell the tangy smell.
>
> Now, take the biggest bite you possibly can out of the lemon. Chew it and taste the lemon juice in your mouth. Squeeze your eyes shut tight. Feel the edges of your mouth sting slightly from the acid. Do the same with the rest of the lemon.

It's likely that your mouth is salivating after you visualize this. Check! Is your mouth watering? What this simple exercise shows is that many parts of your brain and body cannot distinguish between what you see in your mind versus what is real. Your body reacted as if you did bite into that lemon. *Your mind can alter the state of your body.*

Similarly, visualizing outcomes you want can change the way your body and mind react to the environment around you. You see opportunities that you didn't think were there before. You start to behave and think differently. You have a better chance of achieving that outcome.

In this section I first discuss some general visualization principles. We then look at the techniques that support motivation, allow mental practice, and reinforce other techniques.

General visualization principles

Visualization is simply the conscious seeing or thinking through a scenario, task or activity. Other names for visualization include mental imagery, mental movies, eidetic thinking, mental pictures and "seeing with the mind's eye."

Often beginners believe visualization involves seeing images on the back of their eyelids, as if they are dreaming. Most people do not visualize at this level. It's not important. What is important is the concentration on the task and the conscious *thinking through* of what a scene would look like, or the tasks to complete some activity. Sometimes you may get fleeting images of some part of your visualization. If that's the case just accept them and keep going. Don't spend time chasing these images.

The words "visualization" and "imagery" are in some ways misleading. While the dominant sense is usually vision, visualization does not just involve seeing. The more senses you involve, the stronger the effect. Hear a switch click when you turn it on, or feel an engine turn over and the vibrations when you start it. Smell fuel when you check a fuel tank. Feel a rope as you trim the sail, or hear the shutter click when you take a photograph. Hear the applause of an audience after a presentation. All these can significantly improve how you're your visualizations work.

Let's look at three steps for visualization—prepare, visualize and finish. I also provide some general tips.

Prepare

When starting out or when visualizing several chunks of information, write down a script or set of points you want to visualize. This helps keep you on track during the exercise. You may also want to consider recording the steps on to a cassette or computer, and play this while visualizing. This helps when visualizing a complex time-based scenario or task.

Visualization works best when you are in Memletic State. Key parts of state for visualizing include:

- **Clear goals.** Goals and assertions are an important part of visualization. Review your key goals and make sure your visualization fits within those. Also, review some assertions and perhaps add a few more on the specific benefits you wish to gain from this visualization.

- **Concentration.** Your mind may wander during visualization exercises. Review the concentration techniques and use the relevant ones (such as a distraction log) during your visualizations.

- **Relaxation.** The last activity before starting your visualization exercise is a relaxation exercise. Relax your body and brain.

See the Memletic State chapter for more information on these points.

When you are ready, sit down and be comfortable in a straight backed chair. Have the material you are using in your lap. Don't lie down as you may fall asleep.

When you are starting out, plan to spend three to five minutes on a visualization session. You can build up to longer sessions as your concentration improves.

If you have an alarm available (preferably soft), set it to the time you want to finish. If you find yourself easily distracted, you may want to have something beep every thirty to sixty seconds. If you have computer, an easy way is to record the sound of a beep followed by thirty seconds of silence, and then replay the recording in a loop. When you hear a beep, check you are still concentrating on the right content. If not, just bring your attention back to your task.

Visualize

There is no magic or art to visualizing. Simply start thinking through the steps, task or scenarios you wish to visualize. Here are some specific tips:

- **Verbalize the steps or scenarios.** When first starting visualization, in general or a new exercise, verbalize what you want to see. Describe in words the steps or scenario you are visualizing. If you are visualizing a red house, simply say out loud or in your mind: "I see a red house. It has a red tile roof and red brick walls. I am standing out the front on the garden path. It leads up to the front door. I walk up to the wall and run my hand over the brick. It feels rough and cool." Either try to visualize it as you read, or read it and then close your eyes and repeat the content in your mind.

- **Use an internal perspective.** In most visualization, see your actions from an internal perspective. See the scenario from your own eyes. An alternative is the external perspective, where you see yourself through someone else's eyes. Typically the internal perspective works best, especially for mental rehearsal.

- **Use the senses.** As well as seeing, build in as many of the senses as possible. Think of the sounds that would be present in that scenario. Are there any scents or smells you would expect? What forces or sensations would your body or hands feel? Would you have a particular taste in your mouth? You do not physically experience each of these sensual experiences. Rather, you just need to think about what they *would* feel like.

- **See only the correct way.** I once heard that rally car drivers train to look where they want to go, rather than at a tree they could hit, when they are skidding sideways. I like this point because it highlights how powerful our focus is. If the driver looks in the direction they want to go, there is a good chance they gain control and go that way. If they focus on a particular tree, there is a good chance they will hit it.

  Visualization is similar. Only focus on the correct way of doing a task or procedure. If you are visualizing a possible future, focus on the future you want. Don't let possible negative outcomes distract you. If they do arise, write them down for reference and move on.

- **Introduce variability and interference.** In the Task Variety and Task Interference techniques (described below), I discuss how variability and interference in training can help you deal better with unexpected circumstances and strengthen learning. Use these techniques in your visualizations. Introduce some scenarios that may represent a diversion or unexpected event on your way to your objective. Then, visualize yourself dealing with that event in the most positive way.

- **Visualize with compelling inevitability.** Take a moment and visualize something you know is going to happen. For example, getting ready for work tomorrow. Go through the normal routine in your mind. Now change the timeframe and visualize something that is far into the future. Notice the differences between the two. Usually the images of what is likely to happen are brighter, colorful, larger, louder, and clearer in our mind. If we are not sure about a possible future outcome, the images are usually not as clear. They may be grey and fuzzy, smaller or just difficult to even see in a mental image.

  You can use this effect to your advantage. Give your visualizations a sense of compelling inevitability by adding qualities associated with events we know are likely to happen. Imagine your mental pictures are brighter and more colorful. Make them big in your mind's eye. Imagine the sounds as extra loud. Come up with several scenarios that are likely to happen if you achieved your goals. Visualize those scenarios with clarity.

  For example, if your goal is to be an airline pilot, a scenario might go like this. You finish an international flight, leave the airport in a cab, and check in at a hotel. You spend some time preparing for the next day's flight, and then go to bed. All of these are standard activities that you can imagine yourself doing as an airline pilot.

- **Experiment with field of vision.** For many people, their eyes often focus in particular areas depending on the memory they are accessing. If trying to remember events from the past, they typically look up and left. For events happening now or soon, they usually look straight ahead. For possible future events, the usual location is right and up. You may want to try this yourself. Think of examples in each of these categories, while looking in a specific direction. Is it easier or harder for each direction?

If you do find a pattern, use this to your advantage. If you want to bring a possible future event closer, try to visualize it in the centre to mid-right of your vision. If you want to put a recent mistake behind you, visualize it being off to the far left (as well as smaller, in black and white, and fuzzy).

Note that some people have different patterns, or are the other way around (swapping left with right, or up with down). Adjust the directions based on your own patterns.

- **Practice and expand.** You may want to try doing some regular visualizations when first starting out. Use a simple visualization exercise, such as a scenario or task, and visualize it for a few minutes. Do it at the same time each day.

You can also expand your use of visualization away from set exercises. When you are studying or using other techniques, simply relax for a moment and visualize some part of the content or technique. You can visualize anywhere—on public transport, in a meeting, while exercising, or while waiting for an appointment. The more often you do this, the easier and more effective your visualization becomes.

Finish the visualization

Finish the visualization exercise with some positive assertions and a brief relaxation exercise. Bring your focus back into your environment. You may also want to update your notes. Perhaps add some ideas on how to improve the exercise. You could also write down some general comments on how you felt during the exercise (concentrated, aware, distracted, or other feelings).

General tips for visualization

Here are some further visualization tips:
- **Eyes open or closed?** It doesn't matter too much, as long as you stay concentrated. Keeping your eyes open has the advantage that you can refer to notes. Keeping them closed can help with concentration.
- **Don't chase fleeting images.** Sometimes you may get fleeting full picture images while you visualize. Don't go chasing that experience. Simply keep focusing on the task or scenario. If you get more images, simply note them and keep going. If on some days you don't get any, don't worry. You don't need full picture images for the visualization process to work effectively.
- **Use it to supplement real training.** Visualization is a great way to augment physical skills or tasks. You should still do at least the minimum amount of physical training you need to become competent though. Use visualization alongside physical practice. So why visualize? Because even small amounts of visualization can provide larger benefits, as long as you still do the basic physical practice you need.
- **Use the same timeframes as reality.** Always try to do time-based task visualizations in similar timeframes to the real scenario, task or activity. Shortening or lengthening the time it takes in your mind may cause you to

perform the task differently in reality. For example, the touchdown part of landing an aircraft usually only lasts ten to fifteen seconds. If you stretch this out to two minutes in visualization, the motor skills, perceptions and co-ordination will likely differ from the real task.

Creative visualization—see your future

Creative visualization is a way of bringing change into your life through your imagination. You can use creative visualization for many purposes, such as setting goals, changing attitudes, upholding health, and rewriting your past.

There are five basic steps. Set your goal, create a clear idea or picture, focus on it often, give it positive feelings, and congratulate yourself when you have achieved your goal. Let's look at the basic process and specific uses in more detail.

Basic process of creative visualization

These are the five basic steps to creative visualization:

1. **Set your goal.** Your goal may be a short term or long term outcome. When you are starting out, you may want to start with goals that are reasonably easy to achieve. You can add longer term goals as you progress.

2. **Create a clear idea or picture.** Create some scenarios as if you have already achieved your outcome. Think of them in the present tense. You may want to script some of these scenarios (see scripting in the Verbalize techniques), then summarize those scripts into bullet points you can use during a visualization.

3. **Focus on it often (but not too hard).** Set aside some time each day to focus on the goals you currently have. It doesn't have to take long. Five minutes every day is better than half an hour a week (however both are better than none at all!). If you think of your goal during the day, simply relax a moment and expand that thought into a quick visualization then and there. Avoid trying to force the visualization.

4. **Give it positive feelings.** Use assertions to give your goal a sense of compelling inevitability. Use strong positive statements such as "this exists here and now" or "what I see I create." Finish with a statement such as "life creates this, or something better, for me and for the highest good of all involved."

5. **Congratulate yourself when achieved.** When you achieve your goal, congratulate yourself. Find a way to celebrate. Add the experience to a list of positive outcomes you've achieved. You can review this list later as a positive assertion that you achieve your goals.

You may notice that I've mentioned both scripting and assertions above. These are techniques I discuss in more detail soon. Visualization and verbalization are even more powerful when you combine them.

Example uses of creative visualization

While the main purpose of creative visualization is to support you in achieving specific goals, you can use creative visualization for many other purposes. I've listed here just a few. Don't let this list limit you though. You can find a wide variety of applications if you let your imagination guide you.

- **Confirming goals.** You can use visualization to imagine what a goal might be like, and whether it's right for you. You may find, after you go through some possible scenarios, the goal you have in mind may not be so worthwhile or desirable after all.

  For example, many people like the idea of "retiring early, living on the beach and doing nothing." Do they know what that is like? Try a visualization exercise where all you do is wake up, have breakfast, lie on the beach, walk, have lunch, lie on the beach, eat dinner, and go to bed. It may sound good at first, but then visualize yourself after doing this for six months, a year, and two years (or more). Do you still feel like it's what you want?

  Use creative visualization to reduce the risk that a goal you have set out to achieve is not what you expect when you get there.

- **Changing attitudes and behaviors.** Many of our attitudes and behaviors come from a mental picture we hold of ourselves within our subconscious. We can use visualization to make changes to those mental pictures, which then filter through as changes in our attitudes and behaviors.

  The way to do this is to visualize yourself already acting with those attitudes, or behaving in a certain way. See yourself going through scenarios where you have a choice of the old and new attitudes, and choosing the new attitudes.

  At first, you may feel what I call *creative dissonance* when you have a choice between an old mental attitude and a new one. This tension is natural and is a step in changing those attitudes. Sometimes you may fall back into the old one, in which case just accept it and do some more work with the visualization. Have an expectation though that you *will* change. It's *certain*.

- **Maintenance of health.** Visualization and imagery are now a legitimate part of western medicine. Medical researchers have approved specific uses of imagery in such conditions as psychological distress, chemotherapy related distress, pain control, insomnia, and immune system improvement.

  There is much information out there on using visualization for both dealing with injuries and pain, as well as upholding good overall health. A basic visualization for general health would involve seeing your body and mind as being healthy, strong, and fit. You could then focus on any areas of concern.

- **Rewrite your history.** Another creative way to use visualization is to rewrite your history. Much of our view of our own history is less to do with accurate recollection of events, and more to do with how we reacted to those events. Our memories are just one of many subjective views that could have formed from an event. Feel free to change and edit your view of your history. Make some negative events further away, more distant, or non-existent. Exaggerate positive events or even invent new events in the past to support the goals you have in the future.

Mental practice or rehearsal

Mental practice is rehearsal of an activity without physical movement. Much of its application in recent times has been in sport. Examples include popular programs such as "Inner Golf" or "Inner Tennis." However, you can also apply mental practice or rehearsal to other learning objectives.

You could imagine that, given its importance, researchers would be able to explain how and why mental practice works. Unfortunately they cannot. Recent research has cast doubts on three of the most popular theories, however these persist in various books and references. These theories are:

- **The psychoneuromuscular theory.** Mental practice stimulates the same muscular pathways as physical practice does.
- **The cognitive learning theory.** Mental practice helps set up counterpart mental nodes to physical nodes in the brain.
- **The symbolic learning theory.** Mental practice is a coding system for new skills.

Regardless of how it works, mental practice *does* improve task performance. Let's look at some of the key findings.

Most reliable research literature shows that physical or real practice is still more effective than mental practice. For example, if you practiced twenty landings in an aircraft your performance would be better than if you practiced ten landings in the aircraft and ten landings mentally.

However, if you practiced twenty real landings, plus twenty mental landings, your performance would be statistically better than if you just did twenty real landings alone.

So why do mental practice? There are two key reasons. Firstly, combined mental and physical practice is usually more time and cost efficient. The second is that mental practice allows a wider range of training scenarios. For example, it can go places where real or physical practice is too dangerous or prohibitive. Let's look at these points in more detail.

More time and cost efficient

One instance or repetition of real or physical practice is better than one instance of mental practice. However, that one instance of real or physical practice usually takes more time, is more expensive or is more mentally taxing. This limits the number of iterations that you can do in a set time period or with a set budget.

Let's look at an example that highlights this point. If you were training to land an aircraft, you can typically do a maximum of six to seven landings in an hour at a moderately busy airfield. In two hours, you could do say sixteen iterations.

Using combined mental practice, visualizing the landing phase may take say two minutes, which would enable you to do thirty repetitions in that one hour (with enough concentration).

Let's compare two scenarios. On scenario involves the two hours of real practice. The second is one hour of real practice with a one-hour mental practice session. With the second scenario, you get a 230% increase in the number of repetitions, at half the cost. If you split that one hour mental practice session into six twelve-minute sessions over a week, you also improve repetition timing. This increases learning efficiency again.

The same principle applies in other activities. You can use visualization in golf to achieve far more rounds in the same time period. You can use visualization for more brain-based activities as well, such for as selling or negotiation training.

Wider range of training scenarios

As well as being more efficient, mental practice can take you to places too dangerous or expensive to go to during real or physical practice. For example, you could use imagery to practice scenarios such as detecting and dealing with the symptoms of hypoxia, hyperventilation or carbon monoxide poisoning while flying an aircraft.

The same again applies in dangerous or risky activities. This may be getting out of a rally car quickly in an accident in various scenarios (rolled over, door jammed, and others). Another scenario might be reacting to a collision in a yacht race. More common examples may be visualizing a car coming through a red light towards you, or someone approaching you on the wrong side of the road. These examples may be visualizations you want to try now. What would you do?

These scenarios may be too dangerous to try in real training, however mental practice can help you perform correctly should the need arise.

How to apply mental practice

There are two main periods when mental practice can help you. You can use mental practice to help improve how fast you learn a new skill or task. You can also use mental practice to refine or improve your performance of an already learned skill.

The general principles of visualization apply to mental practice. The main focus is on performing a series of steps. When starting out on a new task, it's helpful to verbalize those steps, and use an external reference if necessary. As your competence increases, you should move to direct visualization without these cues.

Good mental practice includes:

- **Vividness.** Increase your vividness by recalling as many parts of the task as possible. Your vividness can increase as you do more real or physical practice. You become aware of the nuances and subtle cues present. Build these into your visualization.

- **Controllability.** Controllability refers to forming consistent images. You need to be able to repeat the visualization consistently and accurately. Again, using scripts and other external cues can help you achieve this in the early stages. Move away from these though as you move from learning to refining the skill (as you probably won't have these when you perform the skill or task).

- **Exactness of reference.** The steps you follow in your visualization have to represent the correct performance of the task. Correct instruction first is important. If you practice the wrong images, you may perform the task wrongly in real or physical practice. Usually you need to have a minimum skill or task competence before mental practice is effective.

- **Timing.** The timing in your visualization should be similar to the timing of the real performance. Significantly slowing down or speeding up the visualization may introduce interference. An exception may be when there is a delay between the steps in a task. You can usually skip to the start of next step.

- **Concentration.** Being in Memletic State helps mental practice. Concentration is crucial though. Be mindful of concentration and distractions, and use the techniques described in the section on concentration to deal with distractions quickly.

Strengthening other techniques

Visualization increases the effectiveness of many of the other techniques in this book. Here are some examples:

- **Associate:** In my view you at least double the effectiveness of association if you take a moment to visualize each link.

- **Visualize:** Use visualization to increase your ability to visualize! Take a moment sometimes to visualize yourself as having good visualization skills. Visualize yourself with strong visual images, strong sensory impressions, good concentration, and following good visualization principles. Like some other techniques, you can use the technique to improve how you use the technique!

- **Verbalize:** Again, your assertions and scripting are more powerful if you visualize the outcome you want as you recite them.

- **Simulate:** All forms of simulation can benefit from visualization. Basic simulation still relies on you to visualize the cues you are responding to. You can get more from advanced simulators, such as flight simulators, by incorporating visualization into scenarios the software doesn't support. Include visualization in role-playing to place yourself more deeply in the role.

- **Perform.** Visualization can still play a big role while you are performing tasks and activities. You may need to work on visualizing with your eyes open though! Visualization plays a key role in the "shunt" technique for changing habits. Visualization can also make anchoring and modeling more effective.

- **Repeat.** Try to build in some form of visualization even while rote learning. For example, visualize flashcards as you see them. Visualize material you review in SuperMemo.

Verbalize—assert your learning with words

In the Memletic State chapter, I discussed in how your internal dialogue influences your overall performance. This is because your internal dialogue influences your self-talk, self-esteem and self-image. You often act in a way that matches your self-image.

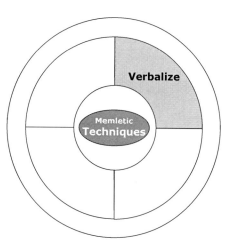

In this section I discuss three techniques you can use to adjust, improve and protect your self-talk. These have a direct effect on your self-image, and therefore your behavior. Assertions are simple statements of something you want to uphold or achieve. The Mental Firewall helps you control self-talk. Scripting involves writing down a story that reflects a learning objective. Let's go through these in more detail.

Three key reasons for using the Verbalize techniques are:

- **Changing negative patterns into positive patterns.** A key step in achieving good learning and task performance is to ensure your internal dialogue supports your activities. Use these techniques to change your internal dialogue from negative to positive.

114

- **Set a positive context.** You can use these techniques to set an overall positive context to your activities. This includes setting a positive context for general and specific goals. This also includes setting positive expectations for mental abilities such as learning, concentration, proactive behavior, discipline and attitudes.

- **Learn and support specific behaviors.** You can apply these techniques while learning new skills and behaviors. For example, during flight training I built up a list of eighty assertions based on previous flight reviews. These were positive statements such as "I check map scale when looking for features" and "I ensure I engage the park brake before starting the engine." These had a significant impact on my learning performance.

Verbalize techniques also allow you to keep full control over the process and content, which is different to techniques such as hypnotism or subliminal messages.

Assertions—assert it's already so

Assertions are strong, positive statements that something is already so. Another name for assertions is affirmations. Assertions can help reduce negative self-talk and help build new, positive self-talk. Examples of assertions to help achieve this include:

- I learn and remember quickly and easily.
- I have a positive mental attitude.
- I live my life to the fullest potential.
- I lead a healthy, happy life.
- I am open to change and new experiences.
- I am now enjoying everything I do.

You can also use assertions to learn and change specific behaviors related to your training objectives. For flight training, assertions might include:

- I easily recall checklists.
- I make clear radio calls.
- I make perfect landings.
- I have the information I need to pass this test.

Assertions can change the way you behave and the way you see yourself. As little as five or ten minutes a day can have an impact after a few days. You can see significant effects after twenty days. Once you change your behavior, you don't need to do much more work.

When you create assertions, write them in first person, be positive and present, keep them short, if possible be rhythmic, and be sure to record them.

Reciting assertions involves relaxation, starting and ending with supportive assertions, saying them aloud or mentally, reciting them often and anywhere, and visualizing them. In the next few pages I'll cover all these points in more detail, as well as some general tips

> Assertions are related to sayings such as "believe and you will achieve," "ask and you shall receive," and "fake it 'till you make it."

Creating assertions

Many books out there can give you a good start on assertions for various areas of your life. They are often more effective though if you create them yourself. This allows you to tailor assertions specifically to support the learning and training you are doing.

These are some general principles for creating assertions:

- **Use first person.** Use "I" and "my." Phrase your assertion so you are the focus.
- **Be positive.** Use firm, powerful statement that something is already so. Avoid using negatives. For example, use "I make eye contact with the audience" rather than "I never forget to make eye contact with the audience." The mind has an uncanny ability to ignore the "never" part of your phrase, and it becomes "I forget to make eye contact with the audience."
- **Be present.** Phrase all your assertions like you have already achieved the outcome you want. For example, use "I make clear and correct radio calls," rather than "I *will* make clear and correct radio calls."
- **Use short and medium length assertions.** Short assertions such as "I am an expert surgeon" and "I learn quickly and easily" provide an overall positive approach to your training. You can use longer assertions to focus on specific training needs. For example, "During presentations I have good eye contact with all parts of the audience." Try to keep assertions to less than four to five seconds when read aloud.
- **Be rhythmic.** For shorter assertions, using rhythm and rhyme can help you memorize the assertion and increase its effectiveness. For example "Better every day in every way."

Reciting assertions

Once you have created your assertions, its now time to use them. Here are a few points on how to use them:

- **Relax.** Take a few moments to relax. Do a more complete relaxation exercise if you have time, or just take a few deep breaths and clear your mind.
- **Start (and end) with some general assertions.** Create some assertions that affirm your ability to change your life via this technique. Similar to visualization, you want to create an air of "compelling inevitability."
- **Visualize the outcome.** As you recite the assertion, visualize yourself in a scenario where you can use the assertion. For example, if your assertion is "I learn easily," visualize yourself in a classroom or during study. See yourself easily understanding the material, and feeling good about being able to.
- **Say them aloud or mentally.** It doesn't matter too much, however saying them aloud can help ensure you read the assertion fully, rather than brushing over it (as your mind may do).
- **Recite them often.** Keep a copy of your key assertions in your wallet. Put them on small cards in different places at home. Set aside a few minutes each day during the week before key flights or exams and review them. It is far better this way, rather than setting aside an hour on a weekend to do them only once. Use the repetition principles from the Memletic Process.
- **Recite them anywhere.** At home, on public transport, in the car, anywhere you like. If you memorize them using peg words, you can recite them anywhere

without references. This is powerful. For example, I memorized key training assertions during preparation for my private license, and then recited these assertions when I was jogging or swimming!

- **Record them.** For extra impact, record your assertions on tape or CD then listen to them regularly (and relax at the same time!). At minimum, write down your assertions for later use and review. Consider using SuperMemo to track and manage your assertions.

General tips

Further tips include using assertions to enable positive dialogue, say them even if you don't believe them, start small and build, take action, and they only work on you. Let's look at these tips:

- **Use assertions to support positive internal dialogue.** Positive assertions sure beat internal dialogue such as "I can't remember anything," or "I stuff up my radio calls and everybody hears it." If you keep these negative thoughts in your mind, your mind helps you justify them by continuing the behavior. Assertions help you change negative self-talk and improve your positive internal dialogue.

- **Say them even when you don't believe them.** A common concern when some people first use assertions is "how can I say something about myself that I don't believe? I'd just be deluding myself." The right time for an assertion is exactly when you don't believe it. When you have that negative thought, immediately replace it with the assertion. Sure, in the beginning it's hard to say. Soon saying it becomes automatic, even if you have some doubts. After a short time you start to act in ways that match and support what you have been saying. The key point is to say the assertion regardless of how difficult it may seem or whether you believe it at the time.

- **Take action when you need to.** If you want to lose weight, assertions alone won't help. They will however provide you with motivation to take action. That action might include changing your diet or getting regular exercise. Recognize that assertions help you take action, they don't replace action!

- **Start small and build up.** When you are starting out, select assertions that are achievable in a short to medium timeframe. For example, if you are physically unfit, it's unwise to start with "I am the world short-distance sprint champion." Start with small steps and build up to your potential—giant leaps!

- **They only work on you!** Lastly, assertions can only be effective on yourself. You can't use them to change someone else's behavior directly. For instance, an assertion like "person X likes me" doesn't work as it relies on something changing in that person. However, you can use assertions to help you change parts of your behavior or environment. Those changes may make it more likely that person X will like you. If they don't, someone else may!

Mental firewall—filter unwanted thoughts

A firewall is a computer that many businesses use to protect their internal computers. A firewall sits between the Internet and the internal network, so all Internet traffic has to go via the firewall. A firewall provides a *checking and filtering service*. This serves many purposes, including:

- It allows safe or trusted network traffic through.
- It stops hackers or other unwanted network traffic from reaching sensitive internal computers.
- It can stop internal users attacking the internal network (as many hacking attacks come from inside the company!).
- It alerts people when there is an attack or suspicious activity.

Why am I telling you about firewalls? One way to help clean up your internal dialogue is to install a *checking and filtering service* in your mind. I call this a mental firewall.

Install your mental firewall

Fortunately, installing a mental firewall does not need any form of surgery. It relies on assertions and visualization. Here is the basic process of setting up your mental firewall:

- Imagine a set of unused neurons in your brain now have the role of your mental firewall. They immediately start to grow out dendrites (the detectors) and axons (the messengers that create the alert in your mind).

> Check the diagram on page 16 for an overview of the different parts of a neuron

- Visualize the dendrites growing out into your frontal lobe, where most conscious thinking occurs. They grow out and around some of the other primary nerves, such as the acoustic nerves where sounds (such as voices) enter the brain. These dendrites bring back information on the messages traveling through those areas, and your mental firewall checks this information to see if it should give you an alert.
- Also visualize the axons wiring themselves back into your frontal lobe. When your mental firewall detects something it needs to alert you on, these axons fire. When they fire, they interrupt your thoughts. Those thoughts may be starting to think about the content of the message that triggered the alert.
- Set up your alert. Your alert could be a red flashing light in your mind, with a buzzing tone similar to a fire alarm. When you hear it, mentally say "stop!" Practice a few negative statements, and seeing and hearing the response in your mind.

Configure your mental firewall

Now that you have your mental firewall in place, it doesn't do much until you provide it with *rules*. The rules control what the firewall will and won't alert on.

By default, your firewall allows though anything you don't have a rule on. The rules that trigger an alert are *deny* rules. Examples of the kinds of statements that you want to set up a deny rule for may be:

- Internal thoughts such as "I'm hopeless," "I forget everything," "I crack under pressure," or "I make poor radio calls."
- External messages such as people saying "you can't do that," "that's impossible," "you'll never finish," "that's stupid."

The process of configuring follows the same principles as the shunt technique. Here are the basic steps:

1. Choose the negative thought or message that you want a deny rule for. Also choose a replacement assertion. For example, if the negative thought was "I'll never finish this," the positive replacement assertion may be "I finish what I start."

2. Breath out, hunch your shoulders, get in a low state and repeat the negative thought in your mind.

3. Visualize your firewall triggering an alert, and the mental alert going off. See a red flashing light going off, hear a buzzing sound and say "stop!"

4. Now breathe in fully, pull back your shoulders and sit up straight. Smile, and say the positive replacement assertion from step 1.

5. Lastly, affirm the role of your mental firewall by finishing with an assertion such as "My mental firewall is working and checks all my thoughts." You can drop this assertion once your firewall is working without you consciously thinking about it.

You can use this technique in many ways. You could use it to help oversee your own internal dialogue if you have many self-defeating thoughts. You may want to try it if you have people around you who do not support your goals. It could also be useful in sports where the competition uses negative comments as a strategy against you.

My last comment though is a small caution. Only set up deny rules for *unconstructive* thoughts and criticism. Make sure you allow through *helpful* thoughts, criticism and suggestions. A simple example involving flight training would be to deny self-defeating thoughts such as "you will never be a pilot." However, you should allow through helpful or important suggestions from your instructor, for example. Examples might include "you need more training" or "to be a successful pilot, you need to do X, and you are not doing it yet." Blocking out those kinds of thoughts may result in you taking longer to reach your goal, or not reaching it at all.

Scripting—turn a story into reality

Scripting is a powerful tool you can use to strengthen both assertions and visualization. The core idea is to write a story-like script of an outcome you want in the future. You can also use it to strengthen knowledge you want to learn. The key point is to *write it down*.

Scripts are similar to assertions. Most people write them in first person. Some write them in third person, referring to themselves by their first name. They are positive. They are in present tense. They are reasonably concise, although they may still be long. You should relax before writing or reviewing them, and you can read them aloud or mentally. Review them often and anywhere, and be sure to visualize each section *as if you were there*.

The more you can include of the senses in your script, the more effective the script is for visualization. Remember that visualization is not just visual. It can include any of the senses.

You can use scripting for many purposes. Let's look at two ways you can use scripting. You can use it for goal setting and for strengthening learning.

Example creative script

I wrote this script about five years before commencing my flying training, so some of the details were incorrect. However, it helped me set a goal that was real and concrete, rather than "I'd like to get my license sometime."

After finishing work early in the afternoon, I catch a taxi to the airfield. Upon arrival, I proceed to the hanger where my Lancair aircraft is stored. The airport staff have refueled and performed the initial checks, and the plane is prepped and ready to go.

I quickly change in the restroom at the hanger, before throwing the small amount of luggage I have behind the two seats in the cockpit. I pull the aircraft out of the hanger and onto the tarmac. I jump in and settle into the seat, buckle my harness carefully, and then pull the hatch shut.

Once sealed inside the cockpit, I do my own pre-flight before starting it up. The engine catches and then runs smoothly. Oil and other gauges show normal. I complete my checks, establish contact with tower, and then proceed down the taxiway to the end of the runway. Bringing the plane around, I turn the nose down the runway.

After I receive final clearance from the tower, I open the throttle to full. The small plane accelerates quickly down the runway. I ease back on the control stick, and the plane leaves the ground. I follow the circuit for a while before turning the plane north, heading for home...

Use creative scripting for goals

Scripting is a great way to define and explore your goals. Writing down specific points helps you clarify what you want from your goal, and gives it more definition. More definition allows you visualize your goal more accurately, and this then increases your ability to make it happen.

For example, if you are training for a pilot's license, I'd suggest you take half an hour and write a script. Describe your first flight after you have gained your license. Where do you fly to? Who goes with you? How do you feel when you first take off, knowing you have achieved something that many aspire to do? What's the weather like? How do you feel when you land?

In the text box titled "Example creative script" I've included a short example of a script I wrote five years before I started my pilot's license. I knew back then it was something I wanted to do, however I had no idea when or how I would. Five years later when a work colleague offered to take me up flying, I jumped at the opportunity. I was also in the right place at the right time, with the right resources, to start my license. Three weeks later I was down at the airfield doing my first lesson. Nine lessons later I went solo for the first time, and what a rush that was!

Creative scripting is similar to creative visualization. Using them together is a powerful combination. Create and write your script, and then visualize it.

As with creative visualization, writing out your goals like this can help you clarify what you seek. It can also help you realize that what you seek may not be that exciting or fulfilling after all. It may be better to realize this earlier and refocus your efforts somewhere else, rather than finding out when you get there!

Reinforce learning and performance using review scripts

A second application of scripting involves writing a *review script*. This is a script you can review regularly to reinforce your learning. An example of this is what I

---

call "The Perfect Performance." I use a "Perfect Flight" script. It incorporates many review assertions and much flying information into a story that describes what a "perfect flight" would be like. Review scripts for other activities could be "The Perfect Sale," "The Perfect Race," "The Perfect Game," or "The Perfect Negotiation."

Use the Task Variation and Task Interference techniques in your review scripts as well. For example, where there is much variability in your performance due to factors outside your control, script several scenarios. In a race against competitors, you might script staying out in front when you are in the lead, recovering the lead if you are behind, and other scenarios.

Simulate—use tools and people to stimulate your learning

In the section on visualization we discussed mental practice, or strengthening task performance by visualizing the task in our mind. Simulation instead uses external aids to help you practice tasks and skills. These aids provide varying versions of the full task environment. Simulation works because it provides many of the same cues the real environment does, to which you need to respond to correctly.

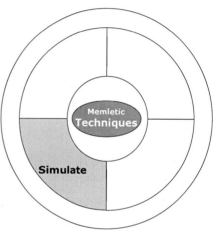

Simulation is effective. This is why airlines spend millions of dollars on simulators to train pilots. However, this section shows how you can gain many of the benefits of simulation by using readily accessible equipment and people.

In this section, I talk about two forms of simulation. Task simulation is one, and this is the focus of this section. I also talk about using role-playing, or "role simulation."

Key benefits and implications of simulation

As with visualization, simulation can provide several benefits to your learning performance:

- **Cost-effective when learning new tasks.** When task performance is expensive or exhaustive, simulation can provide cost-effective instruction. Examples include flight training or practicing surgery.

- **Good training environment.** Simulators often provide a better learning environment than the real equipment or environment. With a flight simulator, it's usually not as noisy. You can more easily carry on a conversation with an instructor. You can pause to focus on some part of a procedure, and many simulators allow you to see a graphical representation of your performance.

- **Variability.** Simulation can introduce variations in training that may be difficult or dangerous to do with the real equipment. It's usually safer. The worst mishap might be falling off your chair!

- **Part task training.** You can focus on individual parts of your training, and then combine them when you've learned each one.

These benefits do not come without implications however. Most simulation is only part task training, meaning you do not get the full task environment. Training on real equipment, performing the real tasks, is usually a full task training method. You still need to do full task training to consolidate what you learned during simulation.

You also need to work with a knowledgeable instructor to get the most benefit from simulation. If you don't first learn the right method for a particular task, you can experience *negative transfer*. Negative transfer occurs when you have to relearn something because you learned or repeated it the wrong way. This can take more time and be dangerous in times of stress.

Here is an example of negative transfer with students that first learn to fly on a PC based simulator at home. If asked to hold a certain angle of bank (lean), students who have first learned on a simulator often look at the instruments to set and hold that bank angle. When learning to fly visually in the real aircraft though, they have to *unlearn* this behavior. They have to learn to look at the horizon to set and hold the correct bank angle.

You may want to use a script to get the steps and timing correct in the early stages of learning a new task or skill. For example, write down the sequential steps of a landing and place this in front of you. Another idea is to work with your instructor and record a series of procedures onto a cassette or computer. Listen to the recording and practice the procedures. This works well with basic simulators.

The role of fidelity

Simulators vary in their *fidelity*, or their likeness to the real task. At the low end of the fidelity scale, for example, is simulating an aircraft cockpit using simple household items. This could be sitting in a chair in your kitchen and moving objects around to simulate the aircraft controls. Another example is simulating the controls of a car using similar domestic objects. At the high end of the fidelity scale are the full motion airliner simulations used by airlines to train their pilots.

High fidelity does not always mean high learning effectiveness though. High fidelity in early training may distract you, and therefore decrease learning performance. Low fidelity simulations, such as the chair example above, can be more effective when first learning new tasks.

What's important is to match the *cueing* (prompting) by the system, and the ability to respond to those cues, with the training level. If the cueing and response is correct, regardless of the automation or sophistication, simulation will be effective.

For example, US army researchers tested personnel training on a complex ninety-two step procedure on a control panel. They compared training on real equipment, on a realistic simulator, and on a mock-up made from cardboard and photographs. They saw no differences in training time or long-term retention across the three methods.

Basic simulator example—the home-based flight simulator

This is an outline of how you could use household items to set up a basic aircraft cockpit. Don't worry if some of the controls are not familiar to you. Just note how I use various objects in creative ways. This cockpit could include such items as:

- **The seat.** Sit in an adjustable chair that you can set to low height, in front of a table or desk.

- **Yoke, throttle and mixture.** A tall glass upside down on the table for the yoke, a smaller upside down glass on the right for the throttle, and shot glass next to that for the mixture (place some red cloth or paper inside the glass to make it look red). Place these glasses on a large sheet of cardboard laid flat on the table, and mark the positions for centre of the yoke and open and closed for throttle and mixture. If you already have a computer joystick, use that for the yoke instead.

- **Switches.** A thin book on the edge of the desk with bulldog clips on the edge for switches such as fuel pump, carby heat, lights, master etc. Place a piece of paper under the clips with markings for what the switches are for. Put a large weight on the other end of the book so it doesn't move too far (or the clock radio, see below).

- **Flaps and trim.** Two saucepans on the floor, placed on their side between a few large books with the handles sticking up, simulating the Piper-style flaps and trim.

- **Radio and Transponder.** An old clock radio for the radio and transponder, placed on top of the switches book. Mark some of the switches for various functions such as on/off, standby/alt, ident etc. Tune your flight radio as you normally do, by turning the dial.

- **The control panel.** Use a large sized photocopy of a standard control panel layout for the plane you are flying in. Mount it on some cardboard, and stand it up in front of you.

- **Your headset.** If you have one already, wear it! If not, just wear some standard headphones.

Use your imagination to think up other ideas to enhance your simulated cockpit. If you have children, you may want to practice your passenger handling skills. They may even come up with ideas you haven't thought of!

Using simulators for learning

Today there are three general types of simulators that you can potentially use for training. There are basic simulators that use simple objects and your imagination. There are simulators running on personal computers. There are full-scale simulators used by advanced training organizations. You can also use the real equipment (for example the aircraft, yacht or car) for simulation. In this section I look at all these simulation methods.

Basic simulators

Basic simulators involve using simple objects around you to simulate your real environment. Your real environment could be the cockpit of an aircraft, the driver's seat of a car, the helm of a yacht, or the side of an operating table. This basic simulation can help you become familiar with the layouts and various controls. It also allows you to practice maneuvers using multiple controls, such as flying an aircraft, changing gears while turning the car, or tacking a yacht. Let your imagination run wild working out the best way to do this. See the text box titled "Basic simulator example" above for one example.

While basic simulation may seem silly, I suggest you get over it and just try it. If you don't have a PC-based simulator, basic simulation is a great alternative. Even if you do have a PC-based simulator, the basic simulator may be more effective for practicing procedural skills. For example, think about reaching down and selecting aircraft flaps, or pulling on the car handbrake using a saucepan beside you. This is far closer to the real task than hitting a key on a computer keyboard.

If you are thinking this training is almost like acting like a child, you are right. Remember that children learn far more in the first fifteen years than most adults do in thirty. I believe a reason for this is they use their imagination well. If you can copy a child's natural imagination and curiosity, learning is far easier!

Personal Computer (PC) based simulators

Flight simulators are the most realistic and complex PC-based simulators publicly available today. However, there are also many other PC-based simulators available that may be relevant to your learning objectives.

A quick look around the Internet found PC simulators for sailing, surgery, photography, marketing, management, military and war, cars, trucks, trains, building and construction, ships, weather forecasting, and more. I even found a stapler simulation, with three different models!

You don't always need specialized software either. Previously I've mentioned practicing public speaking or presentations using the following setup. Find an image of audience from a presenter's perspective (from the stage). Using a computer image projector, project that image on to the wall. Stand in front of the simulated audience and practice your presentation techniques, for example making eye contact with individuals. Unfortunately they may not laugh at many of your jokes!

Seriously though, simulators are powerful training tools. With all powerful tools they can be dangerous if used wrongly. Because they are easily accessible, this also means that you are likely to be using a simulator without a supervising coach, instructor or trainer. Keep the following points in mind:

- **Get the right instruction first.** If you are just starting out in training, get the right training before starting to use the simulator. You may have to unlearn bad habits that you pick up in the simulator. Some of these bad habits may also come back at the worst time, for example in times of stress. Discuss using a simulator with your coach, instructor or trainer as well. They may have some useful information to share with you.

- **Don't become reliant on it.** Don't become reliant on the simulator to complete real-world assignments. An example from flight training: When you start navigation training, fly some of your early training routes in the simulator before the real flight. This can help you become more familiar with the area and procedures, resulting in an easier flight. However, don't become reliant on flying the simulator before each training exercise to feel confident. After your third real flight navigation exercise, start setting your own routes and flying those in the simulator, rather than flying your upcoming training routes.

- **Use as a supplement, not as a substitute.** Using simulators correctly results in improving your skills, and potentially reduces the overall hours needed to achieve your objective. Reducing your training hours should not be your primary motivation though. Always keep in mind that most simulation is still part task training. One hour in the simulator does not always equate to one hour of training on real equipment.

Consider using any training hours saved via simulation to increase your competence and understanding. For example, if you think you have saved an hour or two of core training by using simulation, spend those hours on one or two optional lessons. Use overlearning, task variety or task interference scenarios, or study another related topic.

Full-scale simulators

From the PC the complexity of simulation increases significantly. For example, some flying schools have full-scale enclosed simulators that do not move, and they may include these in their training curriculum. Some driving schools may also provide full-scale driving simulators. Airline training typically involves the full motion simulators costing millions of dollars. If these are outside your financial means, you can still gain many of the benefits of simulation using basic and PC-based simulation, or even the real equipment.

Real equipment

Another way to simulate is to use the real equipment without operating it. For example, for those learning to fly, try sitting in the aircraft before or after your flight. Run through your checklists and procedures without operating the aircraft. If you are learning to sail, spend some time on the yacht before training. Simulate some key maneuvers. If you are learning to drive, just sit in a car before your lessons and practice the activities you are learning. You don't get all the cues that other simulators provide, however you also perform the tasks for real in this environment.

Combine this simulation with visualization, or role-play, for added effect.

Using role-playing, or role simulation

A second form of simulation that is distinct from using objects and technology is role-playing, or role simulation. In this scenario, the tools or equipment you are using to support your learning is other people.

Let's look at some basic tips and example uses.

Tips for role simulation

Here are some specific tips for role simulation:

- Set some guidelines or rules before beginning. Read the rest of these tips and use them as a starting point.
- Be clear on the scenario, the roles each person plays, and the objectives of the exercise.
- Agree to provide each other with practical feedback. Spend some time after the exercise discussing each other's viewpoints.
- Try to keep the role-playing going without interruptions. If someone becomes stuck, others may then prompt.
- Remind everyone involved that it's a training exercise. If someone starts to get too involved, suggest a pause and highlight this objective.

- Be mindful of everyone's time. If you are in a large group, suggest splitting into smaller groups rather than everyone watching two people, for example.
- If the exchange is between two people, perhaps split into groups of three with one acting as the observer and prompter.
- Understand that some people may be reluctant to do a role-playing exercise in front of a larger group of observers. Using the small group approach can work well in this case.
- If you are role-playing a complex exchange, consider splitting the exercise into parts. Use the principles of part task training.
- Another approach may be to videotape role-playing exercises. This way you can see and hear how you perform.

Example uses of role simulation

You can use role-playing to learn a wide range of skills. Indeed, improving communication and negotiation skills is far more effective when you practice those skills with another person.

Here are some examples:

- **Sailing.** Get your crew into the boat and role-play each maneuver you are likely to use that day. Focus on the communication between each other.
- **Flight training.** The most obvious example is for learning radio calls. Have your instructor (or even someone at home following a script) sit behind you and out of sight. Practice all kinds of radio calls, from basic circuit calls right through to mayday calls and complex clearances. Also try to do some of these with some interference, such as noise, other people talking, or even while you perform a complex maneuver on the simulator.
- **Negotiation, sales, or communication training.** Often the only way to learn these skills well is to role-play likely scenarios with someone else. Better yet, find someone who is studying the same material and take turns at the various roles.

Any time that your topic involves exchanges with other people, find a way to role-play it with others.

Perform—for skills and behaviors

The set of techniques described in this section specifically help you learn skills and behaviors. Let's look at these in summary before going into more detail.

Three-stage skill learning is the normal way of learning most skills. To learn complex skills, it's usually helpful to break the skill down into parts. This is "part task training."

You can improve your skill learning by deliberately introducing task variation and task interference into your training, as long as it's "in context." You can also improve retention of skills via a technique called Overlearning.

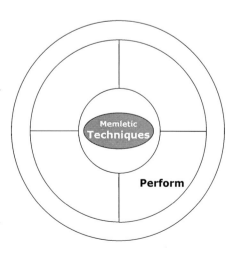

Sometimes you need to change an already learned behavior. This is not as easy as it might seem. You need to follow some specific steps to "shunt" from one response to another. Lastly, you can heighten your overall performance by modeling and anchoring.

This section covers all these techniques in further detail. Read on to find out more.

Note that if you take on a pre-designed training program for complex skills, it's likely the course designers incorporated many of these techniques into your lessons. There is usually still room for you to apply these techniques yourself. If your training program lacks these techniques, you can benefit from adding these techniques yourself.

Three-stage skill learning—how you learn skills

Learning a new skill usually progresses through three stages:

1. You first gain a *declarative* or verbal representation of the steps or rules. For example, "to change gears in a car, I release the accelerator, press the clutch in, change to the new gear, let the clutch out until it engages, then press the accelerator."

2. You then progress to a procedural representation. When you choose to change gears, you think through each of the steps while you do it.

3. Finally, you gain an autonomous action. You change gears without thinking about how.

This is one of the more common skill-learning frames. It involves three stages. These are the cognitive, associative and autonomous stages. Let's look at these stages and how to apply this framework.

The cognitive stage

The cognitive stage is when you build up a mental understanding of the skill. It typically includes understanding the objectives of the skill and recalling the declarations or rules about performing the skill. You "verbalize" these declarations or rules in your mind, however you have not done much real performance of the skill so far.

Let's use the example I introduced in the beginning of this section of changing gears. During the cognitive stage you gain a mental understanding of how to change gears. You understand that you release the accelerator to stop the motor from revving too high. You press the clutch to release the motor from the drive shaft. You use the gear stick to set the new gear, and so on. These are all "declarative" rules in your mind.

The associative stage

The associative stage is when you start turning the declarative or mental rules into procedural or implicit rules in your mind. To do so, you practice the skill. At first you may find it useful to say the steps out loud, however over time you drop the need for this as the skill becomes more automatic.

Using the example of changing gears, you do lessons that focus on changing gears in various scenarios. These may be starting from fully stopped, changing up gears while accelerating, changing down gears when stopping, and starting on a hill.

Each of these helps you discover the overt and subtle movements that allow you to perform the skill properly. For example, you find the balance between letting out the clutch and pressing the accelerator for a smooth gear change.

The autonomous stage

You achieve the autonomous stage when the movements to perform the skill are automatic. You don't have to think about them. Once you have achieved this level, you are usually then competent in that particular skill. There may be further skill levels beyond basic competence though. This comes with further time and practice.

Finishing the example of changing gears, you can drive a car and change gears while carrying on a conversation. You don't think that much about changing gears. It's autonomous.

Practical application

You can use your understanding of this process to improve how you learn individual skills. Here are a few points:

- **Use memory techniques during the early stages.** When you are first learning the parts of a skill, you can use various memory techniques (such as association and visualization) to help you remember how to perform the skill. An example of this in aviation training is the acronym PAST. PAST stands for "Power, Attitude, Speed and Trim" and refers to the steps needed before starting a climb.

- **Reduce reliance on memory techniques as you progress.** As you start to practice the skill, reduce your reliance on memory techniques. For example, practice the skill without saying the mnemonic (with your instructor present). Detect and correct any part of the skill you forget.

- **Do not move on until the skill is autonomous.** If you find yourself still thinking through the steps needed to perform the skill, it's likely that you haven't transferred the skill to procedural memory. Continue practice, otherwise you may find it difficult to progress with further training where the mental or task load is higher.

The last point above is important when using any mnemonic technique (such as first letter mnemonics) to help you learn an autonomous skill. Use the mnemonic while you are learning the skill, however you should reduce and remove the mnemonic as you progress. Continual reliance on a mnemonic for a skill that needs to be autonomous may reduce your effectiveness over time.

For example, you might create the mnemonic ACGCA to stand for "Accelerator, Clutch, Gear, Clutch, Accelerator" to help remember the steps for changing gears. This works well when you are first learning the skill, however at some point you should stop using the mnemonic. Continual use interferes with your ability to make the skill autonomous, and may distract you from other important tasks.

Part task training—divide and conquer

Training courses teaching complex skills sometimes use a technique called part task training. This involves splitting a skill up so you can practice each part separately, before bringing all the parts together to perform the overall skill.

If you are learning or training on your own, you may need to apply this technique yourself. Even if your course already uses part task training, you may find that you want to extend this technique yourself to improve your training. For example, if you find learning a particular task or skill challenging, consider using part task training to conquer the challenge.

In this section I provide to you with the three basic steps for this technique. These are to decompose the task into manageable subtasks, practice each of those subtasks, and then recombine the subtasks to perform the overall task. Let's look at these steps.

Decomposing tasks

You first have to break down tasks into subtasks. Two characteristics help you decide how to do this. These are:

- The complexity or difficulty of the task or skill.
- The integration or organization of the task or skill.

Using these two characteristics, you may decide to decompose the task using one (or more) of these methods:

- **Simplifying.** Simplifying involves adjusting or removing certain task demands during practice. Examples include having a flight instructor handle radio calls when first learning to fly, or reducing time constraints of a practiced forced landing by starting at a higher altitude. Simplifying works well when both the complexity and integration of the skill are both high.

- **Fractionating.** Fractionating involves separate practice on all parts, before integrating them into full performance of the task. An example of this from photography may be to first practice how to compose a photograph, and then practice getting depth of field right without worrying about composition. Fractionating works well when there is high integration between the parts of a skill.

- **Segmenting.** Segmenting involves splitting a task into time-based or location-based parts. An example of this is using a flight simulator to practice landing the aircraft from five hundred feet, separately from practicing the takeoff, circuit and landing. Another example may be to first practice the opening of a sales call, and then only practice the investigation stage. Segmenting works well for sequential or procedural tasks. Segmenting however is not usually effective for tasks that occur over short timeframes.

If subtasks occur within a few seconds of each other, you usually need to practice all parts of the task at the same time. Examples include the last few moments when landing an aircraft, or steps to tack (turn) a yacht. The same applies where there is overlap between subtasks. For example, learning to use the brakes in a car separately to using the clutch (in a manual or stick-shift) may not work effectively. This is because you often need to use the clutch while braking.

Where there is greater than ten seconds between task parts, you can usually practice parts separately.

Practice the subtasks

Once you have decomposed the tasks into subtasks, you then practice each of those subtasks. Use the various Memletic Techniques to help you learn those subtasks quickly. For example, follow the general principles of three stage skill learning, or use simulation to practice each subtask.

Once you have learned each subtask, you can then look at how you recombine each subtask into the full task performance.

Recombine the subtasks

Once you have practiced the subtasks, you then need to recombine those subtasks into a performance of the overall task. There are a few choices here as well. These are pure part, progressive part, and repetitive part recombination:

- **Pure part.** After practicing each part by itself, combine all subtasks at the same time.
- **Progressive part.** Incrementally add subtasks to a growing combination, practicing each new subtask separately.
- **Repetitive part.** Incrementally add parts to a growing combination, *without* practicing each task separately before adding it.

Here's an easier way to visualize each of these methods. If you have four subtasks, the techniques look like this:

Whole part (compare):   1234 1234 1234...

Pure part: 1 2 3 4 1234 1234...

Progressive part: 1 2 12 3 123 4 1234 1234...

Repetitive part: 1 12 123 1234 1234 ...

One variation on the progressive part and repetitive part methods is to reverse the order you add back the subtasks. This is *backward chaining*. Using the example above, backward chaining looks like this:

Backward chaining, progressive: 4 3 34 2 234 1 1234 1234...

Backward chaining, repetitive: 4 34 234 1234 1234...

Backward chaining often works well when a task involves preparation for and then execution of a particular objective. Examples include landing an aircraft or tacking (turning) a yacht. In the yacht example, learn the tack first, and then learn more details of the steps in leading up to the tack.

Performance variation—use contextual variety and interference

Two ways you can increase your learning performance and gain longer-term retention of skills is to use the Task Variation and Task Interference techniques. Let's look at these in more detail.

- **Task Variation technique.** This technique involves performing a task with certain variations. These variations are *in context*. They could occur during performance of the task. Examples may include varying a starting point, the method of achieving the objective, or changing the objective itself.

  For example, variety in landing an aircraft may involve doing landings that are starting from too high or low, with the engine at idle, or on to a short runway. Another example may be docking a yacht under sail or under engine power, with help or without.

- **Task Interference technique.** This technique involves performing the same task but with contextual interference. The interference is from elements that do not necessarily vary how you perform the task, but may make it more difficult to complete.

Using the examples of landing the aircraft or docking the yacht above, interference may come in the form of rain, a low sun, or time pressure. You need to perform the same task while dealing with interference from any or many of those elements.

Task variety and task interference need to be "in context." Use variations and interference from real world scenarios that are likely to occur during or after your training. For example, landing an aircraft in rough turbulence (right context) would improve performance whereas reciting lines from "Romeo and Juliet" (wrong context) may not.

Using task variety and task interference during training may have a temporary negative effect on training performance. The benefit however is better longer term performance and retention. What does this mean? Let's assume the accuracy of landing an aircraft is scored on how close to the start of the runway you land. While you practice scenarios involving variety and interference, it's probable that your scores are lower than if you just did normal landings. However, once you've completed these exercises your scores are likely to increase (and will stay higher), compared to doing the same number of normal landings.

Overlearning—go beyond standard performance

We remember a skill or procedure better if we are good at it. If an expert pilot and novice student both stop flying at the same time, the expert pilot will later have better recall of how to fly.

We can use this principle to improve retention with a technique called *overlearning*. Overlearning involves learning material past the point of general understanding or standard performance. This applies both to theoretical knowledge, such as learning a particular topic in more detail, as well as performing skills and procedures.

If, for example, it normally takes ten practice interviews to become competent in interviewing techniques, overlearning involves doing say an extra five past this basic competence. This is *fifty percent* overlearning. Not only do you perform better immediately afterwards, but you also recall the technique for longer. Spread out those extra repetitions over time as well, rather than doing five repetitions together.

Obviously there is the need for balance here. Overlearning has benefits, however you should balance these against time and cost. Also, be wary of boredom. Avoid further repetitions if you become bored in a potentially dangerous environment. Find ways to further challenge yourself during repetition, for example by using task variety and task interference. Simulation can also help here because you can do many more repetitions without significant increase in cost or set-up time.

The Shunt technique—change habits and behaviors

Sometimes you develop behaviors and habits that you want to change. Changing an existing behavior is not always easy, however the shunt technique can help you do so. The shunt technique consists of five steps (highlighted in the diagram on the right):

1. **Inspection.** Identify that you have a behavior or habit you want to change. It's difficult to change behavior if you don't know you are doing it! Triggers for these may come from your instructor, coach, friends, colleagues, or your own reviews.

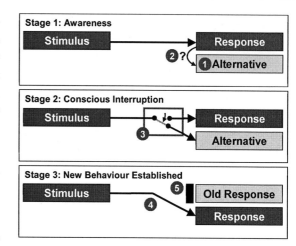

2. **Comparison.** Compare the old behavior with a new behavior that you want to replace it with. Explore what is clearly different. Explore what the benefits are of the new behavior. Go through what the benefits might be with your instructor or interested party.

3. **Correction, or the "shunt."** Practice the new behavior alongside the old. Do as much as you can to contrast the old behavior with the new. Practice the new behavior like you have already changed your behavior. Whenever you accidentally invoke the old behavior, consciously stop and rehearse the new behavior, as if it was the behavior you followed first.

4. **Pre-correction.** Eventually your brain automatically selects the new behavior in response to the stimulus. This is the goal. You have successfully changed your behavior! This will come with repetition.

5. **Reinforcement.** Sometimes you may lapse back into your old behavior. Watch for this. If it does happen, immediately practice the new behavior again. Don't be negative on yourself and believe that you have failed. Simply accept this happens sometimes, replay the new behavior and move on. If it's more serious, you may need to go back through some of the previous steps in more detail.

Example—chipped fingernails

We'll use a simple bad habit, biting fingernails, to explain how to use the shunt technique. To help with the shunt, I've adapted a "swish" technique used by other trainers.

1. **Inspection—identify the old behavior:** Identify the behavior you want to stop. Create a visual in your mind of yourself in that behavior. For example, imagine yourself picking at or biting your nails. See this behavior as if through your own eyes. Make it dull and uninviting.

2. **Compare the new behavior:** Now create a different visual, one in which you display the new behavior. For example, imagine yourself stopping your picking, or taking your fingers away from your mouth. Put some pressure on that finger with another. See yourself with perfect, clean nails. See yourself as well dressed, in control, and more confident.

3. **Set up the shunt:** This visualization will help you "shunt" your behavior from the old response to the new one. Start by making a big picture in your mind of your old state, picking your nails. Feel yourself in a low state, unhappy, with slouched over shoulders and hunched back (physically put

yourself in that posture). Push all the air out of your lungs. See the image in black and white.

Now, make a small picture of the way you want to be in bottom left corner of the big image. Then, explode that small image up and over the big old image. The new image is bright, happy and colorful. As you do so, say "wooosh" while breathing in fully. Pull back your shoulders, straighten your back, and pull your chin up. Smile and feel excited. See yourself in that confident, happy state *with perfect nails*.

Stay in that state for a few moments, then open your eyes briefly. Now go back and do the swish again, starting from the big picture of the old behavior, and replacing it with the new. Do it five or six times in a row, quickly (but have fun doing it!).

Now take a deep breath and bring back that first image of the old behavior. It should almost feel unnatural. Your mind automatically wants to replace it with the new image. If not, go back and repeat the process, making the visuals clearer, and holding that positive state for a few moments before opening your eyes and repeating the process.

4. **Test the pre-correction.** Start to pick or bite your nail. You should feel a trigger or urge to stop. Visualize that high state for a moment. From now on, the next time you are about to pick or bite your nails, you should realize it and can catch yourself. Visualize that high state for a moment, and feel confident that you have changed the behavior.

5. **Reinforce over time.** You may want to add a reminder to your review calendar to reinforce the swish over the next few weeks. Check yourself and if you find you start to lapse back into the old behavior, do a few short "swish" exercises again.

Improving performance state

Often our mental state influences how we perform tasks and procedures. We often do well when we are in a good state of mind. Similarly we often don't perform well when we are in poor state. Many people believe they have little influence over the state they are in at any particular time. This is not true.

By overtly changing your state, you can change how you think and perform. For example, when you are happy you typically smile. When you are feeling down though, if you force yourself to smile it usually triggers happier thoughts. Forcing yourself to smile also affects your physical and mental state, often for the better.

There are two common methods for managing the state you are in during task performance. These are anchoring and modeling. Anchoring allows you to change your mental and physiological state for a short time. Modeling not only helps manage state, it also helps you manage overall task performance. Let's look at these two in more detail.

Anchor previous states

Our state during performance of a skill, task or activity often varies. The word *state* itself can represent functioning of many parts of our body and mind. Physically, your posture, muscle tension, hormones, your heart and breathing rate are all part of your overall state at a given time. Mentally, your self-talk, mental images and other mental activities also form part of your overall state.

Think of how you feel when you are performing a task you know well. Typically you relax more, your shoulders are back, and you think about just the task (or can think of other topics at the same time). Now think about a task you have difficulty with (such as perhaps public speaking). Your whole state is different. You are likely to be breathing fast (or holding your breath), with hunched shoulders, and all these negative thoughts running through your mind. Your state often reflects how you feel about the task.

Our state can change quickly. You might be performing a task well in a good state, however one small mistake (or even just a negative thought) can change your state, if you allow it. That can then result in more mistakes.

Anchoring is a way to help you change your state into one that is suitable for the task. It helps you instantly recall a more resourceful state, simply by squeezing part of your hand or tapping your skin somewhere.

States that you may wish to anchor could be:

- **Confidence.** Think of times when you have felt confident. It could be after passing a hard exam, or while playing a sport, or while doing some activity at work.

- **Peak performance.** Think of times when you have felt like you are performing at your peak. Everything is "clicking." You are performing well, breathing well, alert, and relaxed. It could again be while playing sport, during some activity at work, or perhaps during a recreational activity.

- **Strength.** Think about times when you have felt strong and powerful. Have you ever done some gym work? What about a time when you were fit?

- **Happiness.** When have you felt happy? It could be after receiving some good news, or when life has been going well for you.

The anchoring technique is good for changing your state for short periods of time. It doesn't change long-term beliefs or issues. For example, if you are deeply upset about some part of your life, triggering a positive mood anchor every ten minutes is not going to address the underlying issue. Triggering confidence may help you start working on resolving that issue though.

There are number of steps involved in creating an anchor. Follow these steps to create state anchors:

1. **Design the anchor.** Think of a previous state you have been in that you would like to recall at will. Or, think of what such a state would be like. Also decide what to use as your anchor. It could be squeezing a particular finger or earlobe, or tapping your finger against your skin somewhere. Anchors should be specific and unique. It could be squeezing your index finger between your first and second knuckle, tapping your glasses, bouncing the ball a certain way, or even just squeezing your earlobe.

2. **Relax.** Do a short relaxation exercise. Put everything else out of your mind.

3. **Get in the state you wish to anchor.** Close your eyes and try to recall as much as possible about the state you wish to anchor to. Pick a particular time when this state was at a maximum, and put yourself "in the moment." Recall the sights, sounds and smells at the time. Think of your body posture and your state of mind at the time.

4. **Set the anchor.** At the height of the experience, for that short period of time you are "in the moment," perform the anchor stimulus several times. It needs to be the exact sequence or pressure each time.

5. **Repeat and reinforce.** Relax, breath deeply and then redo steps 3 and 4 several times. Do some repetitions over a few days. Put yourself in another state (for example think about work for a few moments), and then trigger the anchor. Deliberately feel yourself going into the new state. Repeat this a few times as well.

6. **Test.** Now that you have created your anchor, try it out during performance. Trigger the anchor and test that it automatically brings back the state you designed. It should instantly trigger the same physiology and thought patterns you experienced during the anchoring process.

You can use anchoring for a wide variety of purposes. Some common ones include public speaking, exchanges with the opposite sex, and overcoming issues from poor past performances. Here are some more specific examples:

- **Before and during exams.** Use a confidence anchor to help keep your state positive and confident. Repeat it during the exam if you run into some difficulties. This doesn't help overcome issues if you have not prepared for the questions. It however does help keep a confident state if you do run into some issues that might otherwise lower your confidence.

- **During performance.** You can use a peak performance anchor before performing complex or difficult procedures. You might use the anchor when you start to feel stressed. Again, it may not solve underlying problems (such as being behind), however it should put you in a better state to catch up.

- **Pre-performance patterns.** A pre-performance pattern is a specific *ritual* or series of steps that athletes perform before a particular task. Examples are tennis players bouncing the ball a certain way before serving, or golf players visualizing their play, or archers and shooters "zoning out" before a shot. You can use anchors during these pre-performance activities to improve your state.

Model good state

Modeling involves mirroring an expert's performance in a particular area you wish you excel in. You model as many parts of their performance as you can. Such parts include:

- **Physical:** Breathing (including rate, volume and pauses), heart rate, posture, muscular tension, eye movements, voice, body language, general movement, and more.

- **Mental:** Level and focus of attention, relaxation, awareness, reaction time, mental steps and procedures they follow, and more.

While some of these are easy to see, other times you may need to *elicit* (extract) them from the expert. This usually involves asking them how they think or feel at various times during the performance. This is not always easy. Often the response from experts is "it just happens." In this case you may need to ask more direct questions. Where are they looking? Do they feel relaxed or tense? How to they react to some event happening?

Modeling is especially good for transferring general behaviors and attitudes. For example, let's look at the differences between the state of a student pilot and an expert (the instructor) while landing the aircraft:

Aspect	Student	Instructor
Breathing	Almost stopped.	Breathing normally, perhaps pauses at touchdown.
Muscular tension	Tense all over. Gripping yoke in a death grip.	Relaxed. Easy and natural grip on yoke.
Movement	Jerky, large movements.	Small, smooth and deliberate movements.
Attention	Focusing attention in specific places too long.	Moving attention between big and small picture.
Voice	Forced.	Talking naturally. Can instruct while performing the landing.
Overall Tension	High, very tense. Trying to "force the landing."	Low, relaxed. "Guiding the landing."

Modeling in this case would involve looking at how the instructor is performing during this phase, and then modeling that as closely as possible.

It's more difficult to model cognitive, perception and motor-skill parts of performance. Using the example above, we can easily model some parts of the instructor's performance, however it would be difficult to model the specific behaviors needed to land the aircraft. For example, modeling doesn't transfer judgment of when one is too high or low, or when to cut the aircraft engine just before landing. These usually come from direct observation and experience.

See modeling as a fast way to gain good overall state for performing more specialized activities.

Follow these basic steps to create and use performance models:

1. **Find or create the expert.** You can gain models for expert performance in many ways. Perhaps the easiest is to work directly with someone who is already an expert. For flight training, this is usually the instructor. In other areas you may need to seek out an expert.

    You may not have direct access to an expert though. In this case you may use experts you can read about, or even create your own. You can often find out about the way experts think or work by reading their biographies. You may wish to create your own expert who is a composite of many people you know or have researched.

2. **Elicit their strategy.** Spend time with the expert, or do research, and find out about as many parts of their performance as possible. Ask questions about

each of the parts of performance listed above. Watch them while they perform the skill (or visualize them). Write down specific points and observations.

3. **Model the performance yourself.** Once you have the various elements, put yourself in that state. Act as if you were that expert.

4. **Anchor it.** Once you have a good feeling for that performance, use the process in the section on anchoring above to lock as many parts as possible into a specific trigger.

5. **Integrate and Test it.** Try the performance again, trying to keep up as many parts of the performance model as possible. If you are doing this with your instructor, perhaps do some part task training. Have your instructor take over some of the tasks so you can focus on running your performance model. If you were doing the landing example above, you might have the instructor fly the approach and landing while you have your hand resting near the yoke. Act like you were doing the landing, but focus on your breathing, relaxation, small smooth movements, and moving your attention around. Repeat the exercise while taking on more parts of the task, while still upholding your performance model.

6. **Use it.** Use the anchor until you can perform the task while upholding your performance model automatically. You might also choose to use the anchor as a pre-performance activity, in much the same way that expert tennis players use anchoring at the world championship level.

Repeat—techniques to lock in content

In the reinforce step of the Memletic Process, I discuss how important repetition is to the overall learning process, with some specific guidelines for incorporating repetition. While we aim to rely less on repetition as a learning technique, it's still an important ingredient in any learning program.

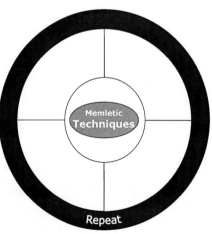

In this section I outline four specific techniques that rely mainly on repetition. These are rote learning, flashcards, scheduled review and programmed repetition. The first three are standard techniques in use today. Programmed repetition is a relatively new technique that I believe provides great benefits for many learning objectives. Read on to find out more.

Rote learning—a standard technique

Yes, sometimes repeated review of information is the most effective learning technique. Examples include the alphabet and the multiplication tables. In my view, you should be able to keep rote learning to a minimum by creative use of the other techniques in this book.

Flashcards—repeat using cards

Flashcards are usually pieces of cardboard with content written on one or both sides. For example, on one side of the cardboard is a word, and on the other side the word's definition. To use them, you simply go through the cards one at a time, *flash* it in front of you, and then repeat what you believe is on the other side. If you don't remember, you can check the reverse side of the flashcard.

Another name for using flashcards is Paired Associate Learning (PAL).

You can use flashcards for two main purposes. First, you can use them as an extension of rote learning. For example, for when you are learning content for the first time. You can also use them as a trigger for review. For example, you may have words on them that trigger visualizations or associations. I believe flashcards are more useful for reviews.

Here are some tips for using flashcards:

- Review them often. Perhaps carry them with you.

- Prepare cards well before any tests on the content.

- Break large groups of cards into smaller groups, especially when learning for the first time.

- Shuffle the cards regularly and flip through them rapidly. This prevents you from learning the cards in a certain order.

- Study the cards that you have more difficulty with. As you flip through, sort them into two or three groups based on how well you respond to the card. Review the difficult cards two more times, the moderate cards once, and don't worry too much about the easy cards.

- Use the other techniques and learning styles where possible. For example, visualize the content, read them aloud, or review the cards while walking around.

Scheduled review—review content regularly

As you can imagine, keeping track of all the review you should be doing can get difficult. You can make this easier by using a review calendar or a spreadsheet.

- **Review calendar.** A review calendar simply involves using a standard or electronic (preferable) calendar to schedule regular reviews. Schedule as you go, rather than set up repeating appointments, as you may want to change the schedule based on how well you remember the content.

- **Spreadsheet.** You may want a more advanced approach, use a spreadsheet to track key review points. Depending on your programming skills, you could enter dates manually, or you could work out an algorithm that automatically tracks and updates review dates.

Programmed Repetition technique—a step forward in learning?

A more powerful way to manage the repetition process is to use some specific software. One example of this software is *SuperMemo.*☾

In SuperMemo, you enter knowledge in a question-answer format, and then it replays that material back to you regularly. The time (in days) between those repetitions depends on how well you recall the answer.

You can set a "percentage retention level," and the software works out the right review calendar to help you preserve your knowledge at this level. The default is ninety-five percent!

You aim to use the tool once a day for a few minutes. The time varies depending on how much new material you are learning and how challenging it is.

How does it work? The software uses complex algorithms that model how a typical person remembers and forgets knowledge. Based on how well you feel you answered a question, it works out when to next ask you the question again. If you recall the answer "well" or "brightly," then it increases the time it waits until it asks you again. If your recall of the answer is "OK," "poor" or "complete blank," then it asks you more often until you do start to remember it. The software also adjusts its algorithms to match your particular learning performance and the difficulty of the material you are learning.

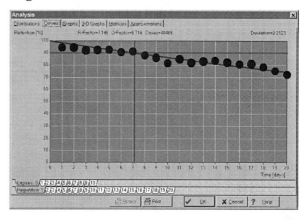

Using a tool like this does take some work, however I believe this to be one of the most effective ways to remember information for the long term. Given our current understanding of the brain, I believe we will rely more on software like this in the future. We will use it to help us both learn and remember new information. One day we may see using tools like SuperMemo as important as regular exercise. The difference between those who do and don't "work out" will be obvious!

Tips for using SuperMemo

The online documentation that comes with SuperMemo is more than enough to get you up and running quickly. Here are a few more tips from my own use of the software:

- **Start early.** Start using it earlier, rather than later, in the Memletic Process. For example, start capturing key points into SuperMemo during the Explore step, and build up the knowledge as you progress.
- **Include review material.** Incorporate the outcomes of your reviews into SuperMemo. If you are having difficulty with a particular topic, break down that topic into more detail.
- **Use it as a reminder tool.** Use it to remind you to review certain topics, such as reminding you to use a simulator and practice a particular procedure.
- **Use it for assertions.** You don't have to use it as just a question-answer tool. You can also use it to help you repeat assertions. Rate each assertion by how well you have achieved the outcome you want. You may want to keep your assertion collection separate from your general learning collection. This is

because you rate an assertion differently to how you rate an answer to a question.

- **Use for goals.** Include scripts, images, photographs, sounds and videos that remind you of your goals.
- **Include techniques as well as content.** Build in your associations, visualizations and other techniques as well, not just the core content you are memorizing.
- **Don't go overboard!** Build up your use of the tool over time. Find what works and doesn't work for you. Don't try to load in one thousand items in the first week for example.

A rollerblading cat? Potential issues with techniques

When we discussed the Associate techniques, I asked you to visualize a cat rollerblading over the Golden Gate Bridge. This example highlights the simple nature of association, however many of the techniques I've described in this book need practice and experience to make them work effectively for you.

Sometimes you may find that a technique doesn't work as well as what you expected. Or, your associations are not so easy to recall when you need them. While these techniques help remember content far longer than usual practices, they still need review. Lastly, it's important not to go overboard.

Let's look at some common issues with using these techniques.

A technique doesn't work

When a technique doesn't work as well as you expect, you have the opportunity to look at why. You can also discover alternative ways of learning. Some of my most effective learning occurred after having to use an alternative technique because the first technique didn't work as well as I wanted.

Some questions to ask yourself when a technique does not work as well as you expect include:

- Have you fully understood the intent, process and use of the technique? Re-read the descriptions, or try to find further information on particular techniques using the references ☺.
- Have you set the foundations? For example, peg words need an investment of effort to memorize at least the first ten words. Recalling the first ten peg words has to be as easy as counting to ten. Some of the techniques that extend on these basic ten words don't work effectively if you cannot immediately recall the correct peg words.
- Have you associated or visualized effectively? Sometimes I came up with a creative association that linked two pieces of content I was trying to memorize. However, I didn't take a moment to visualize it. I discuss this problem in more detail below.
- Perhaps the technique you are trying doesn't work well for your learning style. See the Memletic Styles chapter for more information on the various learning styles.
- Perhaps the technique doesn't work well for the content you are learning. Some techniques do not work so well when you are under pressure. Other techniques

work well for checklists but not learning about weather, for example. In the Memletic Process (the Arrange step) I outline which techniques are good for the various knowledge types, however you may need to vary your choices for your own use.

If you find you still can't get a technique to work for you, whether in general or when applying to a specific learning objective, try another approach. If you find that one technique works for you, use it more often. If you have difficulty with another, try different techniques. The important point is that you should try to find what works for *you*.

Association not complete

Association works as long as you follow some basic guidelines. The section on the Associate techniques describes these in detail, however here are a few pointers if you find your associations are not working as well as you would like.

Not linked from first to second

When you are linking two items together in sequential order, try to link from the first item to the second item. Sometimes you might want to use some part of the second item to link to the first. This can cause problems. Later when you have the first item in mind and are trying to recall the second item, you can become stuck. You don't yet have the second item in mind, so you can't see the link to the first.

Let's look at an example. Imagine one of your review items is to remember to take a camera with you. This item is number 90 in your review list. Therefore, you are trying to link a bus (the peg word for 90) and a camera.

You could visualize a big camera taking a photo of a bus, however this means you visualize the big camera first. When you are trying to recall what you "stored" with the peg word for 90, you first remember that "bus" is the peg word for 90. You may then find it difficult to recall the camera because the camera is the centerpiece of your original visualization, not the bus.

Instead, visualize the bus, and then something about the bus that makes you think of a camera. For example, imagine a bus standing on its rear wheels in a massive photographic studio. The bus is holding a camera (oversize as you may well expect), and it's taking photos of another bus doing a modeling shoot. Squint each time the huge flash (from that camera) goes off. Imagine seeing the bright lights and flash reflect off the bus windscreen.

You more easily remember the association because the bus is the centerpiece. Your mind goes from 90, to bus, and then to the camera.

Not creative enough

Creative associations are easier to remember. Keep in mind the features outlined in the section describing association, such as using the senses, exaggeration, combinations, and more. If you include more features of good association, your associations stay longer in your mind and they reappear faster when you need to recall them.

Created the story, but didn't visualize it

Using the bus example above, you often need to do more than just create the idea of a bus using a camera in a photo shoot. You need to close your eyes for a moment and see it in your mind's eye. See the photographer-bus moving around, and hear it asking the modeling bus for various poses. Feel the heat from the bright lights, hear the camera clicking, and hear a bus-related song playing in the background.

Sometimes it's easy to think you have done enough just to invent the association. It isn't. Until you do the visualization, you haven't locked it into your memory. Close your eyes for just a moment and see the visualization.

No review

Did you know a computer is forgetful? It has to refresh its main memory hundreds of times each second, otherwise it loses the stored data. The human brain is similar, however thankfully it doesn't need as much refresh as that. Using Memletics significantly improves your retention. If you don't use the information you have stored though, it's eventually lost.

Write down the techniques you use to learn content, and then add the important topics to your review schedule. Review your content as you need to. If you use the material regularly, you can skip over some parts of your review. Focus on the material that you have not used or reviewed for a while.

Review the eNquire step of the Memletic Process for more ideas on reviewing content.

The "WOW" factor

Just because you can memorize anything you want to, that doesn't mean you should! Some people go too far after realizing that they now have the ability to memorize anything they want.

You may well be able to memorize every specification of an aircraft or boat. It's often better though to find a balance between what you need to memorize and what you can reference in a non-time-pressured environment. For example, it's unlikely that you need to recall the battery serial number! Memletics aims to improve the speed and quality of your learning, not necessarily the quantity.

Also, there are many techniques in this book. This does not mean you need to try or use every one of them from the beginning. Pick the ones that suit your training material, and come back to others as you need to.

Use the website

On the Memletics website you can post your questions on techniques to other readers of the book. You can also browse the site for previous discussions on how to deal with particular challenges. See the Closing chapter for more information on what's on the website.

Chapter summary

In this chapter you saw over thirty techniques you can use to memorize information and skills. I grouped them into the six categories so you can remember them more easily. These are the associate, visualize, verbalize, simulate, perform and repeat categories of techniques.

You saw that association is a fundamental memory skill. It underlies many of the other techniques, and works well because it uses basic memory principles. I described for you the basic rules of association, as well as some techniques that use it. These include basic mnemonics, linked lists, peg words and events, method of loci, and chunking techniques.

Next we discussed visualization. You read about general visualization principles, and then we considered how you can use it for visualizing goals and strengthening the other techniques. You can also use visualization for mental practice.

The Verbalize techniques rely on using words, both spoken and written, to change your internal dialog. You saw how to create and use assertions, scripts and a mental firewall to change your self-talk and behaviors.

Simulation helps you practice skills and procedures using external aids. We looked at basic simulators that use household objects to help you learn. We considered PC-based simulators, and saw that you can use PC simulators for a wide range of activities, not just flight simulation. We also reviewed simulation using other people, or role-playing.

We use simulation to help learn skills, and the next section on Perform techniques covered skill-learning in much detail. I gave you an outline of how we learn new skills using a "three stage skill learning" model. You then found out about part task training, a technique often used for learning complex skills. We discussed Task Variation and Task Interference techniques, what overlearning means, and the shunt technique for changing behaviors. You also saw how to use anchoring and modeling to manage state during performance.

Repetition is fundamental for learning, and so the last techniques, the repetition techniques, gave you ways to use repetition effectively. We quickly looked at rote learning and flashcards, and then looked in more depth at repetition techniques such as scheduled repetition and programmed repetition. You saw how software like SuperMemo could change how you remember information for the long term.

Lastly, we covered some potential issues that may arise when using these techniques. We looked at what to do if a technique doesn't work, what can happen if you don't associate correctly, and two other points that can help you fix technique problems.

In the next chapter, we look at Memletic Styles. You will discover you own learning styles using the styles questionnaire. The rest of the chapter looks at how to make the most of both your dominant and secondary styles.

Chapter

Adapt with the Memletic Styles

Each of us learns using preferred learning styles. This chapter helps you discover your stronger and secondary learning styles, and the range of styles available to you. It also provides you with strategies for improving your learning by using your dominant styles and developing your secondary styles. These strategies help you adapt Memletics to suit your preferences, while challenging you to increase the range of styles you can use. The result is you can apply your new-found abilities to many more varied goals.

Memletics recognizes that each person prefers different learning styles and techniques. Learning styles group common ways that people learn. Everyone has a mix of learning styles. Some people may find that they have a dominant style of learning, with far less use of the other styles. Others may find that they use different styles in different circumstances. There is no *right mix*. Nor are your styles fixed. You can develop ability in less dominate styles, as well as further develop styles that you already use well.

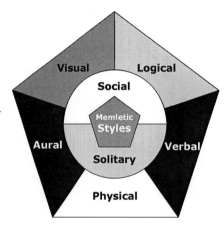

Using multiple learning styles and "multiple intelligences" for learning is a relatively new approach. This approach is one that educators have only recently started to recognize. Traditional schooling used (and continues to use) mainly linguistic and logical teaching methods. It also uses a limited range of learning and teaching techniques. Many schools still rely on classroom and book-based teaching, much repetition, and pressured exams for reinforcement and review. A result is that we often label those who use these learning styles and techniques as "bright." Those who use less favored learning styles often find themselves in lower classes, with various not-so-complimentary labels and sometimes lower quality teaching. This can create positive and negative spirals that reinforce the belief that one is "smart" or "dumb."

By recognizing and understanding your own learning styles, you can use techniques better suited to you. This improves the speed and quality of your learning.

In this chapter, we first look at the basis of learning styles and their influence on learning. Following that, I have an exercise for you. The exercise is a questionnaire to help you discover your preferred Memletic styles.

We then look at each of the Memletic Styles in turn. In summary, these are:

- **Visual.** You prefer using pictures, images, and spatial understanding.
- **Aural.** You prefer using sound and music.
- **Verbal.** You prefer using words, both in speech and writing.
- **Physical.** You prefer using your body, hands and sense of touch.
- **Logical.** You prefer using logic, reasoning and systems.
- **Social.** You prefer to learn in groups or with other people.
- **Solitary.** You prefer to work alone and use self-study.

Lastly, we look at how you can improve your learning by using learning styles. One obvious way is to use more of your dominant learning styles. An interesting feature of learning styles is that you can also improve your learning performance by using styles you do not often use. If you are a mainly visual person, then you can make a lesson more memorable by using some aural content in your visualizations. If you like to use logic, then use some physical learning techniques occasionally.

Why Styles? Understand the basis of learning styles

Your learning styles have more influence than you may realize. Your preferred styles guide the way you learn. They also change the way you internally represent experiences, the way you recall information, and even the words you choose. We explore more of these features in this chapter.

Research shows us that each learning style uses different parts of the brain. By involving more of the brain during learning, we remember more of what we learn. Researchers using brain-imaging technologies have been able to find out the key areas of the brain responsible for each learning style. Refer to the "Brain Regions" diagram and read the following overview:

- **Visual.** The occipital lobes at the back of the brain manage the visual sense. Both the occipital and parietal lobes manage spatial orientation.
- **Aural.** The temporal lobes handle aural content. The right temporal lobe is especially important for music.
- **Verbal.** The temporal and frontal lobes, especially two specialized areas called Broca's and Wernicke's areas (in the left hemisphere of these two lobes).
- **Physical.** The cerebellum and the motor cortex (at the back of the frontal lobe) handle much of our physical movement.
- **Logical.** The parietal lobes, especially the left side, drive our logical thinking.
- **Social.** The frontal and temporal lobes handle much of our social activities. The limbic system (not shown apart from the hippocampus) also influences both the social and solitary styles. The limbic system has a lot to do with emotions, moods and aggression.
- **Solitary.** The frontal and parietal lobes, and the limbic system, are also active with this style.

I've based the Memletic Styles on two brain models you may have heard about. The first is "Multiple Intelligences" by Howard Gardner. I've broadened his model and made it more applicable to learning. You may know the other model as "VAK," or the Visual-Auditory-Kinesthetic model. Neuro-Linguistic Programming (NLP) books also describe this model as "modality preferences."

Brain Regions and Functions

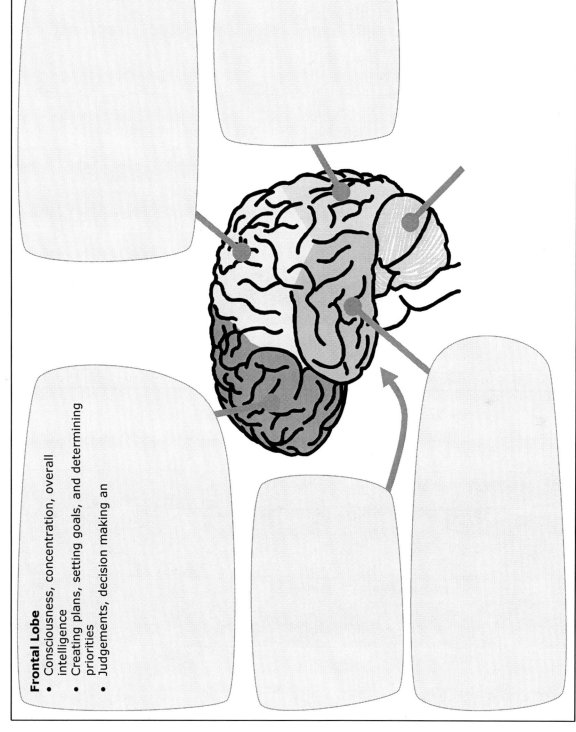

Frontal Lobe
- Consciousness, concentration, overall intelligence
- Creating plans, setting goals, and determining priorities
- Judgements, decision making an

You may have also heard about the "left brain / right brain" model. In this model, the "left brain" is more logical, calculating and knowing, whereas the right brain focuses on emotions, feelings, and the visual sense. Recent research shows the brain is more complex than that simple model allows. Some activities are more commonly on the left or right sides, such as language on the left and music on the right. However, most of our brain's functions are a rich interplay between both the hemispheres.

Profile yourself—use the Memletic Styles questionnaire

Before we look at the various learning styles, let's discover what learning styles you prefer. In the following questionnaire, you first estimate your learning styles. You then answer seventy questions about how you interact with the world. Following that, you complete a scoring sheet that then gives you a score for each learning style. Lastly, you graph your results and compare against your estimate.

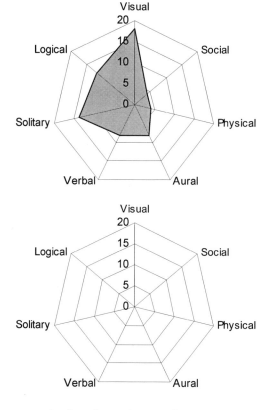

The outcome from the questionnaire is a personalized Memletic Styles graph similar to the one on the right.

You can write in the book (or take a photocopy if the book belongs to someone else) or use the spreadsheet from the website 🌏. The spreadsheet has the benefit that it calculates your scores and graphs them for you.

You will find this questionnaire valuable. Doing this questionnaire helps you better understand your own learning styles. It also makes the following descriptions more relevant to you.

Do the pre-test graph

Before you start the questionnaire, fill out the blank graph on the right. Review the basic descriptions at the start of the chapter if you like.

For each axis, estimate on a rating of zero to twenty how often you use that particular learning style. Score zero if hardly ever, twenty if you use that style often. Draw in the score on each style axis (the lines starting from the centre), then join the dots like in the example Memletic Styles graph above.

Answer the questions

Answer each question by circling one of the numbers on the right. You could also write zero, one or two directly into the scoring sheet further below, or print out a sheet from the spreadsheet on the website 🌏. If you enter your scores into the score sheet while you answer the questions, hide the bottom of the score sheet so you don't see the styles for each column.

The scale is as follows:

0. The description sounds nothing like you.
1. The description sounds partly like you.
2. The description sounds exactly like you.

Take as long as you like. Afterwards we rate your answers. Remember there are no right or wrong answers. Usually the first response that comes into your mind when you read the question is a good answer.

Questions

1	You have a personal or private interest or hobby that you like to do alone.	0 1 2
2	You put together itineraries and agendas for travel. You use detailed lists, such as to-do lists, and you number the items and set priorities.	0 1 2
3	Jingles, themes or parts of songs pop into your head at random.	0 1 2
4	You preferred math and science subjects at school.	0 1 2
5	You are happy in your own company. You like to do some activities alone and away from others.	0 1 2
6	You enjoy learning in classroom style surroundings with other people. You enjoy the contact and it helps your learning.	0 1 2
7	You read everything. Books, newspapers, magazines, menus, signs, etc.	0 1 2
8	You can easily visualize objects, buildings, scenarios etc. from descriptions or plans.	0 1 2
9	You are goal oriented and know the direction you are going in life or work.	0 1 2
10	You prefer team games and sports such as football/soccer, basketball, netball, volleyball, hockey, and baseball.	0 1 2
11	You navigate well and use maps with ease. You rarely get lost. You have a good sense of direction. You usually know which way North is.	0 1 2
12	You prefer to study or work alone.	0 1 2
13	You like being a mentor or guide for others.	0 1 2
14	You spend time alone to reflect and think about your life.	0 1 2
15	In regular conversation, you often use references to other topics or events you have heard about or read.	0 1 2
16	You enjoy finding associations, for example between numbers or objects. You like to classify or group things to help you understand the relationships between them.	0 1 2

17	You keep a journal or personal diary to record your thoughts.	0 1 2
18	You communicate well with others and often act as a mediator between them.	0 1 2
19	You love sport and exercise.	0 1 2
20	You like to listen. People like to talk to you because they feel you understand them.	0 1 2
21	You like listening to music - in the car, studying, at work (if possible!), or anywhere. You love live music.	0 1 2
22	You can balance a checkbook. You like to set budgets and other numerical goals.	0 1 2
23	You have some very close friends.	0 1 2
24	You use many hand gestures or other physical body language when communicating with others.	0 1 2
25	English, languages and literature were favorite subjects at school.	0 1 2
26	You like making models, or working out jigsaws.	0 1 2
27	You prefer to talk over problems, issues, or ideas with others, rather than working on them by yourself.	0 1 2
28	Music was your favorite subject at school.	0 1 2
29	In school, you preferred art, technical drawing, and geometry.	0 1 2
30	You love telling stories, or using metaphors or anecdotes.	0 1 2
31	You like identifying logic flaws in other people's words and actions.	0 1 2
32	You like using a camera or video camera to capture the world around you.	0 1 2
33	You use rhythm or rhyme to remember items, for example phone numbers, PIN numbers, and other items.	0 1 2
34	In school, you liked sports, wood or metalworking, craft, sculpture, pottery and other similar subjects.	0 1 2
35	You have a great vocabulary, and like using the right word at the right time.	0 1 2
36	You like the texture and feel of clothes, furniture and other objects.	0 1 2
37	You would prefer to holiday on a deserted island rather than a resort or cruise ship with many other people around.	0 1 2
38	You like books with many diagrams, illustrations, or pictures.	0 1 2
39	You easily express yourself, whether it's verbally or in writing. You can clearly explain ideas and information to others.	0 1 2

40	You like playing games with others, such as card games and board games.	0 1 2
41	You use specific examples and references to support your points of view.	0 1 2
42	You pay attention to the sounds around you. You can tell the difference between instruments, or cars, or aircraft, based on their sound.	0 1 2
43	You have a good sense of color.	0 1 2
44	You like making puns, saying tongue twisters, making rhymes.	0 1 2
45	You like to think out ideas, problems, or issues while doing something physical.	0 1 2
46	You read self-help books, you've been to self-help workshops, or you've done similar work to learn more about yourself.	0 1 2
47	You can play a musical instrument or you can sing on (or close to) key.	0 1 2
48	You like crosswords, scrabble and other word games.	0 1 2
49	You like logic games and brainteasers. You like chess and other strategy games.	0 1 2
50	You like getting out of the house and being with others at parties and other social events.	0 1 2
51	You occasionally realize you are tapping in time to music, or you naturally start to hum or whistle a tune. Even after only hearing a tune a few times, you can remember it.	0 1 2
52	You solve problems by "thinking aloud." You talk through issues, questions and possible solutions.	0 1 2
53	You enjoy dancing.	0 1 2
54	You prefer to work for yourself, or you have thought a lot about it.	0 1 2
55	You don't like silence. You would prefer to have some background music or other noise to silence.	0 1 2
56	You love theme park rides that involve much physical action, or you dislike them because you are sensitive to the physical forces on your body.	0 1 2
57	You draw well. You find yourself drawing or doodling on a notepad when thinking.	0 1 2
58	You easily work with numbers, and can do decent calculations in your head.	0 1 2
59	You use diagrams and scribbles to communicate ideas and information. You love whiteboards (and color pens).	0 1 2
60	You hear small things that others don't.	0 1 2

61 You would prefer to touch or handle something to understand how it works.   0 1 2

62 You don't mind taking the lead and showing others the way ahead.   0 1 2

63 You easily absorb information through reading, audiocassettes or lectures. The actual words and phrases come back to you.   0 1 2

64 You like to understand how and why things work. You keep up to date with science and technology.   0 1 2

65 You are a tinkerer. You like pulling things apart, and they usually go back together! You can easily follow instructions represented in diagrams.   0 1 2

66 Music evokes strong emotions and images as you listen to it. Music is prominent in your recall of memories.   0 1 2

67 You think independently. You know how you think and you make up your own mind. You understand your own strengths and weaknesses.   0 1 2

68 You like gardening or working with your hands in the shed.   0 1 2

69 You like visual arts, painting, and sculpture. You like jigsaws and mazes.   0 1 2

70 You use a specific step-by-step process to work out problems.   0 1 2

Score your responses

Now that you have completed the questions, use the score sheet further below to assign your answers to the correct styles. In the shaded box for each question, write in your score from the questions above—zero, one or two.

1							*1*
2					*2*		
3			*1*				
4					*2*		
5							*1*
6						*0*	

Once you have filled out all the boxes, add up each column and write the totals at the bottom of each column.

33	*2*						
34			*1*				
35				*0*			
Total	*8*	*3*	*2*	*2*	*7*	*3*	*7*

Finally, add the totals of each style from the two columns and write your overall totals in the bottom box.

Overall Totals (add total lines above):

Visual	Verbal	Aural	Physical	Logical	Social	Solitary
18	5	4	4	14	8	14

Graph and analyze

Lastly, graph your scores on the blank Memletic Styles graph on the right. As you may have done above before answering the questions, draw in the score on each axis, then join the dots.

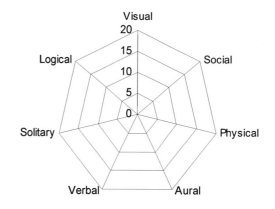

The graph shows which styles you use more often, against those you use less often. You might also like to compare your graph back to your estimate of your learning styles. Look at the differences and try to understand them.

Keep your results in mind and continue to the next section, where I give you some more information on each of the learning styles.

	1	2	3	4	5	6	7
1							▓
2					▓		
3			▓				
4					▓		
5							▓
6						▓	
7		▓					
8	▓						
9							▓
10						▓	
11	▓						
12							▓
13						▓	
14							▓
15		▓					
16					▓		
17							▓
18						▓	
19				▓			
20						▓	
21			▓				
22					▓		
23						▓	
24				▓			
25		▓					
26				▓			
27						▓	
28			▓				
29	▓						
30		▓					
31					▓		
32	▓						
33			▓				
34				▓			
35		▓					
Total							

	1	2	3	4	5	6	7
36				▓			
37							▓
38	▓						
39		▓					
40						▓	
41					▓		
42			▓				
43	▓						
44		▓					
45				▓			
46							▓
47			▓				
48		▓					
49					▓		
50						▓	
51			▓				
52		▓					
53				▓			
54							▓
55			▓				
56					▓		
57	▓						
58						▓	
59	▓						
60			▓				
61				▓			
62						▓	
63		▓					
64	▓						
65	▓						
66			▓				
67							▓
68				▓			
69	▓						
70					▓		
Total							

Overall Totals:

Visual	Verbal	Aural	Physical	Logical	Social	Solitary

Add total lines from the columns above.

The Visual style—images, colors and spatial skills

If you use the visual style, you prefer using images, pictures, colors, and maps to organize information and communicate with others. You can easily visualize objects, plans and outcomes in your mind's eye. You also have a good spatial sense, which gives you a good sense of direction. You can easily find your way around using maps, and you rarely get lost. When you walk out of an elevator, you instinctively know which way to turn.

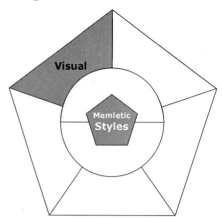

The whiteboard is a best friend (or would be if you had access to one). You love drawing, scribbling and doodling, especially with colors. You typically have a good dress sense and color balance (although not always!).

Some pursuits that make the most use of the visual style are visual art, architecture, photography, video or film, design, planning (especially strategic), and navigation.

Common phrases

You may use phrases like these:

- Let's look at it differently.
- See how this works for you.
- I can't quite picture it.
- Let's draw a diagram or map.
- I'd like to get a different perspective.
- I never forget a face.

Learning and techniques

If you are a visual learner, use images, pictures, color and other visual media to help you learn. Incorporate much imagery into your visualizations.

You may find that visualization comes easily to you. This also means that you may have to make your visualizations stand out more. This makes sure new material is obvious among all the other visual images you have floating around inside your head.

Use color, layout, and spatial organization in your associations, and use many "visual words" in your assertions. Examples include see, picture, perspective, visual, and map.

Use mind maps. Use color and pictures in place of text, wherever possible. If you don't use the computer, make sure you have at least four different color pens.

Systems diagrams can help you visualize the links between parts of a system, for example major engine parts or the principle of sailing in equilibrium. Replace words with pictures, and use color to highlight major and minor links.

The visual journey or story technique helps you memorize content that isn't easy to "see." The visual story approach for memorizing procedures is a good example of this.

Peg words and events come easily to you, however you need to spend some time learning at least the first ten peg words. Afterwards, your ability to visualize helps you peg content quickly.

The swish technique for changing behaviors also works well for you, as it relies on visualization.

What if you're not very visual?

If you are reading this and thinking that visualization is only good for those who use the visual style, think again! While visual people do have some advantages over the other styles for visualization, the other styles have much to gain from visualization.

The word "visualization" is inaccurate. The visual sense in visualization *is only one of five senses you can use*. Visualization is just as powerful when you use it with your non-visual styles. If you use the aural style, focus on the sounds within a scenario. If you use the physical style, focus on the movements, textures and sensations.

Here's an example. You want to use visualization to help you to remember to set the throttle to idle as you land an aircraft. How can you apply each of the styles to visualize this action?

- **Visual:** See your hand pulling the throttle down to idle.
- **Aural:** Hear the engine slow down as you set the throttle to idle.
- **Verbal:** Say "Cut Throttle" as you set the throttle to idle.
- **Physical:** Feel the friction in the throttle as you set it to idle. Feel it stop at the bottom.
- **Logical:** Understand that to land an aircraft you need to set the throttle to idle. Say to yourself "I want to land, therefore I set the throttle to idle."

The social and solitary styles aim more at the environments in which you learn, however even in this scenario you could add to your visualization by:

- **Social:** See three other pilots in the aircraft with you, encouraging you to set it to idle.
- **Solitary:** Visualize yourself being the solo pilot, deliberately setting the throttle to idle without prompting from anyone else.

Having said all this, the visual style is still a powerful style for visualization. If you don't often use visual style, it's worthwhile spending some time to develop it further.

The Aural Style—sound and music

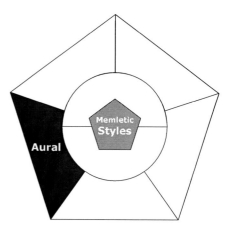

If you use the aural style, you like to work with sound and music. You have a good sense of pitch and rhythm. You typically can sing, play a musical instrument, or identify the sounds of different instruments. Certain music invokes strong emotions. You notice the music playing in the background of movies, TV shows and other media. You often find yourself humming or tapping a song or jingle, or a theme or jingle pops into your head without prompting.

Some pursuits that use the aural style are playing, conducting, or composing music, and sound engineering (mixing and audiovisual work).

Common phrases

You may use phrases like these:

- That sounds about right.
- That rings a bell.
- It's coming through loud and clear.
- Tune in to what I'm saying...
- Clear as a bell.
- That's music to my ears.

Learning and techniques

If you are an aural learner, use sound, rhyme, and music in your learning. Focus on using aural content in your association and visualization.

Use sound recordings to provide a background and help you get into visualizations. For example, use a recording of an aircraft engine running normally, playing loudly via a headset, to practice flight procedures. Use a recording of the sound of wind and water when visualizing sailing maneuvers. If you don't have these recordings, consider creating them while next out training.

When creating mnemonics or acrostics, make the most of rhythm and rhyme, or set them to a jingle or part of a song.

Use the anchoring technique to recall various states that music invokes in you. If you have some particular music or song that makes you want to "take on the world," play it back and anchor your emotions and state. When you need the boost, you can easily recall the state without needing the music.

The Verbal Style—spoken and written words

The verbal style involves both the written and spoken word. If you use this style, you find it easy to express yourself, both in writing and verbally. You love reading and writing. You like playing on the meaning or sound of words, such as in tongue twisters, rhymes, limericks and the like. You know the meaning of many words, and regularly make an effort to find the meaning of new words. You use these words, as well as phrases you have picked up recently, when talking to others.

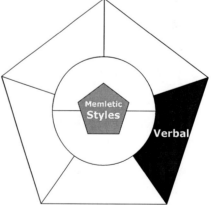

Pursuits that use the verbal style include public speaking, debating, politics, writing and journalism.

Common phrases

You may use phrases like these:

- Tell me word for word...
- Let's talk later.
- The word you're looking for is...
- I hear you but I'm not sure I agree.
- Let me spell it out for you.
- In other words...

Learning and techniques

If you are a verbal learner, try the techniques that involve speaking and writing. Find ways to incorporate more speaking and writing in techniques. For example, talk yourself through procedures in the simulator, or use recordings of your content for repetition.

Make the most of the word-based techniques such as assertions and scripting. Use rhyme and rhythm in your assertions where you can, and be sure to read important ones aloud. Set some key points to a familiar song, jingle or theme.

Mnemonics are your friends for recalling lists of information. Acronym mnemonics use words, focusing on the first letter of the word to make up another word or memorable sequence. You can also make up phrases using the items you want to memorize.

Scripting is also powerful for you. You don't just have to write them down. Record your scripts using a tape or digital audio recorder (such as an MP3 player), and use it later for reviews.

When you read content aloud, make it dramatic and varied. Instead of using a monotone voice to go over a procedure, turn it into a lively and energetic speech worthy of the theatre. Not only does this help your recall, you get to practice your dramatic presence!

Try working with others and using role-playing to learn verbal exchanges such as negotiations, sales or radio calls.

The Physical Style—touch and sensations

If the physical style is more like you, it's likely that you use your body and sense of touch to learn about the world around you. It's likely you like sports and exercise, and other physical activities such as gardening or woodworking. You like to think out issues, ideas and problems while you exercise. You would rather go for a run or walk if something is bothering you, rather than sitting at home.

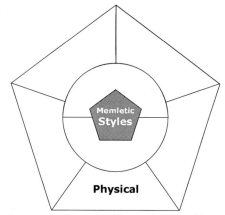

You are more sensitive to the physical world around you. You notice and appreciate textures, for example in clothes or furniture. You like "getting your hands dirty," or making models, or working out jigsaws.

You typically use larger hand gestures and other body language to communicate. You probably don't mind getting up and dancing either, at least when the time is right. You either love the physical action of theme park rides, or they upset your inner body sense too much and so you avoid them altogether.

When you are learning a new skill or topic, you would prefer to "jump in" and play with the physical parts as soon as possible. You would prefer to pull an engine apart and put it back together, rather than reading or looking at diagrams about how it works.

The thought of sitting in a lecture listening to someone else talk is repulsive. In those circumstances, you fidget or can't sit still for long. You want to get up and move around.

Pursuits that involve the physical style include general physical work, mechanical, construction and repair work, sports and athletics, drama and dancing.

Common phrases

You may use phrases like these:

- That feels right to me.
- I can't get a grip on this...
- Stay in touch.
- Get in touch with...

- That doesn't sit right with me.
- I have good feelings about this.
- My gut is telling me...
- I follow your drift.

Learning and techniques

If you use a physical style, use touch, action, movement and hands-on work in your learning activities. For visualization, focus on the sensations you would expect in each scenario. For example, if you are visualizing a tack (turn) on a sailboat, focus on physical sensations. Feel the pressure against your hand as you turn the rudder, and the tension lessening on the ropes. Feel the wind change to the other side, feel the *thud* as the sail swaps with the wind, and feel the boat speed up as you start the new leg.

For assertions and scripting, describe the physical feelings of your actions. For example, a pilot might script as follows: "I feel the friction as I push the throttle forward to start my takeoff run. The controls start to feel more responsive as I check the airspeed, oil pressure and temperature. At takeoff speed, I pull back slightly, and I feel the vibrations of the wheels stop as the plane leaves the ground. After a few moments, I reach down and set the gear selector to up. I feel the satisfying bump as the gear stops fully up."

Use physical objects as much as possible. Physically touch objects as you learn about what they do. Flashcards can help you memorize information because you can touch and move them around.

Keep in mind as well that writing and drawing diagrams are physical activities, so don't neglect these techniques. Perhaps use big sheets of paper and large color markers for your diagrams. You then get more action from the drawing.

Use breathing and relaxation to focus your state while you learn and perform. Focus on staying calm, centered, relaxed and aware. If you want to gain more control over your physical state, look up some references on *Autogenics*. This was a secret behind the great Russian athletic performances over the past few decades. You can find more on relaxation in the Memletic State chapter.

Use role-playing, either singularly or with someone else, to practice skills and behaviors. Find ways to act out or simulate what you are learning.

The Logical Style—logic and reasoning

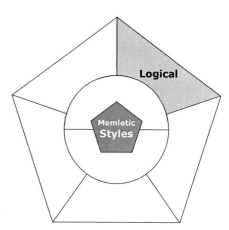

If you use the logical style, you like using your brain for logical and mathematical reasoning. You can recognize patterns easily, as well as connections between seemingly meaningless content. This also leads you to classify and group information to help you learn or understand it.

You work well with numbers and you can perform complex calculations. You remember the basics of trigonometry and algebra, and you can do moderately complex calculations in your head.

You typically work through problems and issues in a systematic way, and you like to create procedures for future use. You are happy setting numerical targets and budgets, and you track your progress towards these. You like creating agendas, itineraries, and to-do lists, and you typically number and rank them before putting them into action.

Your scientific approach to thinking means you often support your points with logical examples or statistics. You pick up logic flaws in other peoples words, writing or actions, and you may point these out to people (not always to everyone's amusement).

You like working out strategies and using simulation. You may like games such as brainteasers, backgammon, and chess. You may also like PC games such as Dune II, Starcraft, Age of Empires, Sid Meier games and others.

People with a strong logical style are likely to follow such pursuits as the sciences, mathematics, accounting, detective work, law and computer programming.

Common phrases

You are more likely to use phrases that reflect your most dominant style out of the visual, aural or physical styles, however you may also use phrases like these:

- That's logical.
- Follow the process, procedure, or rules.
- There's no pattern to this.

- Let's make a list.
- We can work it out.
- Quantify it!

Learning and techniques

If you are a logical learner, aim to understand the reasons behind your content and skills. Don't just rote learn. Understanding more detail behind your compulsory content helps you memorize and learn the material that you need to know. Explore the links between various systems, and note them down.

While you study, create and use lists by extracting key points from your material. You may also want to use statistics and other analysis to help you identify areas you may want to concentrate on.

Pay attention to your physical state, for example your breathing and stress level. It's possible that you isolate your own body from your rational thought. Remember that you are just as much a part of the "system" as any equipment you may be using.

Also remember that association often works well when it is illogical and irrational. It doesn't matter how logical two items are together. You have a better chance of recalling them later if you have make the association illogical. Your brain may protest at first!

In your scripting though, highlight logical thoughts and behaviors. Highlight your ability to pick up systems and procedures easily, *and* that you can detect when you need to change a set procedure.

Make use of "systems thinking" to help understand the links between various parts of a system. An important point here is that systems thinking helps you understand the bigger picture. Often the whole is greater than the sum of the parts. For example, you may understand the individual aircraft systems and flight surfaces, but you may not have a view of how all those systems support flight in equilibrium. Systems diagrams can help you gain that understanding.

You may find it challenging to change existing behaviors or habits. You can rationalize all you want to about why you should change a behavior, but you may find it persists. Try the shunt technique to understand what behavior you currently have and what behavior you want to have. When you understand those behaviors, use the technique to divert from the old behavior to the new.

You may sometimes overanalyze certain parts of your learning or training. This can lead to *analysis paralysis*. You may be busy, but not moving towards your goal. If you find you are overanalyzing which school to start with, or you are over-planning your course maps, stop and refocus on activities that move you forward. Consider how much "bang for buck" you get from spending more time than necessary. Measure your activities by your speed towards your goal. Planning exactly how much time to spend on each chapter of theory doesn't help learn it anywhere near as fast as starting on the theory!

If you often focus from analysis paralysis, write "Do It Now" in big letters on some signs or post-it notes. Place them in strategic places around your work or study area.

The Social Style—communication, groups, and synergy

If you have a strong social style, you communicate well with people, both verbally and non-verbally. People listen to you or come to you for advice, and you are sensitive to their motivations, feelings or moods. You listen well and understand other's views. You may enjoy mentoring or counseling others.

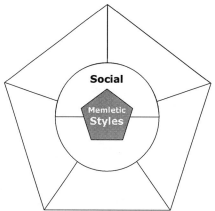

You typically prefer learning in groups or classes, or you like to spend much one-on-one time with a teacher or an instructor. You heighten your learning by bouncing your thoughts off other people and listening to how they respond. You prefer to work through issues, ideas and problems with a group. You thoroughly enjoy working with a "clicking" or synergistic group of people.

You prefer to stay around after class and talk with others. You prefer social activities, rather than doing your own thing. You typically like games that involve other people, such as card games and board games. The same applies to team sports such as football or soccer, basketball, baseball, volleyball, baseball and hockey.

Some examples of pursuits that people with a strong social style may follow include counseling, teaching, training and coaching, sales, politics, human resources, and others.

Common phrases

As with people with the logical style above, you are more likely to use phrases that reflect your dominant style out of physical, aural and visual styles. Here are some other phrases you may use:

- Let's work together on this.
- We can work it out.
- Tell me what you are thinking.

- Help me understand this.
- Let's pull some people together to discuss.
- Let's explore our options.

Learning and techniques

If you are a social learner, aim to work with others as much as possible. Try to study with a class. If this is not available then consider forming your own study group with others at a similar level. They don't have to be from the same school or class. If you like, introduce them to some of the techniques from this book. It may be easier for you to try some of the Memletic Techniques in a social setting, and work with the feedback from others.

Role-playing is a technique that works well with others, whether its one on one or with a group of people. For example, in aviation training, role-play the aerodrome area. Have people walking around in "circuits" making the right radio calls with the tower co-ordinating everyone. Another example might be to role-play with one person being the instructor and the other being the student.

Work on some of your associations and visualizations with other people. Make sure they understand the principles of what you are doing though, otherwise you may get some interesting responses! Others often have different perspectives and creative styles, and so the group may come up with more varied and imaginative associations compared to the ones you might create yourself.

Rather than reciting assertions to yourself, try sharing your key assertions with others. By doing so, you are almost signing a *social contract* that your assertion is what you do. This strengthens your assertions.

Share your reviews, review checklists and "perfect performance" scripts with those in your group as well. By listening to how others solve their issues, you may get further ideas on how to solve your own issues. Try sharing the work of creating a "perfect performance" script. Each person writes the script for the areas they want to work on the most, and then the group brings all the scripts together.

Mind maps and systems diagrams are great to work on in class. Have one person be the appointed drawer, while the rest of the class works through material and suggests ideas. The group may have varied views on how to represent some ideas, however this is a positive part of learning in groups. If you can't agree on something, just take a copy of what the group has worked on and add your own thoughts. Often there is no right answer for everyone, so agree to disagree!

Working in groups to practice behaviors or procedures help you understand how to deal with variations. Seeing the mistakes or errors that others make can help you avoid them later. As well, the errors you make are helpful to others! Whether it's via role-playing, a simulator or other technique doesn't matter too much. Be imaginative. Two chairs in the middle of a classroom to simulate an aircraft cockpit can be just as good as computer simulation and the real activity.

Lastly, if you are working in groups it may help to have everyone do the learning styles questionnaire. This may help everyone understand why each person has different viewpoints. It can also help with assigning activities to people. Individuals may volunteer for activities based on either the styles they currently have, or the styles they want to learn. Remember the classroom is a risk-free environment. It's often safer to experiment, try out new techniques and make mistakes in the classroom than in the real activity.

The Solitary Style—private, introspective and independent

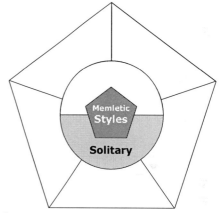

If you have a solitary style, you are more private, introspective and independent. You can concentrate well, focusing your thoughts and feelings on your current topic. You are aware of your own thinking, and you may analyze the different ways you think and feel.

You spend time on self-analysis, and often reflect on past events and the way you approached them. You take time to ponder and assess your own accomplishments or challenges. You may keep a journal, diary or personal log to record your personal thoughts and events.

You like to spend time alone. You may have a personal hobby. You prefer traveling or holidaying in remote or places, away from crowds.

You feel that you know yourself. You think independently, and you know your mind. You may have attended self-development workshops, read self-help books or used other methods to develop a deeper understanding of yourself.

You prefer to work on problems by retreating to somewhere quiet and working through possible solutions. You may sometimes spend too much time trying to solve a problem that you could more easily solve by talking to someone.

You like to make plans and set goals. You know your direction in life and work. You prefer to work for yourself, or have thought a lot about it. If you don't know your current direction in life, you feel a deep sense of dissatisfaction.

Those that have a strong solitary style include authors, researchers, park rangers and security guards. Peak performers in any field often have a good solitary style behind other more dominant styles.

Common phrases

Again you are more likely to use phrases that reflect your other dominant styles. Here are some other phrases you may use:

- I'd like some time to think it over.
- This is what I think or feel about that.
- I'd like to get away from everyone for a while.
- I'll get back to you on that.

Learning and techniques

You prefer to learn alone using self-study. When you spend time with an instructor or a teacher, you often only clarify information you haven't be able to clarify yourself. You may dislike learning in groups.

Don't be afraid to ask questions like "What's in this for me?" "Why does this matter?", "How can I use this idea?" Be aware of your inner thoughts and feeling towards various topics. This is because these inner thoughts have more of an impact on your motivation and ability to learn than they do in the other styles. Here are a few ideas to help this along:

- **Spend more time on the "Target" step of the Memletic Approach.** Set your goals, objectives and plans. Define ultra-clear visualizations or scripts of what life is like once you've achieved your goals. Understand your reasons for undertaking each objective, and ensure that you are happy with your learning goals.

  Align your goals and objectives with personal beliefs and values. If there is misalignment, you may run into issues with motivation or confidence. It's not always obvious what the underlying cause is. If you suspect a misalignment, try some of the techniques like "five whys" and "seventy by seven" to flush these issues out. Scripting and assertions also help highlight issues. If you script your goal and you find you don't like certain parts of it, that's probably a hint that you have some misalignment.

- **Create a personal interest in your topics.** An example for pilots might be to learn more about other aviators, both current and past. Why do others find aviation interesting? What is in it for them? What keeps them motivated? Why do they work in the field?

  You may also want to look at the people behind your books or material. What was their motivation to create it? Why do you think they organized the material in the way they did? Can you ask them?

- **Keep a log or journal.** You may want to keep one separate from your normal journal or training log. Include extra information about your thoughts and feelings. Outline your challenges, ideas on how to overcome them, and what worked. Write down what works well and doesn't work well for you. While you are studying, be aware of thoughts or concerns that arise. Write them down and come back to them. Discuss with others later if needed. Bear in mind it may be more efficient to put something that confuses you aside, and ask others later. This is often better than spending too much time trying to work it out yourself.

When you associate and visualize, highlight what you would be thinking and feeling at the time. You may want to do most of your visualization and association in private. I suggest you also try talking to others with more experience to get some idea of what thoughts and feelings they have in various circumstances.

Assertions are important for you. You drive yourself by the way you see yourself internally. Assertions are a good way to ensure your internal self-image matches your learning objectives. This also applies to the scripting techniques, so include your internal thinking and feelings in your scripts.

Modeling is a powerful technique for you. Don't just model behaviors and appearance. Try to get "inside their heads" and model the thought patterns and feelings you believe they have in various circumstances. You can gain ideas by talking to people or reading biographies. Remember you don't have to find a single perfect model. Create a model that combines several people.

Be creative with role-playing. You don't always need other people to role-play with, because you can create plenty of people using visualization! For example, you can visualize your instructor beside you, or a colleague and you practicing a procedure or skill. Work with them and talk to them while you visualize. An advantage of this form of role-playing is that you can control their behavior!

When changing behaviors and habits, you need to have a strong desire to make the changes you want. Explore the benefits of making a change, and visualize scenarios in which you've already made the change. If you don't believe strongly in the benefits, you may find it difficult to change the behavior.

Your thoughts have a large influence on your performance and often safety. Your thoughts are just as much part of a system as is the physical equipment you are using, such as an aircraft, car or boat. In addition, other people are also part of those systems, so be aware that their thoughts and feelings can affect the overall system.

Years of refinement have made physical equipment, such as aircraft and boats, safe and reliable. For example, aircraft failure causes less than ten percent of all aircraft accidents. The largest percentage is pilot error, more than seventy percent. This is likely the case in many other fields. It's just not as visible when accidents happen. It's well worthwhile spending some time refining the reliability of your own systems.

Expand your use of styles

Understanding your current learning styles can help you improve your learning performance. Expanding your learning styles helps even more. You can expand your learning styles by strengthening your dominant styles and using more of your secondary styles.

The Memletic Style graphs below show these two ideas:

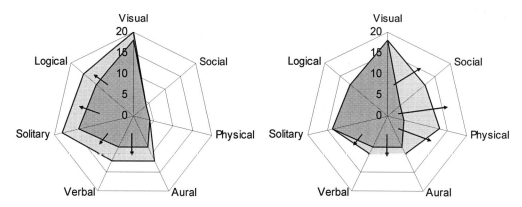

Expanding your styles helps learning because it supports strong neural networks that are already there, as well as extends networks that you don't use often. By doing both, you increase the range of styles you can apply to your content. You can use a style that's most suitable at the time. You may use a technique that's powerful for one particular style, or simply involve more of the senses when using another technique.

You improve your learning and retention by using styles you don't often use. If you are a mainly visual person, you can make a lesson more memorable by injecting some aural content into your visualizations. If you like to work things out logically, occasionally using some physical learning techniques adds variation to your learning. A visualization that involves sight, sounds, movement, sensations and logic is more powerful than a visualization involving sight alone. All these aid learning.

You might think your learning styles don't change. "That's who you are." That's not true—you *can* alter and improve your learning styles. For example, when many of us were younger, we preferred a physical learning style. As we grew older, many of us changed to prefer a visual learning style. Our learning styles change and adapt over time.

Your current learning styles are just a neural network that can alter and expand like any other. You can rewire even the strongest neural networks. For example, when a pilot does instrument training (flying in clouds) one of the key behavior changes is to ignore signals from their body. These signals, such as the sense of balance, try to signal the body's orientation and movement in space. They are often unreliable while flying. The pilot has to learn to ignore those senses and only use the instruments on the control panel. The neural networks that form part of the sense of balance are deeply inbuilt, and yet we can still alter them through training. Your preferred learning styles are no different.

Don't fall into the trap of believing you are a *one style person*. Some learning systems try to label people with a particular style, and then radically change the learning curriculum to meet the needs of that style. The studies on these systems have not been encouraging. I suggest you accept the brain's appetite for diversity and make the most of all the styles.

Lastly, don't consider these descriptions or scores to be limits. These are just the start. If you can improve your score in a few styles, then you increase your ability to learn. What I haven't told you is a score of twenty is just a starting point—you can go much further. With the power of the brain, there may also be learning styles we haven't discovered yet!

Let's look at some specific ways you can make the most of these learning styles, by strengthening your dominant styles and expanding your secondary styles.

Making the most of your dominant styles

Look at your questionnaire results. In which styles did you score well? These are your dominant styles. Work to understand which parts of your dominant styles you don't use that often. Read the descriptions of your dominant styles. Use your answers to the questions for each of your dominant styles. The questions for which you scored zero or one could show you ways to build on your dominant styles.

For example:

- If you use a visual style, but have never tried mind mapping, read about the technique and give it a go.
- If you use a verbal style, but have never tried verbalizing your thoughts aloud, try doing so next time you are working through an idea or issue.
- If you prefer a physical style but haven't done much role-playing or drama, try it next time you want to get another person's perspective.
- If you prefer the logical style, but haven't tried to analyze you how solve problems, write some points on the steps you follow. Compare your approach to other problem solving strategies.

Look at some of the techniques other people with similar styles use, and try them out yourself. It's like the websites that say, "People who bought this book also bought these other books..." You may find that some techniques may not work well for you, perhaps because of a stronger conflicting style. When you find ones that do, you then have a stronger arsenal of techniques that match your already strong learning styles.

Use your secondary styles

Go back and look at your lower scores in the learning style questionnaire. You can expand your range of learning techniques by using more of the styles you don't use often. Again, go back through the questions, the style descriptions above, and the techniques themselves. Look for ways you can further develop your secondary styles. For example:

- If you use a visual style, try verbalizing your thoughts aloud next time you work through an issue.
- If your preference is an aural style, think more about how you approach and solve a problem. Write down a few notes.
- If your preference is to use a physical style, try mind mapping on big pieces of paper using oversize pens or markers.
- If your preference is a logical or solitary style, try some role-playing or drama— especially with some other people!

You can go further and create a model of someone, real or visualized, who mostly uses one particular learning style. Try using more of the phrases the other styles use. Practice them. Say them aloud. Try doing visualizations and associations using the style of your model. Try to experience the world through their style for a while.

Chapter summary

In this chapter you first discovered your learning style preferences using the style questionnaire. This helped you identify you dominant and secondary styles.

You then read about each of the styles—the visual, aural, verbal, physical, logical, social and solitary styles. For each style, you saw common traits, occupations and phrases. You then discovered how you can adapt Memletics to suit your personal learning styles.

Lastly, we considered how you can expand your learning styles. You can improve how you use your dominant styles, as well as develop your secondary styles. Both of these increase how well you can use your learning styles to improve your learning performance.

In the next chapter we examine the last part of Memletics, the Memletic Approach. You will learn how to target your goal, plan your path, manage the journey and remember to enjoy the goal.

Manage using the Memletic Approach

The Memletic Approach provides you with an overall strategy for achieving your learning goals. This strategy helps you plan and start your goal, track progress, and keep you going in the right direction. The Memletic Approach also helps remind you to enjoy the journey as much as reaching the goal. When you use this strategy, you can be confident you have a much stronger likelihood of success.

Over the previous four chapters I've covered much detail about the various ways you can accelerate your

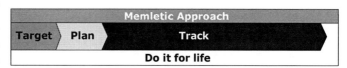

learning. In this chapter, we step back from specific learning methods to cover an overall strategy for running your learning program. The Memletic Approach helps you plan and manage your learning activities.

The following diagram shows the steps of the Memletic Approach:

As you can see, the four steps of the Memletic Approach are as follows:

- **Target.** Choose and clarify your goal.
- **Plan.** Decide your approach to achieve the goal.
- **Track progress.** Track your progress along the way.
- **Do it for life.** Enjoy both the journey and the goal.

You usually work through these activities in the order listed, however you may also work across two or more at the same time. For example, you may go back and clarify your goals further once you have done some planning. You may also alter your plan once you start learning.

How much planning and managing you do for any activity varies according to the size and importance of the goal. The Memletic Approach is no different. The activities I suggest in here are mainly relevant if you are targeting an effortful learning goal. If you are planning a longer-term goal, such as gaining a university diploma or a commercial flight license, I suggest you spend more time planning and managing your activities. If you are simply doing a course in public speaking, you may not need to spend as long in this part of Memletics.

A good guideline to start with is to spend about ten percent of your overall effort on these planning and managing activities. You will likely need to spend more time on these activities at the beginning of your journey, with less time towards the end.

Free guide: For examples of the targeting and planning steps of the Memletic Approach, get a copy of the free "Learn to fly guide" ☯. You can apply much of the content in the guide to other training activities, not just flying.

Target—choose and clarify your goal

The first step in any worthwhile activity is to clarify the goal and objectives. I call this  targeting, and it serves several purposes. The targeting step itself helps take the first steps towards your goal. You begin to decide the direction for how to get there. Setting a goal provides you with motivation, and you know your finishing point.

The targeting step has three key tasks. Firstly, find and understand your reasons. Why have you set the goal? Secondly, explore your goal. This means learning more about your goal. Make sure you have a realistic understanding of what life will be like after you reach the goal. Lastly, set your objectives. What are the major objectives you need to complete on the way to your goal?

In a moment we'll look at these tasks in more detail. Before we begin though, you may recall that "Clear, Desirable and Achievable goals" is one part of Memletic State, in particular mental state. While there is some duplication here, it's because this goal-setting activity is critical to both getting your journey started as well as upholding state along the way.

Find and understand your reasons

The aim of this task is to turn vague ideas of why you want to do something into clear reasons. This helps you clarify your goal and why it's important to you.

Often there are two groups of reasons. Some reasons arise from your specific goal. Others may come from a desire to develop the underlying personal skills along the way. As an example, the following table contains a list of potential reasons from someone wanting to learn to fly:

Activity specific reasons	Personal skill reasons
• Knowing how to fly. • Taking friends and family up or away. • Flying as a career. • Networking, business or personal. • Transport.	• Achieving a dream. • Overcoming challenges. • Personal discipline. • Planning and forward thinking. • Decision-making and judgment. • Learning how to learn.

As you can see, the reasons on the left are potential benefits that come from flying itself. The reasons on the right are more to do with underlying personal skills you develop on the way to the goal.

For your own goals, I suggest you find reasons from both groups. Sometimes the "personal skill" reasons motivate you more than the activity reasons. Other times you may not realize you are developing personal skills along the way to a goal.

Sometimes you may have a learning goal you feel doesn't match your personal direction. Often this is the case in a work environment. If this happens, you may want to focus on the personal skill reasons to help motivate yourself. Find your own reasons for achieving the goal. Look for what could help you achieve your own goals later.

A similar case is when you feel that you don't have a clear idea of what you want to focus on. This could be as minor as choosing a training course at work, or it could be as major as choosing a career. My view is that it's often better to set a direction, any direction, rather than wasting time waiting for enlightenment on what you should do. Set a direction that helps you develop your personal skills. When you do find your direction, you will likely get there faster than those who have wasted their time sitting still in one place. Many people do just this, waiting for someone else to hand them their *purpose* or their meaning of work or life.

If you find it difficult to find your own reasons for a particular goal, consider doing some of the next step, explore your goal. If you still struggle to find rational and realistic reasons for a particular goal, you may want to think more about why you are considering the goal. Are the motives of someone else driving you? Perhaps the motives of another individual, group or company are driving you, for example. If you feel that might be the case, be aware that allowing others to continually make decisions for you can harm your Memletic State. When you start on a goal, it's your choice to do so. Make sure you understand your reasons!

Learning Memletics as a goal

You may be thinking about setting a goal to learn Memletics by itself. My suggestion is to find another learning goal you can use Memletics with, rather than only studying Memletics. Your understanding and learning of the system comes more easily when you apply it to different activities. For some examples of activities you may want to try, see the Overview chapter.

You don't learn to drive a car by studying the car itself. You learn to drive by using it. I suggest you follow the same approach for Memletics.

You don't have to learn Memletics all at once either. In the appendix I provide some tips on how to learn Memletics.

Explore your goal

Often when people achieve a goal, they find the outcome is not what they expected. Exploring your goal helps confirm you have a realistic idea of what life might be like after achieving it.

Talk to others, read more widely, and try to involve yourself in the activities you are considering. Get "close to the action" before making a major commitment of time or money.

For example, in aviation you may want to do a trial instructional flight, or even a flight screening course, before committing to flight training. If you are sailing, ask to just be a passenger during a race or cruise. If you are about to start a university degree, how can you spend some time with others who are already in that profession?

You can also try two techniques described in the book to help you further clarify your goals, reasons and objectives. These techniques are creative visualization and creative scripting.

While these examples may involve some added time and cost, consider the time and cost wasted if you achieve your goal and find it's not what you wanted!

Set your objectives

If you now have a reasonably clear picture of your goal, and why you want to achieve it, set some major objectives. In my view, objectives are stepping stones along the way to your goal.

Usually you can take some of the reasons you explored above and turn them into specific objectives. Also, don't be afraid to set some objectives that you still have to understand further. This understanding comes during the research work below.

I strongly recommend you *write down your goal, reasons and objectives*. This act alone significantly improves your chances of success. Writing these down before starting your investigation helps keep you motivated. You may need this when you start to understand what work you need to do. Often you find you have underestimated the effort needed to achieve your objectives.

The brain has an interesting ability to subtlety change your thinking once it realizes it might have more work than it realized. By writing down your objectives, you can later check back to what you were originally thinking. You can also check what has changed. If you are now feeling less excited about your goal, why is that? Is it simply because it's more effort than you thought? If so, is that a reason to change your goal?

Keep your objectives close by while you progress towards your goal, and review them regularly. Update them if you feel they don't match your current direction. Review them if you find you are regularly lacking in motivation. Check whether your objectives are clear enough or whether the goal is compelling enough?

Also feel free to update and change your goals. Be wary though of reducing your vision of what you want to achieve. Peter Senge in "The Fifth Discipline" talks about a "creative tension" that comes from setting a vision that stretches us to achieve it. There are two ways for you to release that tension. You can work to move yourself closer to your vision, or you can lower your vision. The more you reduce your vision, the less you move away from your current reality. Change your vision and objectives due to purpose, and not just an unwillingness or laziness to move from your present circumstances.

Plan—decide your approach

Now that you have your guiding goal, reasons and objectives, you next turn your objectives into a plan

you can use to guide your actions and track your progress. You now extend the research you started in the previous Targeting step. You gather information you need to develop your plan. Once you have this information, the next steps are to create a course map, plan your time and plan your costs. These are three key tools you can use to track your progress.

Keep in mind that you may not need to do these activities to the depth outlined here. If your learning objectives are short term and easy to achieve, you may not need to do much planning at all. The size or importance of the objective should guide you on how much planning and management you need.

Do the research

Doing the research involves finding information you need to plan your course. There are usually three basic questions to answer. These are whether you should learn full- or part-time, the method of instruction, and the location. The following considerations can help you answer these three questions. Take some time to consider:

- **Time.** How much time will it take, versus how much time do you have?
- **Cost.** How much will it cost, versus how much money do you have available?
- **Importance.** How important is the course to you? How important is quality instruction?
- **Restrictions.** Which is your greater restriction, time or cost?

You often start your research with some basic ideas of time and costs, however after further research you may find that you need to change those assumptions. Don't be afraid to take a "point of view" early in your research on what may be the right answer. Change your view though if you gain new information that suggests another answer.

Let's now look at the commitment, method and location questions in more detail.

Commitment—full-time or part-time?

Often the biggest choice that influences your planning is whether to learn full-time or part-time. Both methods have their advantages. Let's look at some:

Full-time	Part-time
• Get to your goal faster. • Less chance of forgetting material between lessons. • Cheaper course cost (usually). • Lets you focus only on the course, with potentially fewer distractions.	• Balance other commitments more effectively. • More opportunity to study and review between lessons. • Can continue normal work. Total cost may be less as you are still earning income.

Sometimes you may not have a choice. If you do have a choice, consider the non-financial impacts of your choice. For example, how could your study impact your family or relationships? Lastly, think about your history. If you have always found it difficult to complete a part-time course, perhaps you should choose full-time instead.

Method—self-study, individual instruction or classes?

The second key question to answer is the method of study. This again affects the time, cost and quality of your training. There are usually three main choices:

- **Self-study.** This is a good choice if you are a self-directed learner. It also has the advantages of being cheaper and you can study at your own pace. You may find it difficult though to stay motivated. You may find it difficult to talk to knowledgeable person. You may not have access to the experience of an instructor, teacher and potentially others.

- **Individual instruction.** Individual instruction usually means you receive one-on-one training or coaching from someone with experience and knowledge. Usually this is the best choice considering time and quality of training, however it's also usually the most expensive choice.

- **Group or class based learning.** Often a better choice considering cost-effectiveness, however you also have to deal with the others in the group. You also need to keep pace with the group. You do have access to a knowledgeable person, although they must split their time across the group. If your learning objective involves working with other people, for example a presentation or communication course, you may find group-based learning a better choice.

Again, sometimes you may not have a choice on the method of instruction, for example when sitting certain qualifications or licenses. In flight training, for example, you must learn flying skills from an instructor. You have a choice for the theory parts though.

Consider how you will get your learning material. Is most of it coming from well-structured books, or do you have to listen to long lectures and extract your material verbally from your instructor? Do you have a choice of which references to use? The answers to these questions may influence which method you choose. For example, I often spend money on a good set of books and use self-study, rather than attend a course or class.

Quick suggestion: If you are planning to use an instructor or go to a class, ask the instructor or class lead if they know of Memletics. Are they are wiling to use it? Do they support you using Memletics during your training? If they have not heard of it, suggest they visit the Memletics website ♠.

Location—local or further away?

For many courses you may have to choose where you want to study, train or practice. You may have to choose between training providers in the suburbs versus the CBD, or in regional or country areas rather than the city. Sometimes your choices may extend to interstate or overseas providers. Often cost drives choices like these, however you may also find there are not many local providers and therefore you need to travel.

If you are thinking of studying further away because those providers are cheaper, make sure you also consider time as well as cost. For example, include the time to travel there and back. Often people find it difficult to put a cost on their time, so here's a simple method. Work out your personal hourly rate. Ask yourself, "how valuable is my time." Another way of asking this is "how much am I willing to pay to save an hour of my time."

Let's use an example to help you answer those questions. You are on your way home from somewhere and you miss the bus. The next one is not for an hour. Assume it's too far to walk. Would you be willing to pay 10 cents to catch a cab or taxi? Would you pay one dollar? Two, five, ten dollars or more? Where you stop is roughly your *personal hourly rate*. Here's another example. Compare the cost of an eleven-hour train trip to a one-hour flight. Divide the maximum cost difference you would accept by ten, and you have another indicator of your personal hourly rate.

How do you apply this to your training? If you could drive to a training provider that's out of town, but it takes an extra two hours to drive there and back, is it worth it? If your personal hourly rate is roughly five dollars, you need to be saving at least ten dollars on *each class* to make the extra travel worthwhile. You may also want to add the cost of fuel to get there and back.

Also consider whether you could better spend that time with your partner, with your children, or on extra study. If you can't avoid a long trip, look at how you can use the time. Perhaps record some of your lesson material on to a tape or CD and play it during the trip.

Use guides to help you decide

Once you have made the high-level decisions on time, method and location, you then need to decide the finer details. For example, which book, instructor, training provider, or school will you use?

Rather than make these choices on instinct or based on your own experiences so far, I suggest you seek out some guides that can help you. For example, the "Learn to Fly guide" I described earlier includes two checklists, with 70+ checks, for selecting both a school and an instructor. It contains lots of information to help you make an informed choice. If you are spending much money, it's likely that someone else has already written a guide to help you make the right choices. If you can't find one, try asking people who have followed a similar path what they think are the key questions you should ask. If all else fails, sit down and brainstorm at least ten questions. Make sure three of them you ask are:

- What are the common questions other students ask before they decide?
- Can I talk to some students already studying?
- How does the provider feel about using learning systems like Memletics?

I suggest you make a preliminary decision on a training provider, however don't sign up immediately. Wait until you finish the planning activities outlined in the rest of this section. Be prepared to walk away if the training provider puts undue pressure on you to "sign up today otherwise you miss out."

Understand your course map

A course map is simply a high-level view of the topics you need to learn to complete an objective. I define a course as "a study or training effort with a clear objective at the end." I break down a course into streams and modules. A stream is a group of modules, and each stream is either theory or practice. A module is a group of related exercises or lessons.

Let's look at an example. Flight training usually consists of a flight practice stream as well as a theory stream, with many modules in each. You can see an example of a course map for achieving one major stage of a flight license below.

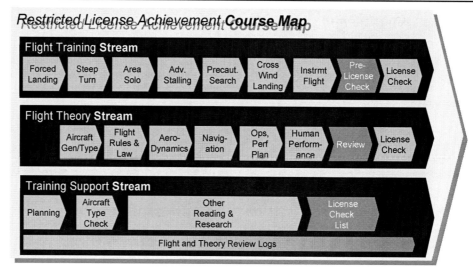

Restricted License Achievement **Course Map**

In this example, others have already worked out a well-defined course map for gaining a pilot's license. Not all goals have a well-defined course map, so you may need to create your own.

You can break down a course in a way that suits you, so don't worry too much about my terminology. The idea is to use it to gain a clear understanding of the entire course. Use what makes sense to you and your objective.

This is usually as far as you go during the planning period. During your lessons or studies, you continue to break down the lessons into individual pieces of knowledge that you learn and memorize.

The depth of your map usually depends on the depth of knowledge you need for your objective or goal. For example, a course map for learning how to drive a car should not have as much depth as a map for an engineering degree.

Plan your time

The next part of planning is to work out the timing of your course. There are three questions that you need to consider:

- **Completion goal.** When do you plan to complete the course?
- **Time needed.** How much time do you need to complete the course?
- **Available hours.** How much time do you have available to spend on the course?

Use this information and the course map to lay out a basic schedule for your course. Then decide whether it's all going to fit. You may need to adjust your answers to the questions above, or your expectations, to make it fit.

Keep in mind though that your schedule is a plan. Events will occur that you don't expect. Come back to your schedule during your training to see how you are tracking. If there are significant variations, look at what is causing those variations. If it's an underestimate in your original plan, update your estimates so you are more accurate in the future. If it's because you are spending too long on some parts of your material, consider whether you need to.

There are two more considerations when planning. One is to build in time to learn Memletics, and the second is to understand the effect of exams and tests.

Include time for learning Memletics

Include some time in your schedule to learn more about Memletics. If you are just starting out, you may want to plan more time so you can explore more of the system. Plan some time to do the Learning State quiz (if you haven't already), and review the Learning Checklist for other ideas ☯.

Understand the effect of exams

People often underestimate the time needed for exams and tests. This may be because most people don't like them and so prefer not to think about them. If this sounds like you, see some of the points I make about exams and tests in the Challenges chapter.

If your training uses tests, make sure you build in time for the pre-test preparation *and* post-test review. You may also want to use these as markers or checkpoints in your plan. Use them to split your goal into a series of smaller objectives.

Plan your costs

Similar to your time schedule above, the cost schedule provides a guide to the financial needs of your course over time. A basic cost schedule shows both the total outlay and the timing of outlays over the course. Compare that back to the money you have available, and address any gaps.

This helps you avoid temporary pauses (or worse, complete halts) in your training due to running out of money. These pauses can cost you more, as you may need to spend time and money reviewing and relearning topics you covered previously.

Review your plan

Now that you have created a basic plan for your study, take a step back and review it all for consistency. Is there anything missing? Are there any areas of concern remaining? Do your time and cost schedules match up? Do you know where all your learning material is coming from?

If you are comfortable with your plan, *get started!* If you still have some issues to address, decide whether you need to resolve them first, or whether you can write them down and start anyway.

If you haven't already, this is a good point to start reviewing your activities. Start your review log now (described in the Memletic Process chapter). Write down a summary of your activities during this planning period. Review what you feel you have done well, and what you felt you could have improved. What would you do differently next time?

Track—manage your progress

After you start your training or study, the Memletic Approach switches from planning to progress tracking. Just like navigating an aircraft, I suggest you pause occasionally and consider how well you are tracking to your plan.

One habit to avoid though is checking your progress too often. There are two key reasons for this:

- **It takes your time away from what you should be doing.** Too much tracking leaves less time for doing what you are tracking! In an aircraft, for example, too much tracking can be dangerous. It takes time away from other important activities. Pilots train to check their location often, but not a minute-by-minute basis. This allows them to do other critical activities such as keeping an eye out for other aircraft, checking the instruments, and communicating on the radio.

- **Regularly seeing how far you still have to go can sometimes be demoralizing.** A good example is a long-distance runner. Often when they are running long distances, they set their next objective as reaching the top of the next hill. They focus all their attention on reaching that objective. When they reach it, they set their next objective as the top of the *next* hill. If they started thinking too much about how far you they still have to go, it's likely their brain would stop them right away!

Tracking your progress is still an important task though. It helps keep you going in the right direction. It helps you realize you may be off track, and helps you understand how to get back on track. It also helps you to celebrate progress.

Key items to track are:

- **Your time schedule.** How well are you meeting your original time schedule?

- **Your cost schedule.** Were your earlier cost estimates accurate?

- **Progress.** What shows you are progressing? Signs include module completion, exam scores, positive feedback from others, or behavior changes.

- **What is coming up?** Are there any exams or tests coming up?

- **What issues are you having in your training?** Who can you discuss these with to help you resolve them?

If any of these items suggest you are off track, you may need to do some replanning. Consider whether you need to get back on track, or whether you should change your track. Either way, you should consider the changes you may need to make to your plan.

While you may not need sophisticated tracking, I suggest you at least keep some basic notes in your review log.

Do it for life—enjoy the journey and the goal

When you reach your goal, be sure to take time to enjoy what you have achieved. Whether it's for

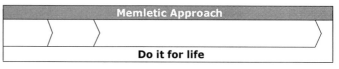

work or recreation, find ways to use what you've learned. When you use your knowledge, you reinforce your self-image as someone who can learn fast, overcome obstacles and reach goals you set for yourself. This often provides a high sense of satisfaction.

Make sure you also enjoy the journey to your goals. As you improve your learning state, for example, you soon realize it has other positive benefits on your life. Enjoy them. As the techniques start working for you, realize you are already reaching small goals by applying what you have learned from this book. Take time to enjoy what you are learning. Look back occasionally at the ground you have covered and the challenges you have overcome. Celebrate your milestones. Often it's the journey that makes the destination worthwhile, so enjoy it as you progress.

When you have reached your goal, remember that you need to review what you've learned if you are not using it regularly. If you want to keep it for life, make sure you put in some effort to create tools and material for faster reviews later. Distractions in life may prevent you from using what you have learned for a while. Having these review materials available makes it easier to refresh your training when you need to.

All these activities can help you continue using what you've learned, and enjoy it for the rest of your life!

Chapter summary

You've now seen how the Memletic Approach gives you a strategy to help you achieve your learning goals. By using these steps, you greatly increase your chances of success.

You read how the Target step helps you choose and clarify your goal. You first find and understand your reasons for wanting the goal. You then explore how the goal could change your life. Lastly, you set some solid objectives to achieve on the way to your goal.

The Planning step showed you how to decide the path to your goal. You learned the basic questions you need to answer. I then discussed three plans you should create. These are a course map, a time plan and a cost plan.

Once you begin your journey, you need to track your progress. In the Track step I gave you some advice on how much tracking to do. We then discussed some key points to track, such as your time and cost schedule, what's coming up, and whether you need to re-plan some parts of your journey.

Lastly, I suggested you take time to enjoy your goal once you reach it. I also suggested you enjoy the journey on the way to the goal.

You've now read about all of the five main parts of Memletics. When you do start on any worthwhile learning journey though, you will run into challenges. In the next chapter, I discuss many common learning challenges and how to overcome them.

Deal with Challenges

Chapter 7

During your pursuit of a worthwhile learning goal, you continually face challenges. Overcoming challenges is one reason achieving a goal is so rewarding. Sometimes though, challenges can seem overwhelming. This chapter deals with some of the common challenges you may face. It also shows you how to use various techniques to help overcome those challenges.

In this chapter, you will find ways to overcome many of the common challenges you may face during your learning journey. Developing a better understanding of these challenges, as well as techniques to address them, helps you move forward faster when these challenges arise. The challenges we tackle in this chapter include:

- **Motivation.** Lack of motivation is often the largest issue that arises when times get tough. However, lack of motivation can also come from other sources as well, such as misaligned goals or internal or external conflicts.

- **Fear.** Fear and nervousness, in many guises, degrade learning performance in several ways. I describe fear's dual nature, and how to combat fear with knowledge, understanding and other techniques.

- **Mistakes.** Rather than seeing mistakes negatively, learn to see them as steps towards your goals. You can learn from your own mistakes, as well as the mistakes of others.

- **Pressure.** I outline some tips on how to deal with the impact of pressure on various techniques, both during learning and at other times.

- **Wrong assumptions.** You can use the ACT model to overcome wrong assumptions.

A tip before we begin. Medical students often develop the symptoms of a disease they are studying. If you read this chapter and suddenly believe that your *lack of motivation* comes from a *deep internal conflict* about *possible success* and the impact a *mistake*, due to making a *wrong assumption under pressure*, would have on that success, stop for a moment! Are you suffering the Medical Student Syndrome? I cover this in more detail at the end of this chapter.

Keep it up—deal with motivation issues

In any challenging exercise you have times when your motivation is low. This is just one more challenge that you need to overcome to continue towards your goal.

In this section, I explore some topics that you may find helpful in identifying and resolving motivation issues.

Issues with goals and objectives, and internal conflicts, are a major cause of motivation issues. Reviewing your own past performance can help. Other people can also be of great help. They can give you feedback and guidance. They can also act as motivators, whether they know it or not. Sometimes you may have some management issues to deal with, such as too much tracking, too many distractions or too many outstanding issues. Lastly, I cover some other points that may help. Let's explore these topics.

Review goals and objectives

As I mentioned, many issues with motivation come back to your overall goals and objectives. You can overcome almost any challenge if you want to, and it's easier if you believe your goal is worthwhile, achievable and relevant to you. Here are some points to check:

- **Use internal motivators.** Internal motivators, such as a belief in a goal, often motivate better than external motivators, such as rewards and punishments. Are external rewards driving you? Are you trying to avoid a negative outcome or punishment? If so, try to find some internal motivators. Find some personal reasons for doing what you are doing. Look at some of the potential self-development objectives outlined in the planning step of the Memletic Approach.

- **Check if the objective appears too difficult**. Motivation difficulties often come because an objective you have set yourself turns out to be more difficult than you expect. Review your reasons behind your overall goal and whether any of them have changed. Can you split your objective into smaller objectives that may be easier to achieve?

- **Check if the objective is too easy.** Sometimes it's difficult to motivate yourself when an objective is too easy. This can be even more of a challenge if the objective still takes a long time to complete. Again consider your goal. If you need to complete this objective to achieve your overall goal, it's still important to finish it. Try to find other reasons to achieve this objective, for example add some self-development objectives to increase the challenge. What else can you learn from the experience?

- **Review your goals and objectives**. Review some of the points you wrote during the targeting and planning steps. Has anything changed? Often a source of low motivation is you no longer believe your goal takes you in the direction you want to go, or it just seems just too far away. Take some time to review your goals and make sure you are happy with the direction you are going. Read (or create) your goal scripts again. Perhaps review the images you may have collected (see the Memletic State chapter).

Understand internal conflicts

Internal conflicts are sometimes difficult to detect. They often show themselves in ways that appear unrelated to the underlying issue. Three common internal conflicts that you may come across are:

- **Anxiety due to change.** Often learning involves some internal and external change. Indeed, would learning be worthwhile if there were not some changes in your life? Change, however, also involves anxiety for many people. There may be some internal anxiety from changing beliefs, behaviors, and responsibilities. External anxiety may come from a changing environment, expectations or even from others close to you who see changes in your behavior. This may be especially the case if achieving your goal needs self-development.

    Understand that anxiety in this form is common, both in yourself and others. Add some assertions stating that you deal positively with change. Keep in mind that your changes may cause others to feel anxious, and they may react negatively. If you need further help in dealing with these issues, I suggest you try searching out books or people who can help you deal positively with these issues.

- **Awareness of risk and fear.** Some motivation issues can arise because of believed or real risk during learning activities. These issues may arise in the form of excuses or self-sabotage. Pilots sometimes experience this after gaining their license. They stop flying for awhile, citing numerous excuses. The underlying issue is a disproportionate sense of risk. Ironically, these pilots are often the safest pilots as they are far more aware of risks. They also understand how to reduce those risks.

    Review the section on knowledge and fear below, and try some of the techniques to help get your sense of risk in perspective. If you still feel the personal risk is too great to continue a learning activity, be sure to at least talk to some people before abandoning it.

- **Learning oriented versus performance oriented.** Some people consider themselves learners. They feel comfortable with making mistakes while learning. Other people consider themselves performers. They consider mistakes and errors as negative outcomes and they strive to remove them from everything they do. If you have a performance orientation, you may feel internal conflict and excessive stress when learning, especially when you make a mistake. Often you unintentionally degrade your performance if you allow this conflict to continue. Review the section on making mistakes below. Let your guard down while learning. You can always put it back up once you have finished learning!

Consider your learning performance

When you feel your learning progress is slow, it's common to doubt or question your learning performance. You may feel nothing is "sinking in." You can help yourself keep moving by:

- **Getting feedback.** If you are not receiving regular feedback on your progress, find ways to get it. If you are working with an instructor or teacher, but they are not giving you feedback, demand it from them! It's as much their responsibility give you feedback as it is to teach you. If you are self-studying, find a mentor or guide who can give you feedback on your progress. Another alternative is to present a short presentation to your friends, family or work colleagues on what you are learning, and then ask them for feedback.

- **Affirming your ability to learn.** Use the anchoring technique to link to experiences when you have learned well. Use these anchors to stay motivated when you feel you are not learning well. Use assertions and scripts to affirm your natural ability to learn, even if you feel you've lost that ability to learn in past years.

- **Looking at how far you've come.** Sometimes it's easy to ignore how far you have already come, especially while dealing with a few large challenges. Take a step back and look at where you are now. Consider the challenges you have already overcome, and use them as a motivator to keep going.

  For example, I anchored back to the experience of my first solo flight to keep me going through the challenges of the latter parts of my license. I still use this anchor today when I'm challenged by some activity I'm trying.

Enroll others to help

Other people can help your motivation in many ways, whether they realize it or not. Here are five ways you can enroll others to help your motivation:

- **Talk to other people.** This can often be your number one weapon against low motivation. Other people can often offer invaluable insights into your current challenges. You may want to explain your issues, or simply ask them about a time when they were suffering from low motivation. Ask them how they improved their motivation. Be sure to pick your confidants carefully though. Avoid those who may prefer to see you fail in your efforts.

- **Use self-inflicted consistency.** *Consistency* in this case refers to the principle that you often act according to the image you want others to hold of you. You can use this principle to motivate yourself by telling as many people as you can about your goal. Tell your best friends as well as your worst enemies. They can both become your support team. Your best friends usually support your activities with encouragement. Your enemies may wish to see you fail, and in doing so they can motivate you to prove them wrong. Either way, you have set an expectation with others that you will succeed. You often go further than you otherwise would to prove that expectation.

- **Help others.** One way to help you stay motivated is to help other people reach their goals. The opportunity to "make a difference" in the lives of others, whether an individual or a whole community, often provokes unprecedented levels of involvement and participation. You can often find small ways to contribute. It may be helping a student along who is further behind you, or writing some notes that others can use later. Helping others can help keep you motivated, and at the same time perhaps reinforce material you've already learned.

- **Understand how your activity affects others.** Consider how your learning activities affect, or will affect, other people. While you are learning, you are likely helping an instructor, author, coach or teacher make a living. You may also be supporting companies that provide you with equipment, as well as all the people who work for those companies. If you are in a class, you help others understand content through the questions you ask and the discussions you have. Most learning activities have a positive effect on many other people, not just you. Use this thought as another way to motivate yourself. Striving to reach your goal helps other people reach theirs.

Check your learning management

Management can be an overhead, especially if there is too much of it or it's not doing its job right. The same applies in your learning activities. Sometimes you can tie yourself up in too much tracking. This distracts you from doing the work that moves you towards your goal. Part of the management task is to also provide you with work space, however sometimes distractions or other responsibilities can clutter that space. Lastly, you need to manage issues that arise during your learning.

Let's look at these points in more detail:

- **Too much tracking?** If you find yourself spending too much time tracking your progress, rather than making progress, this can sometimes be a sign of low motivation. In addition, measuring your progress too often can also lead to low motivation, especially if you keep "looking up" to see how far you still have to go. Keep your tracking activities to a minimum. Allow yourself the flexibility to get "a few degrees off course," rather than feeling the need to track your progress every minute.

- **Manage distractions or other responsibilities**. Low motivation can also be the result of too many distractions from your other responsibilities. One of the management tasks you have is to make sure you have enough *mental space* for your efforts. If you find that space continually crowded, you may need to find ways to rearrange your responsibilities. This may mean you need to suspend your activities if other responsibilities become more important than your goal. Be wary of chasing a goal while ignoring your responsibilities.

- **Manage issues.** I consider distractions as circumstances that arise outside your learning activities. Issues are problems that arise within your learning activities. As you progress, it's likely that you will come across various issues that you need to deal with. One may be that you are having difficulty mastering a topic. Another may be that it's taking you more time or money than you thought, or you are not getting along well with your instructor or a classmate.

  I suggest you use a common project management technique called "issue management." Write down your issues. Work out what impact they have on you. Consider how important it is to deal with them now or at some point in the future. This technique helps you understand your issues and just how large they are. Low motivation may come from an exaggerated sense there are too many issues in front of you. Writing them down can take the emotion out of them and give you a plan for addressing them. Often they don't appear so bad after you've written them down.

Further points

Lastly, here are a few extra points that didn't fit in with the topics above:

- **Focus on something else for a while.** If your learning activities are full-time, it sometimes helps to get away from them for a while. Take a break, go somewhere, or just spend some time relaxing. This helps you get your activities back into perspective. This is also a good time to review your goals and objectives, without feeling the strain of having to "get back into it" immediately.

- **Enjoy as you go.** You can increase your motivation by finding small ways to enjoy what you are doing. For example, go for a flight or a sail just for enjoyment, if that's what you are learning. Celebrate reaching a particular milestone. You may just want to celebrate that you are on the road. This is often easier if you see one of your objectives as the journey itself.

- **Review references on motivation.** The suggestions here are just a few. There are many other references out there that focus on general motivation issues ☾. Before you reach for these, remember you can often trace many motivation issues back to inconsistencies in goals and objectives. "Quick fix" motivation techniques are unlikely to help you keep going if you have major issues with your goal.

- **Get trained help.** If you find it difficult to take even the first steps towards a goal, you may want to consider getting some outside help. See this as just another way to overcome the challenges you face. Talk to your general medical practitioner first and, if needed, get a reference to a trained professional.

Knowledge—your weapon against fear and nervousness

Fear has a dual nature. It's both a protector and an inhibitor. You can use this understanding to help defeat fears that hold you back, as well as learn how to use knowledge to manage fears and stay safe.

In any learning activity involving significant challenges, you may sometimes feel nervous. What underlies this nervousness? It's usually fear. Fear of accidents, not being able to handle an event, not being able to recall information, or even sometimes fear of success.

In this chapter we explore some activities that can help you find the right balance between too little and too much fear. Firstly, I describe a "balanced model" of fear, showing that both too much and too little fear can harm your livelihood. An effective way for controlling fear is to make it known. Accept you have the fear and then find more information. Understand the particular issue causing the fear.

> **Quotes:**
>
> "Fear of failure is the father of failure."
>
> "If at first you don't succeed, try, try again"
>
> "Failure is not the worst thing in the world. The very worst is not to try."
>
> "Wisdom is learned more from failure than from success."

Fear of failure is a common issue, less known though is fear of success. You can use positive experiences to help you work through fearful events. As well, there are techniques to help you disassociate yourself from a past or feared event if it holds an irrational amount of fear.

Lastly, I cover three more techniques and tips that help you control fear. These are how to uncover hidden fears, how to control breathing to control nervousness, and tips for exams and tests.

Let's explore all these topics.

Use the balanced model

While many self-help books treat fear negatively, fear often has a rightful place. *Fear is usually a warning from your body or brain that you may be putting yourself in danger.* Often though we let it control our activities too much. What you need is a balance between too little fear and too much fear. You could look at fear along a scale:

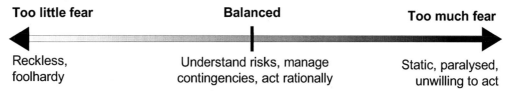

Too little fear

Reckless, foolhardy

Balanced

Understand risks, manage contingencies, act rationally

Too much fear

Static, paralysed, unwilling to act

The balanced model means you accept the dual nature of fear. If you have too little fear you may take too many unnecessary risks. You may put yourself and others around you at risk of hardship, injury or worse. Too much fear can be just as devastating though. It can result in a *life not lived.* You are too afraid to do anything worthwhile. I believe the ideal position on the scale is somewhere near the middle. You take time to understand risks, plan contingencies (see side bar), and then do what you want to do.

The same person can be at different positions along the line for different activities. For example, someone who is careful in business may be reckless when driving. Being too aware of risk in one area of your life may lead you to be less so in other areas. Be aware of where you are along the scale for each major area of your life, and look for differences like these.

> **What is a contingency?**
>
> A contingency is an action to handle a potential future issue. For example, you plan to meet a friend at a restaurant at 7pm. Your friend is often late, so a contingency might be to call them from your cell phone at 7:15 if they haven't arrived. You may need to take some action now to help you use that contingency. For example, you need to take your cell phone with you.
>
> Planning for contingencies involves thinking ahead for possible issues that may arise, and working out what you would do if those issues do arise. You might then do some preparation now to help reduce the effect of those issues.

Your inner dialogue strongly influences your approach to risk and fear. Assertions are a good way to change that dialogue. These are some assertions I use for a balanced approach to fear:

- I work to understand risks before I take them.
- I make the most of the life I have, and this involves taking risks.
- I plan contingencies for the risks I take.
- I work to understand what might be unreasonable fears.
- I consider failure as a necessary part of success.
- I learn from my mistakes.

Remove the fear of the unknown—make it known

Sometimes our fear comes from not knowing what to expect. However, often our fear prevents us from finding out what we should expect. Talking to others and writing our fears down are two ways you can break out of this pattern. Let's look at these in more detail.

Whatever the experience, it's likely that others have been in similar circumstances before you. Reach out and talk to those around you. Talking to others and explaining your fears brings them out in the open, allowing you to then find ways to resolve them.

You may also find it helpful to write down persistent fears. Expand those fears into likely "worst case scenarios," and then decide whether you can live with those outcomes. Also write down how you can reduce the likelihood of those scenarios.

If you feel nervous about an activity or event, find out as much as you can about it. Some examples:

- **Exams and Tests.** Do sample exams. Time yourself doing those samples. Ask your instructor or teacher what to expect. Ask where others usually have trouble. Ask others before you what they found difficult and what they found easy.

- **Finishing your training.** If you have just finished an organized learning program or course, you may now be moving from a comfortable routine into unstructured real life. Ask others how they decided what to do next. What do they do when unsure? Sometimes setting a path and making the most of it is better than staying static and claiming to be "assessing your options" or "biding your time."

- **Journeys into new areas.** Sometimes your activities take you into areas you haven't been before. While you may not be able to find someone who has faced the same situation, it's likely others have faced similar experiences. Talk to others about how they approach new areas. For example, if it's your first time presenting to a particular group, try to find someone who has presented to the same group, or a similar group. If you are sailing to a new harbor, you might call up a yacht club there and ask about the local area.

Here are two assertions that can help remind you to find out more when you have a fear in a particular area:

- I use the light of knowledge to reduce the fear of the unknown.
- My knowledge controls my fear.

Understand fear of failure

Many people have deeply ingrained beliefs about failure. The prevention of failure is a common goal in many societies. In contrast to this, many successful people are those who have failed previously, and who have learned to fail well.

Our fear of failure has created a whole new market of "positive thinking" methods. Beware though—positive thinking can harm your progress, and can result in higher levels of failure. Why? People often apply positive thinking in the wrong place. Let me use an example to explain:

> Imagine you regularly walk along a dark road at night. There are many potholes you can't see. Often you step in one and stumble or fall. It hurts.
>
> One day you read a great self-help book about positive thinking. The next night you start your journey along that road with a big smile on your face, thinking "I shall walk along this road with ease." Imagine your surprise when you step into yet another pothole and hurt yourself. It's likely that you feel even worse

about falling, and believe that all the positive thinking has been a waste of time.

What you need are tools that help you find solutions for avoiding the potholes. For example, perhaps you could buy a torch or flashlight. If not, find a stick and push it along the road in front of you. You could also take a different route altogether.

This is where to apply positive thinking. Affirm your ability to learn from your failures. Assert your ability to find creative solutions to avoid the potholes in future.

While this is a simple example, how many people do you know continue to walk along a similar road in life? They fear the next time they will step into a pothole, and appear unable to learn from their experiences.

Symptoms of fear of failure

There are many ways that a fear of failure can reveal itself to you. Three symptoms are:

- **Escape mechanisms.** You may develop defenses or escape mechanisms. For example, you may find ways to avoid training. You may procrastinate more than usual, or you may spend too much time reading, intellectualizing or watching TV. You may find you want to sleep even when you don't feel tired. You may lose focus during training or study, or you may eat too much, clean too much or shop too much.

- **Anxiety.** Often when you forcibly subdue the fight or flight reflex, it lets you know though anxiety. Symptoms of this may include general anxiety, stress, nervousness, a sore neck or backaches, out of control feelings, sleeplessness, tension, hyperventilation, overreaction to minor events, and more.

- **Irrational self-talk.** You may suffer from excessively irrational self-talk. This includes continually going over worst case scenarios in your mind, or continually doubting your ability to succeed.

Managing the fear of failure

A key way to manage a fear of failure is to learn to fail well. Failing well involves changing your mindset about failure, making your fears known, getting out there and doing what you want, and dealing with the outcomes. Let's look at these steps.

1. **Change your mind-set.** The first step in developing a healthy attitude to failure is to break the belief that success is good and failure is bad. Failure often comes before success, and indeed success without some failure first may be more luck than achievement.

   Use assertions to change your self-talk about failure. Some examples include:
   - I am flexible. I bend when I fail, and I spring back into progress.
   - I handle failure well. I learn the lessons and move on.
   - Challenges and setbacks are what make my goals worthwhile.

   You can expand on these using scripting and creative visualization, affirming how well you handle failure. You may also want to use the mental firewall technique to block any persistent negative thoughts about failure. Only do this after you've documented those negative thoughts as part of the next step.

2. **Make your fears known.** Use the approach outlined above in "Remove the fear of the unknown. Make it known" (page 187). Bring out the facts of a fear, as well as the emotions involved. By openly discussing your fears or writing them down, they immediately start losing their power.

   You may also want to consider using the "seventy by seven" technique below to help draw out some of the reasons behind your fears. Another way to bring these out is by using the Five Whys technique. Ask yourself at least five times why you fear a particular outcome.

3. **Manage the risks.** Consider your fears from step 2. Which ones are rational? Turn them into risks, and then understand whether you can live with those risks or if you need to plan contingencies. Consider this assertion: *I take calculated risks and I make safe mistakes.*

4. **Get out there and do it.** This is the most powerful antidote to fear of failure. Get out there and do what you want to do. Accept mistakes or failures if or when they arise. They are a natural part of the journey. Learn and develop the ability to handle failure, find solutions and keep moving forward.

5. **Deal with the outcomes.** If you do fail or make a mistake, deal with it properly. Document it in your review log, and talk to others about the mistake.

If you find you are making the same mistakes over and over, persistence is unlikely to help. If you keep doing the same thing without varying your approach, don't expect a different result! Take time to analyze what isn't working and then change your approach.

Understand fear of success

Sometimes your fear may not be of failing. It may be fear of success. This may sound silly, however sometimes your underlying fears show themselves in different ways. This scenario is more common than you might think. People suffering this fear can sabotage themselves or find many reasons for why they can't finish their goal. Their fear of success, and moving on past their goal, often drives this behavior.

Many of the symptoms are similar to those outlined in the "fear of failure" above. Here are some questions to explore whether you may have some underlying fears of success. Visualize yourself already at your goal and ask questions like:

- What does it mean now you've reached your goal?
- Are there more responsibilities that you have to take on?
- If you are training for a career or career change, how do you feel about going out and looking for work? Do you have the skills? Do you have a plan?
- Does your life become more complicated or unpleasant for any reason?
- What is your next goal once you have achieved this one? How do you feel about not having an organized training program to follow?
- Will there be extra pressure to stay successful? Are you concerned about decline after success?

If any of these bring out uncomfortable thoughts, you may want to explore them more to see if there are any underlying issues.

Often you can deal with fear of success using a similar approach to what I described in fear of failure above. Change your mindset to accept that it's natural for many people to fear change. Make your fears known by talking to others or writing them down.

The key point though is you now have tools and abilities to deal with issues if they arise. Get out there and do what you want to do, and don't let the fear of reaching your goal stop you.

Use positive experiences as anchors

Your past positive experiences are assets you can use when you find it difficult to move forward. Use the anchoring technique described in the Memletic Techniques chapter. Consider some of your positive learning experiences, or times when you have overcome fears, and create an anchor to those experiences. Recall the anchor when you need a boost to get through a challenge.

Disassociate yourself from negative experiences

When you recall a past event, usually because of your current circumstances, you also recall the emotions and feelings that went with that event. This then colors your view of your current circumstances, sometimes irrationally.

If you've had a significant negative experience that you feel has too much fear associated with it, try disassociation. Disassociation helps you reduce your fear to a more rational level. You may also want to try this technique if you continue to focus on a negative future scenario.

Disassociation is opposite to anchoring. Anchoring ties positive experiences to a trigger. You can use that trigger to improve your current state by recalling a past positive state. Disassociation uses mental imagery to separate the negative emotions associated with an event from the event itself.

Be sure to "learn the lessons" from negative experiences—don't ignore them. Use disassociation though if you feel you've associated too much fear to a negative experience.

Let's look at a disassociation technique. This is the disassociation movie technique:

1. **Recall the experience.** Recall the negative experience. Play it through in your mind to give yourself some of the negative feelings and emotions associated with it.

2. **Go to the movies.** Now go back to the just before the start of the event, before anything happened. Freeze the frame. Now make that picture smaller, and move back from it. Now visualize yourself sitting in a movie theatre or cinema, towards the back. This is a unique cinema that specializes in disassociation. See that frozen frame on the screen.

3. **Replay.** Now replay the movie in black and white, almost like a Charlie Chaplin movie. There is that piano music playing in the background. Turn down the volume of the voices or other sounds so you can hardly hear them over the music. Try to see the humorous side of the events as they unfold. In fact, smile and laugh at various points, even if you are "faking it."

4. **Rewind.** Still in the cinema, imagine the movie running backwards. Do this quickly. The "rewind" should take no longer than two to three seconds, or four to five seconds your movie involves several contributing events. See

everything running in reverse, and hear the sounds like they are going backwards. It's amusing. Repeat this step a few times.

5. **Leave and check.** Still visualizing, get up and walk out into the cinema lobby. There is a camera crew there with an interviewer. You sometimes see these scenes on TV, with the interviewer asking moviegoers what they thought of the movie they just saw. This interviewer asks you "on a scale of one (low) to five (high), how would you rate your fear now?" Briefly recall the negative experience, and give it the rating. If it is more than three, the interviewer says "looks like you are going to have to see it again!" Turn around and go back into the cinema, and repeat the technique in further detail. If it's a rating of one to three, the interviewer says "congratulations, now go out and try it".

6. **Experience—gradually.** If the experience you are disassociating yourself from affects your current behavior, put yourself in some circumstances that used to trigger your fear. See how you feel. Be careful though—start small and build up, and test how you feel as you go.

This process is also good for working with phobias. Replace the movie with the first time you experienced the phobia, or the time when you had a severe reaction from the phobia.

Techniques and tips for common issues

Following are three ways to handle common fear-related issues. The "seventy by seven" technique is useful for uncovering hidden fears. Breathing normally helps you handle nervousness. Lastly, I give some tips on handling exams and tests.

The "seventy by seven" technique: Uncover hidden fears or issues

The "seventy by seven" technique is a good way to explore hidden thoughts. It helps you draw out issues and concerns that you may be hiding or denying.

Here are the basic steps:

1. Create a short positive statement that you feel may have deeper complications. The shorter the better. Some examples may be:
   • I am a successful commercial pilot
   • I am a commercial photographer
   • I am a doctor
   • I am OK with heights

2. On a notepad or on the computer, start writing. Write down or type the statement once. Say it in your mind, and then write down the first thought that follows. Don't try to analyze it. It may seem unrelated. It may be a feeling or emotion, or a recollection of a previous event. Regardless, write a brief note and move on.

3. Repeat step 2 seventy times in one sitting. At the end of the sitting, read through your responses and highlight any themes. Each sitting should take up to an hour.

4. Repeat the process for seven consecutive days. If you miss a day, go back to day one.

At the end of the seven days, review your notes and look at some of the key thoughts. Write those key thoughts up separately on a summary note, and then keep them all together.

This technique involves much time and commitment, so use it sparingly for important issues. What you typically find is a few thoughts come up that help you see what has been causing you difficulty in the past. Some explode into your mind as a sudden realization. Some only come after reviewing your comments. If it didn't bring out anything of value, it may be that you're OK about the statement. Alternatively, it could mean there is something deeper that needs outside help to bring it to the surface. Either way, it's your choice whether to probe it further or to accept it and move on.

Breathe normally—a key to unlocking nervousness

Your breathing often changes when you feel fearful or nervous, usually for the worse. You tense up and either hold your breath or start to hyperventilate (breathe too fast). This is a self-perpetuating loop. Holding your breath or hyperventilating triggers more nervousness.

The key is to get your breathing back to normal. Here are a few exercises that can help you achieve this:

- Simulate or visualize the exercise that makes you nervous. Focus on keeping your breathing calm and steady. See the pressure increasing while you stay calm and steady, handling each event with ease.

- Use the shunt technique. Put yourself into a low state, visualizing the scenario that makes you nervous. Breathe right out and hold it there until you start to feel that urge to breathe in. When you do, think "wooosh," take a breath in, sit up, pull your shoulders back and say to yourself "My breath is calm and normal." Focus on taking four to five normal breaths after that, and then repeat the exercise.

- If you occasionally suffer from hyperventilation, you may want to try a similar swish exercise where you simulate the symptoms of hyperventilation, and then get your breathing back under control. Only do this with someone knowledgeable, like a doctor or coach.

- Find a way to laugh regularly. A good laugh forces you to take a breath and clear your lungs. It also has a favorable neurological effect on the brain. Associate something in your environment with something funny that causes you to laugh each time you look at it. A common tip for those nervous while speaking publicly is to imagine part or all the audience naked. During a test, you may want to imagine the clock falling off the wall on to the teacher. It knocks the teacher out so you can all sneak out of the room. Even if when you look at the clock you don't feel like laughing, force yourself to smile, laugh silently and take that breath.

- Have someone or something nearby remind you to breathe normally. For example, if you are nervous during a presentation ask someone in the audience to smile or tug their ear each time you look in their direction. Use this as a trigger to take a breath and breathe normally.

- Relax your posture and muscle tension. If your body is tense, this often constricts your breathing. Trigger yourself to relax more often. Stretch and move around before an activity to help release some of that nervous tension.

- Use a mnemonic or similar memory technique to remind you to breathe at stressful times. An example from my flight training is the ACE mnemonic, which stands for "Airspeed, Calm, Eyes outside." I linked the mnemonic to the airspeed indicator. Every time I checked my airspeed I thought "ACE." When I said "Calm," I remembered to relax my body and mind (staying alert though) and normalize my breathing.

These exercises are not a replacement for preparation or training. Controlling your breathing doesn't help you remember something you didn't study, or perform something you don't already know how to do.

Excel in exams and tests

Exams and tests may cause feelings of fear and nervousness. These feelings can reduce your ability to perform well. Here are four ways to minimize the nervousness that's sometimes associated with exams and tests.

- **Understand the source of nervousness.** As you progress through a course, you often form your own subjective view on how well you have learned the material. Exams are often a more objective way of confirming your understanding and retention. This realignment of your view is sometimes difficult though. Have you ever walked out of an exam feeling you did well, however when you got the results you find you did poorly? You may blame something about the test, rather than accept that you may have had a different view of your own understanding. It's a common behavior.

  An uninvited change of your personal view often causes intellectual pain. The potential for this pain is often a main cause for nervousness before an exam. You can reduce the nervousness if you accept the potential for the change, and welcome it as further progress towards your goal.

- **Reframe the purpose of the exam.** As a pilot navigates an aircraft, they often spend greater than ninety percent of the flight off course. Navigation involves not only staying on course, but also getting back on course after deviations from plan. One does not suddenly "fail" navigation as soon as one is off course by more than a mile!

  Reframe your exams as progress checks. They are just waypoints to verify your progress along a planned track. If you are off course, then your exam helps you get back on track. Even if you fail the exam, it simply means you have some more work to achieve your goal. It doesn't mean your journey is suddenly over!

- **Reverse roles.** One of the techniques I use when doing check-rides or flight exams is to reverse the roles in my mind. I visualize or model myself as the instructor or examiner, and the person next to me as a new student. I "forget" the new student may have over three thousand hours of experience. I see myself as having years of experience and that this is just another training run. This way the flight becomes a demonstration, rather than a test. You can use this technique in many other ways. For example, reverse the roles in a job interview, where you become the interviewer. You're there to make sure the job is right for you. Apply a similar approach for sales calls. Instead of trying to sell your product, take the role of the buyer. You want to make sure your product is the right one for their needs, so you ask many questions about how they might use it.

- **Relax to move forward faster.** Use the *ninety percent technique.* If you try to do something at one hundred percent effort, you are more likely to fail or make mistakes. This often costs you more time. Instead, relax a little and work at ninety percent effort. You're likely to get there faster.

In the same way, I suggest you don't aim for one hundred percent or perfection in tests. Your first minor mistake may cause undue stress and again cost you more. Instead, aim for between ninety and one hundred percent, and accept the mistakes if they come.

I don't know if it was deliberate, but the instructor pilot who did my first two major flight tests quizzed me harder and harder until I made a mistake. This was before we had even left the ground. Until that point, I felt some pressure to "keep up the perfect test." Once I made that mistake I relaxed and didn't worry about achieving perfection. I passed both times.

Some of the greatest performances by athletes have occurred when they "gave up on the hope of gold." Once they relaxed, their natural instincts and abilities took over. They didn't have interference from wanting a perfect performance. They then came closer to perfection than they ever had before.

A final note

A closing reminder is that *fear is usually a warning from your body or brain that you may be putting yourself in danger.* Sometimes your fear signals real danger. If you are putting yourself into unknown or dangerous circumstances, pause and take a step back. Ask yourself how you can make it more known. How you can discover, understand and reduce the risks?

Mistakes—shortcuts to faster learning

Many people avoid mistakes at all costs, however mistakes are a key part of learning. You progress faster by accepting and making the most of your own mistakes. Another shortcut is through using the lessons from mistakes that others make.

Learning from your own mistakes

Many anecdotes, proverbs and sayings reflect the view that learning and success come from making mistakes. You must make mistakes during your training. I believe that your rate of learning and success depends just as much on making mistakes as it does on positive learning experiences.

There are three key points that influence the impact mistakes have on your learning and success:

- Your **attitude** towards making mistakes.
- How you **react** when you do make a mistake.
- How effectively you **learn** from your mistakes.

Let's look at these points in more detail. While some of these suggestions may be more relevant for higher risk activities such as flying or medicine, you can find ideas to apply in any field.

Attitude towards making mistakes

No matter how good you are, you must make mistakes while you learn. Accept this. Your attitude to making mistakes has a big impact on how you firstly deal with the mistake when it happens, and secondly how you learn from the mistake.

Good training programs should let you make safe mistakes. You should have a *safe* environment so you can explore the boundaries of your topic. Also, avoid trying to be right all the time. Stretch yourself while you are learning. This is the best time to make mistakes as you have someone who can help you correct them and ensure you don't get into trouble.

Consider this example from flight training. You are an instructor and you have two students that are getting close to their first flight alone. One of them has made close to a perfect landing every time. This student has not bounced, landed hard, been too high or too low on approach, or been too fast on touchdown. The other student has done all of those, but is now doing reasonably good landings. Which one would cause you more concern?

I'd have more concern about the first student. Why? The student has not had to correct many mistakes. If one day the first student does bounce a landing, are they going to recover correctly? Perhaps, but the second student has had to recover several times from a bounce on landing. The second student probably has a better chance of a good recovery.

While this may be an extreme example, it shows that part of your training is learning how to recover from mistakes, even if some are not your fault. So get out there, make safe mistakes and don't feel bad about them.

Note that this is not a license to go out and take unnecessary risks though. Don't deliberately make a mistake that puts you in danger.

Your immediate reaction

The next consideration is how you deal with mistakes when they happen. You don't want to be sitting there thinking, "Great, I've made a mistake! I'm closer to my goal!" Depending on the circumstances, you may need to act immediately. Here are some guidelines:

- **Accept the mistake.** Once you realize you have made a mistake simply say to yourself "I've made an error. Now let's work out what to do next." Don't linger too long on the reasons for making the mistake, or the thought that you are a bad learner, or that it's someone else's fault. Accept it and move on.

- **Act immediately if needed.** If the mistake you've made needs an immediate response, do it. Don't waste time. If it's an event you've trained for, then make a firm decision to follow the response your training has taught you.

- **Plan your response.** If you have made a mistake that doesn't need immediate correction, then you are usually better off taking a few moments to plan your response. Often pilots put themselves in worse trouble by reacting to a mistake without much consideration, even when they have time. Take a moment to plan your response, and then act.

  Note that some mistakes may need both an immediate and then a secondary response. For these mistakes, do the immediate response, and then plan the secondary response.

- **Verbalize it.** Once you have corrected the mistake, simply say one or two positive assertions to help you do it correctly next time.
- **Make a note.** Whether it's a large or small mistake, make a small note of it somewhere (if possible). Add it to your review later. This links to the next section on effective learning from your own mistakes.
- **Don't try to hide it.** If you are with your instructor, you are usually better off admitting the mistake. They probably know anyway. If you are not with your instructor, I recommend letting them know afterwards. Explain what happened and your response, rather than trying to hide the issue. You may find that you chose the correct response, or you could have chosen a better one. Either way it's helpful to your learning.

Effective learning from mistakes

Capture those opportunities for further learning as they happen, and then work on how to avoid them in the future. The review technique, described in the eNquire step of the Memletic Process, is a key technique for achieving this.

The technique works better, however, if you make a note of issues you have so you can come back to them later. You may quickly forget the small mistakes along the way, only to continue to make them. Many accidents are due to small mistakes adding up into a bigger one, so capture them early and capture them often. Your training may not be as serious as this, however attention to detail often controls how fast you progress.

The review technique description includes most of the points I would make here, however here are a few more:

- **Ask for help.** If you are unsure of whether you dealt with the mistake correctly, ask for help from someone who knows.
- **Replay scenarios in a simulator, or simply visualize.** If you made a mistake and you want to ensure it does not happen again, try replaying the scenario in a simulator, or writing a brief script. Look at the causes of the mistake, and then replay the scenario making the right decisions.
- **Consider your fears.** If your mistake comes partially from a fear, such as a fear of failure, do some further work to document your feelings. Record what happened, why you think it happened, and how you feel about it. Give some thought to the lessons learned and what you need to change. What will you do differently next time? Add to your review notes and do some work to better understand your fear.

Learn from other people's mistakes

Today's air safety record is a result of the mistakes of others and the following accident investigations. You too can improve your competence in your field by understanding the mistakes that others have made.

"It is necessary for us to learn from others' mistakes. You will not live long enough to make them all yourself." (Hyman George Rickover)

Some good sources to research include:

- Accident and incident reports (sometimes available in different fields).
- Books, magazines, and websites.
- Discussions with others in the field.

- Biographies of individuals and companies.

Some of the best accident reports are from aviation. Many of these reports highlight mistakes that others in different fields could make. The lessons learned are just as valuable in other fields as they are in aviation.

Let's look at an example. A passenger aircraft crashed into a Florida swamp in December 1972. The entire flight crew of three was focusing on changing a faulty undercarriage light in the cockpit. Everyone thought the plane was on autopilot, and nobody noticed the aircraft descend into the swamp. This highlights the danger of fixating on one issue for extended periods, while not looking after "the bigger picture."

As you read about the mistakes made by others, both in your field and outside, think of your current training or activities. Could you make similar mistakes? Consider adding items to your assertion lists to help reduce the likelihood of such mistakes.

Lastly, try using a simulator or visualization to replay circumstances that have led other people to accidents. Try to recreate some common mistakes that others make. What would you do differently?

Under pressure—impact on techniques

A technique may work well when you practice it in the comfort of your home or classroom. When you get out and try it in the real environment though, you may find it doesn't work as well as you expect. This is often due to pressure.

I've found that pressure causes issues with techniques both during learning as well as after you've learned something well. Let's look at both these situations.

Experiences during learning

During my flight training, I sometimes had to change a technique I used to memorize content. This was usually because the technique did not work well while I was under pressure. Two examples include:

- I tried to memorize a forced landing procedure using an acronym mnemonic. When I was under pressure in the aircraft, I couldn't remember where I was up to in the mnemonic. I changed techniques and instead used an acrostic mnemonic, "In planned trouble, make brief plans, short plans, approach and land." Each word stood for a step of the procedure. I then repeated the procedure several times just sitting in a chair, timing each instance. Once in the aircraft I found it much easier to remember where I was up to in the phrase.
- I tried to memorize radio calls also using first-letter mnemonics. Trying to recall the mnemonic during call interfered with what I was saying. I found the mental journey technique much more effective in remembering each part of the radio call.

When you come to use a technique in the real environment, don't worry if it doesn't work well for you. There are multiple ways to learn and memorize content. They all have their strengths and weaknesses and these vary from person to person. If something doesn't work well, try a different technique or approach.

Experiences after learning

After I had finished my flight license, I sometimes neglected to complete a checklist even when I knew the entire checklist back to front. It was usually when I was under pressure for other reasons, for example when I was running late. This also sometimes happened if one of the individual checks took longer than usual. It was easy to become distracted.

I picked up this issue in my reviews and added some assertions to counter this behavior. The key one was "I consciously start and finish each checklist." Now when I start a checklist I briefly focus on the last item. As I finish the checklist I "destroy" the last item. This reminds me I've finished the list.

ACT! Recognize and act on assumptions

Wrong assumptions are a problem in many fields. You can improve the assumptions you make by becoming more aware of when you make them. Recognizing assumptions can be challenging in any environment. This section helps you recognize assumptions and deal with them.

There are two main kinds of assumptions:

- **Conscious assumptions.** You consciously accept a piece of information as a fact, while understanding that it may not be.

- **Unconscious assumptions.** You unconsciously accept a piece of information as a fact, without questioning whether it is. These are the dangerous assumptions, however they are also difficult to detect because they *are* unconscious!

We all make many assumptions about the world we live in. In our time pressured society, making assumptions allows us to be as effective as we are. Imagine if every day we had to check that each part of the car worked before starting it. Imagine if we had to call the local transport office to make sure the train is coming that day. Think about having to ring the bank every day just to check our money is still there.

There are two parts of assumptions to consider:

- **Strength.** Our assumptions become stronger with experience. The car starts most of the time. The train usually arrives. Our money stays where it is (well, if we don't touch it). The more we experience the expected outcome, the more we treat the assumption as fact.

- **Impact.** The need to question assumptions usually arises when the impact of our assumption being wrong has an effect we would rather avoid. However, this is difficult if you don't realize you have made an assumption.

Unfortunately, wrong assumptions cost our society much time and money. Wrong assumptions by pilots (and others) cause accidents and loss of life. Many aircraft accident investigations show the pilot made an assumption that led to the accident or incident. Some of the most common are "I can get through the weather" and "I have enough fuel."

The key to staying safe is to turn unconscious assumptions into conscious assumptions. Once they are conscious assumptions, you can then use a simple process to decide whether the assumption is safe.

In this section, I provide you with a technique I call the *assumption buster technique*. This technique is a good way to deal with unconscious assumptions. You can apply this assumption buster technique to check assumptions you make in any field, not just aviation. You can train yourself to recognize and act on assumptions before they become issues or problems.

There are two steps. The first is to set up triggers for common assumptions. Assumption triggers are visualizations and assertions you can review that help pull your assumptions from the unconscious to the conscious mind. The second step is to ACT on them when they arise. ACT stands for Assumption, Contingency, and Test.

Let's look at these two steps in more detail.

Creating assumption triggers

Assumption triggers help pull your assumptions into your conscious mind. You do this is by associating assumptions with ACT.

Here are the three steps.

1. **Find the important assumptions.** Below I've listed some assumptions that pilots sometimes make, grouped into a few areas. You could treat this as a starting point if you are a pilot, or you could extract a few from these for your own field. You can also add to your list based on assumptions you find you make in your own experiences, or after learning about other's experiences. Once you have a list, rank them according to likelihood and possible impact. Focus on the high likelihood and high impact ones first.

2. **Visualize the assumption and swish it.** For each of the assumptions listed, you then use the swish technique to visualize yourself in a scenario where you might be saying or thinking that. Get into the low state and say the assumption, either aloud or in your mind. Then straighten up, smile, take a deep breath and say "but first, I'll ACT on it!" Then follow through with the ACT steps below.

   Repeat this step a few times for each assumption. Also, be careful to only do the visualizations while in a low state, otherwise the assumptions may act as assertions (which you don't want).

3. **Back them up with assertions**. Write a few positive assertions for each category. Add them into your review list. This also helps trigger you when you make an assumption that's inconsistent with your assertions. Add in ACT somewhere in the assumption, for example "The weather is always variable and unpredictable, so I ACT on it."

From conscious assumption to ACT

Once you trigger to ACT on an assumption, use the mnemonic to verify your assumption. Remembering that ACT stands for "Assumption, Contingency and Test," here are the three steps:

1. **Assumption:** When you trigger yourself with ACT, follow the assumption with a statement like "that's an assumption, so I ACT on it!" This helps confirm in your mind that it is an assumption and so it's open to question.

2. **Contingency:** What is the impact if the assumption proves wrong? What could you do to either reduce or deal with the impact? To work these out, try

to think of the top two or three "worst case" scenarios. If they are significant, like running out of fuel, spend more time here. You should also pay more attention to the "Test" step next. If the worst case is that you are going to be ten minutes late, you may not need to worry too much about contingencies and testing.

3. **Test:** What are one or two tests you could do now, or at some point in the future, that could prove your assumption was correct? You can use these tests as decision points where you may choose to use a contingency plan.

Example—weather in Aviation

In private aviation, poor weather judgment in pilots is a problem. Often pilots go flying even when there is an approaching cold front. Cold fronts often bring heavy rain and thunderstorms—poor flying weather. Let's use the trigger statement "that cold front won't be here until later this afternoon" as an example.

1. **Assumption:** See yourself in a flight planning room on a bright sunny morning, planning for a flight to another airfield. You're taking some friends, and you plan to return later that afternoon. There is a cold front due at your destination airfield two hours after you leave, according to the forecast. Visualize yourself in the "low" state saying, "That front won't be there until after we leave." Then straighten up, smile, take a deep breath in and say (or think) "That's an assumption, so I'll ACT on it!" Repeat this step a few times before doing the contingency and test steps.

2. **Contingencies.** Continue the visualization, and think of two worst case scenarios. One might be you are halfway there and you realize your destination airfield is already under the front. See yourself in flight looking at a huge bank of black cloud ahead. Another might be that you can't leave the destination airfield because the front arrives early.

   What are your contingencies? Your first one may be to locate some alternative airfields on the way to your destination, in case you have to divert. The second may be to tell your friends of the risk of having to stop at the other end for a night, and check what impact that has on them.

3. **Test.** Now that you have worked out some contingencies, decide two tests that you can do either now or later. One may be to call the weather office before departure and ask if there has been any change to the estimated arrival time of the front. The second may be to look up an airfield thirty miles past your destination airfield, towards the approaching front, and take their telephone number with you. On arrival at your destination airfield, you could give that airfield a call and confirm the front hasn't arrived there yet.

While this example is aviation specific, you can apply the same principles in many other areas as well.

Example triggers

Here are some example triggers from aviation. I've included these particular ones as you could apply many to other fields. For example, weather, fuel and location are just as important for sailing, boating and perhaps four-wheel driving. "I'm OK" is important for fields where your personal performance is critical. Let's look at the examples.

Weather

Use the following triggers to ensure you are aware of the assumptions you make about the weather:

- That front won't be here until later this afternoon.
- Those thunderstorms are still far away.
- The weather will be clear or clearer when we arrive.
- I have enough time before last light.

Fuel

A pilot once took off from a country airstrip and almost immediately crashed because of lack of fuel. He had fuelled the aircraft within the previous twelve hours, and didn't bother checking again. Between fuelling and takeoff, someone stole the fuel from the aircraft. In an aircraft and other equipment, fuel helps keep you alive, so make all fuel assumptions conscious.

- Someone else refueled the aircraft. It's full.
- It was full when I checked a few hours ago.
- I should have enough fuel to make it home.
- The gauge must be faulty.

Location

Misidentifying landmarks is a fast way to become lost. If you are in any doubt be sure to ACT.

- That must be the right town.
- I must be "here" (pointing to a map).
- I've departed in the correct direction.
- My compass must not be working properly.

I'm OK

A pilot's internal systems are part of the whole system that makes an aircraft fly. The system can't work correctly if the pilot's internal systems don't work correctly. The same applies to other equipment. This may also be relevant in other fields where good personal performance is important. Use these triggers to make sure "you're OK."

- I'll be more awake once I get going.
- I'll be OK, or I'll be all right, or I'll be fine (with that nagging feeling that maybe you won't be).
- I got enough sleep last night.
- It's been eight hours since my last alcoholic drink. It's out of my system by now.

Other people's actions

People can be as unpredictable as the weather. You can often rely on your own actions, however others may have a different understanding of what you expect from them.

- (Someone) closed that door or hatch properly.
- (Someone) knows what I'm doing.

- (Someone) is going to be there when I expect them.

The Medical Student Syndrome

Another variation on wrong assumptions is one I briefly discussed in the introduction to this chapter. This is the *Medical Student Syndrome*, where medical (and sometimes psychiatry) students start to believe they suffer the disease or disorder they are studying. These students then make a second mistake. They do not try to test their thinking, for example by discussing it with a doctor or specialist. There have been many cases where students have convinced themselves they suffer the disease, only to have tests prove them wrong.

I've included this anecdote because you might do something similar as you read about the challenges in this chapter. After reading this chapter, you may feel there are one or two issues relevant to you. That's fine. Reread the information on those issues, try the techniques to resolve them, and keep moving forward.

However, you may find yourself rationalizing why it's so difficult to move on while you suffer from several of these challenges. If so, try talking to someone or at least write down your thoughts. You may be suffering a similar syndrome to those medical students. Talking to someone else or putting pen to paper often highlights mistaken assumptions. Be open to them! If you get defensive, that behavior may show you are defending thoughts that you want to believe are true.

Lastly, be aware you may also talk yourself into believing something to justify inaction. If you have a history of procrastination, review the section on motivation to help you keep moving.

Chapter summary

In this chapter, you've seen some of the challenges that may arise on the journey to your goals. These can happen to anyone. Now you have some tools and techniques you can use to resolve those challenges faster.

The first challenge we dealt with was motivation. Motivation issues are often the key cause of people giving up on their learning goals. You have now seen some of the common motivation issues so you can deal with them more effectively if they arise.

The next challenges were nervousness and fear. Fear is often an issue when there is some danger or risk in a training course, or when there is significant personal change. You now have some ideas for balancing your fear, dealing with fears, and handling positive and negative experiences. We've also covered some further techniques for uncovering hidden fears, controlling breathing, and excelling in exams.

The last part of the chapter dealt with some other common challenges that arise while learning. Mistakes often concern people, however you now know that both your mistakes and the mistakes of others are often valuable lessons that help you along the way. Pressure also has an impact on some techniques, so be prepared to try others if this arises. Wrong assumptions can sometimes be inconvenient, if not dangerous. Using the assumption buster technique, you can bring unconscious assumptions out so you can deal with them properly.

Closing Comments

You've come a long way through much detail, and your journey though the Memletics Manual is nearly at an end. I hope though your Memletics journey is just beginning. You now have a far greater understanding of how to learn faster and remember more. Let's finish with an overall summary, some thoughts on further work, and some final words.

In this last section of the book I summarize what you've read, look at some ideas for further exploration, and then finish with some final words.

Book summary

The first chapter of the book, "Overview of Memletics," introduced you to the five parts of Memletics, the Memletic State, Process, Techniques, Styles and Approach. Having this high-level understanding made it easier to see links between the five parts. We also saw many activities in which you could apply Memletics.

In Memletic State, you saw there are many contributors that support good learning state. There are three layers. These are the cell, physical and mental layers. Good cell state supports the basic needs of cells, including neurons. The physical layer supports our body-mind systems. The mental layer provides ways to support and improve mental functions.

You then read about the Memletic Process. This process consists of five activities, and the mnemonic for these is LEARN. These activities are Locate, Explore, Arrange, Reinforce, and eNquire. Locate means finding the information to learn. Explore is to understand the material. Arrange is to prepare content for long-term memorization. Reinforce applies the various techniques to lock in content. Lastly, eNquire reviews your learning performance as well as how you use the overall system.

Next were the Memletic Techniques. There are six categories of techniques. The categories are Associate, Visualize, Verbalize, Simulate, Perform, and Repeat. Association links new knowledge with knowledge you already have. Visualization involves replaying scenarios in your mind using all the senses (not just vision). The Verbalize techniques use words to help you affirm your goals, content and abilities. Simulation uses external tools and people to reproduce parts of the real environment. The Perform techniques give you ways to learn skills and behaviors. Lastly, the Repeat techniques provide you with more techniques to reinforce content over time.

The Memletic Styles followed Techniques. These seven styles are the Visual, Aural, Verbal, Physical, Logical, Social and Solitary styles. The Style questionnaire gave you a picture of your current stronger and secondary learning styles. You saw that you can improve your learning by better understanding and using both your stronger and secondary styles.

The final part of Memletics we discussed, the Memletic Approach, gave you a series of activities you can use to plan and manage your overall learning journey. You start with targeting your goal and planning your effort. You then track your progress, while remembering to enjoy both the journey and the destination.

In the "Challenges" chapter, we reviewed some of the common challenges you may face on the journey to your goal. Motivation is important. We discussed how ensuring your goals and objectives match your direction in life helps support your motivation. We also discussed fear and nervousness and how to combat these issues when they arise. Lastly we covered some further challenges. We discussed mistakes, the impact of pressure on techniques, and assumptions.

The last chapter of the book, "Closing Comments," is the one you are reading now.

You may now see some of the links between the parts of Memletics. Your learning styles, for example, influence how you explore new material as well as the techniques you choose. Getting your goals right in the approach influences your mental state. Your learning state underpins your ability to concentrate on your learning activities. Your improved learning performance contributes to better mental state. The list could go on. The power of Memletics grows from these mutually helpful links.

Even though you have now read about all the parts of Memletics, you probably don't remember much of the detail. That's normal, and there are some tips on how to start learning Memletics in the appendix.

Further work from here

If you want further develop your Memletic fitness, in this section I discuss a few suggestions on how to start. Firstly, visit the memletics.com website. It contains a wide range of further material, references and links to more web and book based information. You could spend some time researching more detailed references on the topics in this book, or try some of the more advanced learning topics. Lastly, I encourage you to share your experiences.

Visit the memletics.com website

The Memletics website is a great place to continue with your learning about learning. In this section I discuss some of the ways you can use the site.

You can find the site on the Internet at **http://www.memletics.com/**

Also on the Memletics website, you'll find:

- **Memletics Statistics**. See some interesting statistics on Memletics users.
- **Instructor-led training**. Learn about upcoming instructor-led training for Memletics.
- **Testimonials**. Don't just take our word for it. See some comments from readers and reviewers of Memletics.

- **Resources**. See some of the additional resources that are available to Memletics Members.
- **Accelerated Learning Research Projects**. Find out about some of our current research projects, including information on Memletics VR (Virtual Reality).

You can also learn more **about us**.

Other resources you may be interested in

Here are some additional Memletics resources you might be interested in.

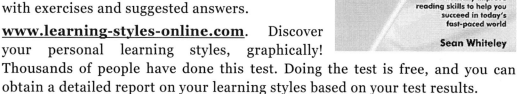

- **Speed reading course**. Our new speed reading course provides in-depth information on how to improve your reading speed. Visit Memletics.com to learn more about this resource.
- **Concept mapping course.** This course provides you with detailed information on each of the major types of concept mapping techniques. Over 10 are covered in detail, along with exercises and suggested answers.
- **www.learning-styles-online.com**. Discover your personal learning styles, graphically! Thousands of people have done this test. Doing the test is free, and you can obtain a detailed report on your learning styles based on your test results.

Memletics for organizations & businesses

Representatives of organizations and businesses may be interested in the following programs:

- **Volume license program.** This program is ideal for organizations that want to provide the Memletics products to many students or employees.
- **Partner certification program.** For individuals and training organizations wanting to conduct training specifically on Memletics, or create new products or services based on the Memletics content.
- **Affiliate program.** If you would like to receive rewards for referring visitors to our sites, the affiliate program is for you.
- **Reseller program.** If you would like to resell Memletics, for example as reference with your existing training program, you can obtain the Manual at a discount.

For more information on these programs, please visit
www.memletics.com/support/programs.asp

Registering on the site

I strongly suggest you register on the site. We can then keep you up to date with any changes or updates to the book through our newsletter. You can also access more references and resources that are not available to general users of the site.

Try the references

You may notice that I haven't included any references in the back of this book. This is because I've chosen to keep them all on the website. This allows easier additions and updates. There are notes, references to books, web articles and links to websites.

You can access these at **http://www.memletics.com/manual/references**

Try some learning software

In various sections of this book I've discussed specific software relevant to learning. On the reference pages there are links to other sites so you can download full or trial versions, where applicable☻.

Explore the Memletics Forums

The Memletics Forums are discussion groups on the website where you can discuss various topics with me and readers of the book. Feel free to use these to ask questions, get more guidance or post your feedback on specific or general topics.

Further features

Over time we'll add more features to the website to make it even more useful to you. Be sure to visit occasionally, or register to stay in touch with what is happening through the newsletter!

Try further references

If you want to examine some topics in more detail, there is much information out there. Here I provide a few general suggestions on further references such as books, the Internet and courses.

Books

There are many other books out there that cover many of the topics in this book to far more detail. If there are topics that interest you, you may want to get your hands on some of those. I suggest you spend a month (at least) on each one. Read it. Use it. Reread it. See what works for you, and what doesn't. Do not put it down until you have at least tried some of its suggestions.

The Internet

There is much content out there on the Internet. I've suggested some starting points on the book's reference pages. Take care though. Keep an open mind, but also be aware of the content source.

Sometimes the library or bookstore is still the best place to go for information.

Courses

There are some courses out there that focus on particular topics included in this book. I haven't seen too many though that focus on the wide range of skills involved in being a good learner. It appears that since we made it past school, everyone assumes we must already know how to learn well.

If you want to use courses, you may need to put together your own curriculum that involves several courses covering different topics. Use the Memletic Forums on the website to tell others about courses related to Memletic topics. I'm sure there are others who would like to know if you've found relevant training.

Also keep an eye out in the future for training providers offering courses either teaching Memletics, or using Memletics to teach other topics.

Try advanced memory techniques

Memletics includes a wide range of memory techniques from various sources. There are other techniques out there as well, some of which are more advanced or more specialized than the ones discussed in here. Often they are just extensions of those we have already discussed. Be wary when anyone claims to have found a "completely new technique" or claims to have made a breakthrough. Feel free to post a note in the forums if you find something unique though.

One of the more advanced memory techniques is "SEM3" or the Self-Enhancing Matrix. It's from a book called "Master Your Memory" by Tony Buzan. I'll let you follow it up, however in summary it takes association and the peg word technique to a whole new level. It provides "pegs" for potentially over ten thousand items!

Another variation is the Dominic System created by Dominic O'Brien. Instead of using Peg Words, the system is uses "Peg People." You associate numbers with well-known people. This again needs a significant investment of time, however it does provide advantages to some people. You may find it easier to associate using people rather than the objects that make up the peg word system.

As you can see, these systems simply extend existing memory techniques. If you find new and innovative techniques, be sure to let us know!

Share your experiences

If you haven't already realized, I am keen to hear from you. I'd like to hear about your experiences, feedback, criticisms, and suggestions. All are welcome. Memletics is not a one-off book. It's an ongoing project to discover more about learning faster. You're comments can influence the project's direction.

Please post your comments into the Memletics Forums, rather than writing directly to me. This allows others to join in and potentially add to your comments or answer your questions.

Final words

My aim from the start was to give you an easy-to-understand system you can apply to improve the way you learn and remember. The Memletic processes, tools and techniques come from a combination of experience and research. All these parts together help you start and achieve many different learning goals.

I now encourage you to start, or continue, with your Memletic training. If you like what you have read, commit to beginning. Try the system. Start small. Don't take on too much to begin. If you don't have a topic to learn, find one! Flying is a great self-development course, however there are so many other choices out there. Try developing your work skills, relationship skills or recreation skills. Review the Overview chapter for more ideas on getting started. If you do have difficulty getting started, reach out to others. Try the website or just talk to those around you.

Don't be one of those people who read material such as this, think "that would be great to do," but never do! If you find you are reading more and more books (or attending more and more courses), without doing any work, be careful. Don't fall into the *self-help trap* of having to read every book on the topic before you start. If you find you are reading one book after another, ask yourself: Are you just exercising your eyes, or are you *developing your skills?*

If you are having difficulty deciding on specific activities, keep in mind that it's sometimes better to set a direction, any direction, rather than staying in the same spot. Don't wait for enlightenment on the direction you should take. Once you get moving, you gain new perspectives. You gather speed and experience. Even if you eventually find you want to go in the opposite direction, you pass others still waiting in the middle for that enlightenment to come.

The direction I've set for Memletics is to *use technology to help us learn faster*. In this first version of the book, technology has helped me find information, prepare the book, and share it with a wide audience. Technology allows me to publish this book without a publisher. This means more of the revenue from sales can go back into research and development, instead of to shareholders of some multinational publishing company. Technology allows us to share our experiences across the globe, for example through the Memletics Forums. Sharing our experiences helps everyone develop their skills and helps guide the future direction of Memletics. Lastly, technology is driving new discoveries about the brain and how we learn, and hopefully these will lead to further improvements. I'll tell you more about these in future versions of the book.

We live in exciting, and sometimes challenging times. The world now changes faster than ever before. If you focus on developing your learning skills, you can see and take advantage of more opportunities than those who avoid change. I suggest you develop your Memletic fitness. Aim to be a lifelong, self-directed learner. Keep an eye on developments, and pass your experience on to others.

Good luck on your journey.

Appendices

Additional information referred to from the chapters in the book.

This section contains some further content and examples. The additional content includes:

Tips for learning Memletics

Memletics is a system for learning more effectively, however it also takes time to learn how use all the parts of Memletics together. In this section I'll give you some pointers to help get your Memletic training program underway.

My first suggestion is to learn Memletics with another learning goal. As you know I developed Memletics out of my flight training, however flying is just one way to learn Memletics. You may want to try applying Memletics to some topics that help your work or career. Communication, presentation or negotiation skills are often helpful in a wide variety of areas. You may want to apply Memletics to a recreational activity, such as sailing, photography or orienteering. You can apply many of the topics to sports. School and college students can find many opportunities to apply Memletics to their studies. The key point is that Memletics is far easier to learn if you are applying it to a personal learning goal.

If you want some ideas on learning programs to kick off your Memletic training, review the Overview chapter. In this chapter I outline many activities in which you could learn and apply Memletics.

Another suggestion I have is to get a hold of the Memletic Learning Checklist. This checklist is available from the website🌑. It contains a few pages of notes that you can review as you start each learning objective. This checklist covers many of the points below.

Let's look at some more specific details on learning the various parts of Memletics.

- **Memletic State.** You can apply some parts of Memletic state immediately before or during a learning activity. Other parts may take weeks or months to develop. I suggest you review each part of Memletic State and decide the priority areas you need to work on. If you find there are many, you may want to select only the key areas to work on in the beginning. Don't go out and change your diet, change your sleeping habits, start an exercise regime, stop smoking, start mediation, start Neurobics and do a stress reduction course all in the first week, while also starting a challenging learning goal! Start small, address a few areas at a time and build on successes.

- **Memletic Process.** Use the checklist to guide you through each of the steps. Use the "quality not quantity" approach. Don't worry about trying to follow every step to the letter. Instead, understand the basic principles and use them a lot! Over time you can integrate more of the ideas to further improve your learning.

- **Memletic Techniques.** Use the technique selection matrix in the Process chapter to select the techniques that may be relevant for each lesson you undertake. Don't try to use them all. Try a few at the start and see which ones work for you. Keep in mind your preferred styles when choosing the techniques too.

- **Memletic Styles.** Do the style questionnaire to understand your current learning styles. Review the descriptions of your strongest and weakest styles, and then decide on a few ways to expand both of those areas. Remember to start small. You have plenty of time to try the other areas!

- **Memletic Approach.** Spend more time in this part as you begin the course. As your goals have a big impact on your motivation, spend some time exploring those goals using visualization and scripting. Get a hold of the "Learn To Fly guide" ☯, even if you are not learning to fly. It gives you an idea of some of the items to consider during this phase.

- **Challenges.** Don't try to learn or memorize the entire challenges chapter. Instead, keep in mind some of the symptoms of common challenges. If you feel you are having some difficulties in those areas, go back into that chapter and see if you can find material that is relevant. If not, get on the website and talk to others.

While you may feel you are training alone, keep in mind that you also have the Memletics website where you can discuss your challenges and successes with others.

Above all, keep in mind that improving your Memletic fitness takes time. It's like physical fitness. You can't go from a long period of unfitness to running a marathon without time, effort and perseverance. The good news is that while your fitness improves, you notice the positive benefits early in your training. Enjoy them and use them as motivation to keep going on your journey.

Association exercise

I reference this exercise from the Memletic Techniques chapter. It proves the power of association. It should take less than 15 minutes.

Let's take a list of fifteen household items. Look at the list and try to memorize all the items in the order I present them (across then down). Do this for two minutes, then cover the list and write down as many as you can remember. No peeking!

Pencil	Microwave Oven	Lamp
Chair	Television	Fork
Toothpaste	Clock	Pizza
Doormat	Apple	Tap
Dog	Grandma	Desk

What score did you get? If you scored fifteen right, well done. If not, let's try a simple way to make sure you remember all fifteen items.

I'm going to present fifteen scenarios for you to visualize. Spend twenty seconds on each, before progressing to the next. Close your eyes, and imagine what the scenario would look like. Be creative! Not only see, but think of what it would sound like, smell like, maybe even taste like. Let's start.

Visualize a pencil that is three feet long, standing in a microwave oven. Not a normal microwave oven, but an oven that's obviously made for microwaving pencils. It's four feet tall, very narrow, and has buttons for "light pencil," "medium pencil" and "dark pencil." See yourself putting this pencil in, pushing the buttons (hear the "beep" as you push them), wait a moment, then take out your "cooked" pencil. Take a bite.

See a normal lamp stand, but instead of a light bulb there is a tiny microwave oven. The light comes from the light inside the microwave oven. It doesn't work well. Turn the light on and off a few times, and every time you do, it beeps at you.

This lamp you were looking at just grew arms and legs, walked across the living room, and sat down in your favorite chair. You are yelling at the lamp, telling it to get off the chair. "Furniture is not allowed on the furniture!" you yell. It doesn't get off and instead sulks and looks insulted.

You feel a tap on the shoulder, and turn around and there is the TV, also with arms and legs, yelling at you to leave the lamp alone! There is a picture of Darth Vader on the screen, and then the TV pulls out from behind it a light saber and starts swinging it around. Hear the sound like in the *Star Wars* movie, and smell the ozone.

You realize its time to fight, and pull from behind you a... fork that's about the same size as a light saber. You fight for a while but realize it's not doing you much good because the end of the fork keeps getting sliced off. It's getting shorter and shorter. You can feel the heat of the light saber getting closer and closer.

The TV is about to slice you up when there is an almighty crash! You open your eyes and through the ceiling has fallen a huge tube of Colgate toothpaste. It's fallen right on the TV! You prod the toothpaste tube with the end of your fork and yes, toothpaste comes out (is it regular or minty gel?).

You walk around the toothpaste tube and see a clock hanging there. But this is no ordinary clock. It's wired up to the toothpaste tube and it looks like a... toothpaste bomb! The clock is ticking (hear it), and it's almost twelve o'clock! You start to run for your life.

But there is a buzz at your front door. It's the pizza man (smell that pizza). The pizza man is also a bomb-disposal expert. He dumps the pizza at the front door, rushes in and disarms the bomb.

The pizza looks so good at the front door you decide to use it as a doormat. You walk in and out of your, feeling the pizza under your feet. Mmmm it still smells good.

You are about to close the door when a big apple rolls in the front door and squashes the pizza. This is a huge apple, and it barely fits through the door. The pizza sticks to the apple, and it rolls around for a while. Every time the pizza goes underneath, it squishes. The pizza doesn't smell so good any more.

You decide to go and clean up at the kitchen sink. As you turn the tap on something weird happens. Instead of water coming out, the tap seems to draw the apple (sitting on the floor) towards it. The tap draws the apple all the way to it and then sucks it in. The apple shrinks as it goes in, and the tap expands like a snake eating a rat. The tap is squeaking and rattling, and then "plop," the apple is gone.

But wait. What's that sound coming from the tap? It sounds like... like barking? Suddenly hundreds of miniature dogs come streaming out of the tap. You manage to turn the tap off and they stop, but you still have one hundred or so tiny dogs running around the sink, barking and yapping.

The dogs make such a noise they wake grandma up. She comes over to the sink, sees all the dogs, and then faints. But instead of fainting on the floor, she faints on the ceiling. You try jumping up to pull her down, but you can't reach.

At that point your study desk comes into the kitchen. It's floating! You jump up on top, and it floats up close to the ceiling. As grandma wakes up, she falls a small way onto the desk. It then floats back down to the ground.

This is a crazy list, so let's call it our "Crazy List." How do you write a crazy list? Obviously with a crazy pencil! Imagine trying to write the list with a pencil that is laughing its head off. This pencil is really loony!

Turn to the next page to start the review...

Review

Review your associations by completing the missing words...

You would write a crazy list with a crazy _____

If you were going to cook one of these you would put it in a

_____, which is also the light bulb for a

_____, which sits in your favorite _____ so

you yell at it until the _____ taps you on the shoulder. It's upset.

It pulls out a light saber so you have no choice but to pull out your trusty

_____. It doesn't do you much good and you are about to be

sliced up but a giant _____ tube falls through the ceiling.

Unfortunately, the tube is also a bomb because it has a _____ ticking

on the other side. Luckily, the _____ man turns up and he happens to

be a bomb disposal expert, but he drops what he was delivering at the front door.

It looks so good there you decide to use it as a _____, until it is squished

by a giant _____ rolling through the front door. No problem, it's

sucked away when you turn the _____ on at the kitchen sink, but

before you can turn it off, miniature _____ come out and into your sink.

These wake up _____. She sees these, faints and falls to the

ceiling. You can get her down because you happen to have a floating

_____.

Turn to the next page to test your recall...

Check

Now close your eyes and review this whole crazy story in your mind. As each item from the list comes into your mind, write it down and continue with the story in your mind.

_____	_____	_____
_____	_____	_____
_____	_____	_____
_____	_____	_____
_____	_____	_____

How did you go? If you missed any, review the scenes that link the items on either side. While this may seem a cumbersome way to memorize a list, with some practice you can create these stories quickly. You now also have a way to memorize any list with great accuracy!

"Memletics Terms of Use" agreement

The following is a copy of the "Memletics Terms of Use" agreement, as at January 2006. You should check the website for the latest version.

Your use of any products or services (materials) provided by Advanogy.com (the publisher) is conditional on your acceptance of this "Memletics Terms of Use" agreement. This is a binding agreement between you and Advanogy.com. Advanogy.com is an Australian-based company, registered in Victoria, ACN 104 198 263.

This agreement was last updated on January 2006. Advanogy.com reserves the right to amend these conditions without notification. You should check back to the website occasionally and review any changes.

By using any material provided by Advanogy.com (and from time to time, demonstrating your acceptance on various online forms), you agree you accept all parts of this agreement. This agreement is in effect from the first time you use the materials.

The parts of the agreement are arranged as follows:

- General conditions
- Disclaimer
- Privacy and data protection
- Intellectual property
- Term, termination and jurisdiction
- Website specific conditions
- Memletics Manual specific conditions
- Contact and questions

General conditions

The Memletics materials contain ideas, opinions, tips and techniques for improving human performance. The materials intend to provide helpful and useful material on the subjects addressed in the materials. Advanogy.com does not provide you with medical, health, or any other personal professional service. You should seek the advice of your medical practitioner, health professional or other relevant competent professional before trying or using information in this material.

It's your responsibility to maintain all legal, regulatory, company and other applicable requirements while performing day-to-day or work responsibilities. These may be requirements relevant to your qualification, the type of activity you are undertaking, or the equipment you are using.

You will only use Memletics materials for lawful purposes. You will not infringe the legal or moral rights of other users. You will not restrict or inhibit the use and enjoyment of the materials by others. This restriction includes unlawful activity, harassment, defamation, causing distress or offence and interruption or attempted interruption of service.

Disclaimer and limited liability

The Memletics materials are provided as is, without representation, endorsement or warranty (express or implied). This exclusion includes implied warranties of appropriate fitness, quality, non-infringement, security, accuracy and compatibility. Advanogy.com does not warrant the materials are complete or free from inaccuracies.

You agree to not hold, nor attempt to hold Advanogy.com liable for any loss, liability, claim, demand, damage, or expense (including legal fees) whatsoever in connection with the use, misuse or inability to use Memletics materials.

In jurisdictions that exclude such limitations, liability is limited to:

- The consideration paid by you for the right to view or use these materials, and/or

- The greatest extent permitted by law.

Indemnification

You agree to indemnify Advanogy.com against any loss, liability, claim, demand, damage, or expenses (including legal fees) asserted by any third party due to or arising from or in connection with your materials usage, or materials usage by others.

Third Party Rights

The provisions in this agreement applicable to Advanogy.com may also be asserted by Advanogy.com shareholders, directors, agents, sponsors, employees, reviewers, moderators, contributors and other third parties under commercial arrangements with Advanogy.com.

Privacy and Data Protection

We are committed to your privacy. Information collected on the site and by Advanogy.com may be used for internal review, to improve and customize content and layout, to notify users about site updates, and for marketing purposes. We will obtain your express permission before providing any data to another organization.

We reserve the right to make site information available to third parties or law enforcement authorities to assist in the enforcement of this agreement or for the investigation of illegal activities.

If you wish to discuss any privacy matter, please contact us.

Intellectual Property

Copyright and Permissions

All material © 2003-2006 Advanogy.com (except where noted). All rights reserved. This includes (but is not limited to) text, images, illustrations, colors, layout, and code. You may view or download publicly accessible materials, or materials for which you have obtained a license, to your local workstation for your personal use (and other uses as provided for under copyright "fair use" provisions). However, you may not further copy or distribute (by any means) any part of the materials, including the Memletics Manual and any derivative or summary material.

The Memletics Manual has been registered with the US Library of Congress. Material may consist of derivative works from the manual. The courts can impose heavy penalties on those who willingly violate copyright provisions

If you wish to use this material for commercial purposes or purposes other than allowed for under fair use, please contact us. We license material for use in instruction, training, education and commercial organizations.

Trademark Information

"Memletics®," is a trademark for an information product in international classes 9, 35 and 41.

This information product is marketed and sold worldwide. Registration pending. Where not currently registered, trademarks are claimed under common law and relevant treaties.

Other trademarks are the property of their respective owners.

Assignment of Intellectual Property

You agree to grant Advanogy.com a royalty-free, non-exclusive, worldwide, perpetual license for any materials and other information you post or communicate to Advanogy.com or memletics.com. This includes rights to sublicense, reproduce, distribute, transmit, derive new works from, publicly display and publicly perform these materials. These materials, and the ideas they contain, may be used (without limitation) for new or improved products or services. This license is applicable to all means and in any media now in existence or later developed.

You agree that you have no recourse or claim against Advanogy.com for any alleged or actual infringement of any intellectual property rights in your communications with Advanogy.com (including both forums and personal email).

Infringements

If you believe any work has been infringed by any materials provided by Advanogy.com, please contact us. Please provide details of the original work and where on the site the potentially infringing material is located.

Term, termination and jurisdiction

This agreement is in effect from the first viewing of any Memletics materials. It remains in effect regardless of whether you continue to use the material. Any claim or cause of action you may have must be commenced within one year after the cause of such claim or action, otherwise you agree that any claim or action is barred.

If Advanogy.com does not act to enforce any provision in this agreement, this inaction does not indicate a termination or waiver of any part of this agreement. In addition, if any part or parts of this agreement are found to be not enforceable, you agree that all other parts remain in full force.

You agree this agreement shall be governed by and construed in accordance with the laws of Australia and/or the United States. Any dispute arising under these terms and conditions shall be subject to the exclusive jurisdiction of the courts of either Australia or the United states. You agree the choice of which court, including which state, is the sole choice of Advanogy.com.

Website specific conditions

Forums and other public areas

If you wish to read or post messages in the Memletics forum, you agree to be bound by the rules of the forum as posted at the top of each forum. Those rules form part of this agreement.

We are under no obligation to monitor user activity, forums or other user posts on the website. We assume no responsibility for errors, omissions, infringements, defamation, obscenities or inaccuracies within these areas.

Site linking to memletics.com

Please advise the webmaster if you wish to directly link to pages within memletics.com. We typically support such requests, however we reserve the right to determine which pages you may link to, if at all.

We do not allow our pages to be loaded into frames or other systems which cause our material to appear alongside material from another site. The pages must load into the user's entire window without modification.

Memletics.com linking to other sites

Websites linked from memletics.com are not under our control. We are not responsible the content, reliability or availability of any linked site. Listing and linking should not be taken as an endorsement or recommendation. We do not guarantee that links are correct, work all the time or that pages on linked sites are available or correct.

Service and defects

The site may not be continuously available or error free. We may not fix some defects. The site, server and content may not be free of viruses or represent the complete functionality, reliability or accuracy of the services and materials provided.

Virus and hacker protection

We make efforts to ensure our materials are virus free. You should take steps to protect yourself from viruses and hackers. We do not accept responsibility for any loss, disruption or damage arising from viruses, hackers and other illegitimate activities.

Licensed product specific conditions

Single reader licenses

Products sold under the single reader license may only be used by the individual who receives a license from Advanogy.com. This license allows the license holder, and their immediate family, to use the product they received a license for.

A single reader licensed product cannot be transferred from one individual to another individual, nor can the associated materials be transferred.

Single reader licensed products cannot not be shared between the employees of a company, nor lent, rented or resold to 3rd parties.

Multi-user and other licenses

Multi-user licensing, content licensing, reseller and other agreements vary in their terms and conditions. They form an addendum to the Memletics Terms of Use agreement.

Contact and Questions

You agree to contact us, and provide us at least 14 days to comply with a request, if you believe we have infringed your rights. This is prior to you making any further requests to Internet service providers, Internet authorities, other authorities or courts.

If you have any questions regarding this agreement, please consult an attorney or other relevant professional. We are unable to give legal advice specific to your situation.

Index

Please note:

- **Bold** page numbers indicate the term is part of a heading.

- Book references are maintained at http://www.memletics.com/manual/references

O

objectives
  and mental state, **51**
  and motivation, **182**
  setting, **172**
  too difficult, and motivation, 182
  too easy, and motivation, 182
objects, in associations, 92
occipital lobes, 146
oil, association example, 93
OK, I'm OK - assumption trigger, 202
omega, fatty acids, 28
OSAID model, 66
other people, helping with motivation, 184
other people's
  actions, assumption triggers, 202
  mistakes, **197**
overlearning, **131**
  during repetition, 77
own mistakes, **195**
oxygen, **26**
  and cell damage, 29
  in a classroom, 35

P

pain control, 111
Paired Associate Learning, 138
PAL, Paired Associate Learning, 138
paragraph marking, 48
parietal lobes, 146
part task training technique, **128**
part-time, **173**
password, memorizing example, 99
PC-based simulators, **124**
peg events, **101**
peg words, **97**
  destroying, 101
  for assertions list, 82
  words for 1 to 10, 97
  words for 21 to 100, 101
  words from 10 to 20, 100
perfect performance script, 121
performance techniques, **126**
performance, improving state, **133**
peripheral vision, and concentration, 49
personal hourly rate, 174
personal skills, examples, 19
physical environment, **35**
physical fitness, **32**
physical relaxation, **33**
  example exercise, **33**
physical state, **30**
Physical style, **158**
  exploration techniques, **65**
planning, **172**
  costs, **177**
  response to mistakes, 196
  time, **176**
PMA, Positive Mental Attitude, **49**
PMR, Progressive Muscle Relaxation, 34
Polar bear, 93
Positive Mental Attitude, **49**
  and health, 31
Post-it notes, for exploring content, 66
pre-performance patterns, 135
presentations
  chunking example, 94
  example content, **55**
  simulating an audience, 124

pressure, **198**
pre-synaptic terminal, 16
principles, knowledge type, 70
procedures, knowledge type, 70
professional training, examples, 20
programmed repetition, 80
progress, tracking, **177**
Progressive Muscle Relaxation
  example exercise, 33
Progressive Muscular Relaxation, 34
progressive part recombination, 130
protein, amino acids (cell state), 28
psychedelic drugs, 32
psychoneuroimmunology, 31
psychoneuromuscular theory, 112
Pubmed, 39
pulse rate, and cell state, 26
pure part recombination, 130
purity, in associations, 94
puzzles, and mental fitness, 45
pyramid, for content, 60
Pyridoxine, 40

Q

questionnaire, for Memletic Styles, 148
questions, for content pyramid, **62**

R

rally car drivers, 108
reaction to mistakes, **196**
real equipment, for simulation, **125**
reasons, for goals, **170**
recombining, in part task training, 130
recommended daily allowances (RDAs), finding, 40
recreational activities, examples, 21
references, where to find, 11
reframing, exams, 194
refresh reviews, 77
rehearsal. *See* mental practice
reinforce step, **74**
relaxation. *See also* mental relaxation,
  See also physical relaxation
  and fast learning, 33
  and light, 35
  and physical health, 31
  and physical state, **33**
  physical example, **33**
repetition
  examples, 75
  in reinforce step, **75**
  lessening over time, 77
  spaced, 75
  spreading, **76**
  tips, **79**
repetition techniques, **137**
repetitive part recombination, 130
responding to mistakes, **196**
responsibilities, and motivation, 185
responsibility, and health, 31
retention, 75
  approach, **72**
retire early, as a goal, 111
reversing roles, 194
review log, **80**
reviews
  formal, **86**
  lesson, **83**
  not done (issue), **142**
  refreshing, 77
  scheduled (technique), **138**

scripts, 120
  system, **86**
rewards, and mental state, **51**
rhythms
  body and brain, 36
  brain, and caffeine, 42
risk
  and motivation issues, 183
  and simulation, 113
  balanced model, 187
role-playing, **125**
  for exploring content, 66, 67
roles, reversing, 194
rollerblading cat, 90, 91, **140**
Roman Rooms technique, **104**
rote learning, 59, **137**
rules, for mental firewall, 118

S

schedule, time planning, 176
scheduled review technique, **138**
schools, and limited methods, 145
scripting technique, **119**
secondary styles, 167
segmenting, in part task training, 129
self-directed learning, 9
Self-Enhancing Matrix, 94
self-esteem
  and mental state, 50
  and verbalization, 114
self-help trap, 210
self-image
  and mental state, 50
  and verbalization, 114
self-inflicted consistency, 184
self-sabotage, 183
self-study, **173**
self-talk
  and mental state, 50
  and verbalization, 114
  irrational, 189
senior years, using Memletics during, 19
senses
  in associations, 91
  in visualization, 108
sensory deprivation, 34
sensory-motor skills, knowledge type, 70
serotonin, 44
setting objectives, **172**
seven, and chunking, 94
seventy by seven technique, **192**
shunt technique, **131**
sick buildings, 35
siesta, and physical state, 37
simplicity, in associations, 94
simplifying, in part task training, 129
simulation, **121**
  and fidelity, **122**
  basic, **123**
  full-scale, **125**
  PC-based, **124**
  role-playing, **125**
  with real equipment, **125**
singing, and mental fitness, 45
situations, in associations, 92
sketching, exploration technique, 63
skills
  learning, **126**
  three stage learning, **127**
sleep
  and body rhythms, 36